MISS WILLMOTT OF WARLEY PLACE

MISS WILLMOTT
OF WARLEY PLACE

Her Life and Her Gardens

AUDREY LE LIÈVRE

faber and faber

This edition first published in 2008
by Faber and Faber Ltd
3 Queen Square, London wc1n 3au

Printed by CPI Antony Rowe, Eastbourne

A CIP record for this book is available from the British Library

ISBN 978-0-571-24352-5

To my family, friends and colleagues
—all of them—
since there is scarcely one who has
managed to avoid being embroiled in
some way in the enterprise
this book is affectionately dedicated

'I am myn owene womman, wel at ese'

Chaucer, *Troilus and Criseyde*

Please to explain Miss Wilmot a
person so conversant with trees interests me

Lord Ducie, writing to Lady Fitzhardinge, 12 January 1896

Contents

Plates

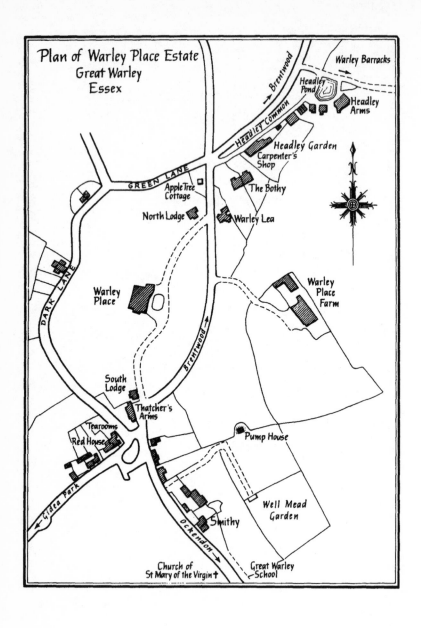

Plan of Warley Place Estate
Great Warley
Essex

Warley Barracks

Brentwood

Headley Pond

Headley Arms

Headley Common

Headley Garden

Carpenter's Shop

The Bothy

GREEN LANE

Apple Tree Cottage

North Lodge

Warley Lea

N

DARK LANE

Warley Place

Warley Place Farm

Brentwood

South Lodge

Thatcher's Arms

Tearooms

Red House

Pump House

Gidea Park

Well Mead Garden

Ockendon

Smithy

Great Warley School

Church of St Mary of the Virgin ✝

Introduction and Acknowledgements

Consulting nurserymen's catalogues for plants which would survive the darkest corner of my small London garden, I came once again on the name. I reached for the telephone and spoke to the Royal Horticultural Society's Lindley Library. 'Who *was* Miss Willmott?' I asked. An interval of a few seconds before the answer came indicated that I should perhaps already have known it. 'Is there a biography?' I asked idly, and hearing that there was not, replied with no hesitation and on heaven knows what inner prompting, 'Then I think I'll write one.' Here is the result. The story of Ellen Willmott's life has been a fascinating one to trace back to its beginnings, but not an easy one to present. For it early became clear that it would be impossible to set off good and bad qualities against each other to produce an average personality—for this would be the least appropriate way of describing her. Extravagant, impatient, brilliantly quick-minded, full of mirth and gaiety, and at the same time absolutely infuriating and quite impossible to deal with, are words which better catch the essence of her personality: nothing cancels out, and so everything, good and bad, has to go into this account. And if the result is untidy and contradictory, that is how her life went, and I hope that this book succeeds in reflecting too some of the brilliance and beauty with which that life was shot through.

I hardly know how to muster the names of everyone who has helped me, for the writing of the book has been very much a communal effort. First I must thank Miss Willmott's family—her great-nephew Mr John Berkeley, Mrs Berkeley, and her great-niece Miss Juliet Berkeley—for the help and hospitality they have given me, for allowing me access to material at Spetchley Park and for giving permission to quote from letters and to reproduce photographs and portraits in their possession.

Next I would like to thank two people who sustained me in the very early stages of writing: Mr James Lewis, then the Group Librarian at Brentwood, without whose encouragement this book would certainly never have left the ground, and Professor W. T. Stearn, who has made some very helpful suggestions about material for the book and about the form and content of the appendix, who very kindly made available to me the text of his article which appeared in *The Garden* in June 1979, and who reminded me, at a time when I was uncertain and flagging, that one learns on the job of writing. Mr Norman Carter, the present owner of Warley Place, has proved a mine of information, and has given generously of his time and much practical help beside: he has patiently answered questions, lent documents, searched archives, checked the part of my manuscript relating to the final sale of Warley Place, and tramped over the estate in all weathers to show me the skeleton of the house and the wraith of the garden. For all this I am deeply grateful.

And then there are the estate children, whose reminiscences have provided some of the most vivid and rewarding detail of the book and whose lives I have tried to record in the 'Leaf-mould Pit' chapter and elsewhere: Mrs Nellie Skinner (*née* Preece), Mrs May Mileham (*née* Hurcombe), Jim Robinson (son of Robinson, the butler) and his sister-in-law Mrs Florence Robinson, Mrs Charles Preece and Miss Eileen Preece, and also the family of Jacob Maurer, especially Max Maurer. Mrs Annie Carter (*née* Cotterell) has enlivened Chapter XI with memories, still clear and fresh, of her time as Miss Willmott's housekeeper, and Mr Hugh Balls has added to the story his experience of the life of a young gardener at Warley Place in 1914.

John Russell and the late Mrs Marjorie Sedgwick (*née* Russell), once of Stubbers, Romford, and David Rolt, once of The Glen, have described, graphically and invaluably, the impact of Ellen Willmott's personality on their own lives and on the community in which she lived. I am grateful to David Rolt too for his permission to use much of the material included in the memories of Ellen Willmott compiled by Mrs Sedgwick, Miss Pamela Russell and himself, and deposited in the Essex Record Office. Cynthia, Lady Sandys, who as a child and young woman knew Ellen Willmott well, has contributed a perceptive and colourful account of her.

Lord Aberconway and the staff of the Royal Horticultural Society have been of the greatest help; and in particular I should like to thank

Mr P. F. Stageman and Dr Brent Elliott of the Lindley Library. The quality of the library service which they have given, and the sympathetic interest which they have shown in the progress of the book, have spurred me on in many a period of doldrums. I am grateful too to Miss Elspeth Napier for advice on plant names and other botanical matters.

My friend Susan Dicks deserves more thanks than she is actually getting for patiently ferrying us both by car to Tresserve and thence to Boccanegra (via 'I Giardini Hanbury'), for standing by at many emergencies and also for acting as official photographer to the expedition. Monsieur André Blin, Mayor of Tresserve, welcomed us kindly and helped with much useful information, accompanying us to visit '*quelques vieilles personnes*' who remembered Ellen Willmott. As a result of this visit I made contact with Madame Yvonne Nicolai (daughter of the schoolmistress at Tresserve) and with Madame la Baronne de Buttet (grand-daughter of the Mayor of Tresserve in Ellen Willmott's time), both of whom have given me valuable information about the Château and its establishment.

Mrs Rona Hurst has helped with constant encouragement, and in providing much explanatory material on cytogenetics as well as on other matters of background interest; and she has suggested many useful contacts. Mr E. F. Allen, lately President of the Royal National Rose Society, has patiently answered many questions in the field of rose work, and Mrs Betty Massingham kindly allowed me to quote from her biography of Miss Jekyll a letter written by Miss Willmott to Mr Cowley. My friend Mrs Ann Morley cheerfully gave time to undertaking searches into the Fell family history, and with her husband helped in providing information on Roman roads and those who travelled on them. Mr Desmond Hill, Director of W. E. Hill & Sons, violin-makers, has kindly given me information on Miss Willmott's Amati instruments, and has traced the ownership of the Willemotte Guarneri. Mr Warren G. Ogden Jnr, Hon. Historian of the Society of Ornamental Turners, has very kindly provided me with extensive information on Holtzapffel lathes. Mrs Fox has allowed me to use material from the thesis she wrote on Ellen Willmott for a City and Guilds examination.

My thanks are due to the staffs of the Royal Botanic Gardens, Kew, the National Botanic Gardens, Glasnevin (especially Dr Charles Nelson), the Royal Botanic Garden, Edinburgh, and the Arnold

Arboretum. The staff at the Southwark Collection in Borough High Street, particularly the Librarian, Miss Boast, have provided many useful suggestions and references to throw light on the Willmott family's Southwark days; and the Essex Record Office have been similarly helpful with later material concerning Warley Place. The kindly welcome and help provided at the University Botanic Garden, Cambridge, by Dr Max Walters and his staff remains a pleasant memory.

The late Mrs Gillian Morris has provided an invaluable source of information on Spring Grove in her College thesis on the district, and generously gave permission for me to make extensive use of the material which it contains. Miss Andrea Cameron, Librarian in charge of Local Studies at the Hounslow Public Library, has been most helpful in providing other material relating to the Spring Grove area.

I must also thank Mr John R. Murray of Messrs John Murray for his help and courtesy in allowing me to see correspondence relating to the publication of *The Genus Rosa*, and for permission to quote from this.

No. 82 Borough High Street has reverted to occupation by a firm of solicitors: Messrs Simpson Millar, successors in title to a firm which may well have been a rival of Messrs Hawks, Stokes & McKewan, have kindly allowed me to see the rooms in which Frederick Willmott and his partners worked.

Shortly before her death in the early summer of 1978 Miss Alice Coats lent me the papers on Ellen Willmott which she had collected for a projected short biography, and gave me her permission to use them, and her blessing on the work. This is now most gratefully acknowledged.

A host of others have helped with information, reminiscences, background material, checking references, and many other things; lack of space precludes mentioning them all but they will, I hope, see from the shape and progress of the story the value of the contribution which they have made.

Finally, it remains for me to thank my publishers for their unfailing support during the last eighteen months while this book has been in preparation: they cannot have had an easy ride with so unfledged a writer.

NOTE ON THE PLANT NAMES

Many plant names have been taken from hand-written records which are not always easily legible, and where the style used is often not according to today's practice. I have tried always to give the correct version, except where using direct quotation. Where plant names have been changed, I have given the modern form in parentheses.

CHAPTER I

Boro' to Spring Grove

> I was so young when the seeds came to Warley that I had
> not the sense to enquire where they came from. I must
> have been about nine at the time. My Father's friend had
> been all over the world and I remember in one letter he
> said 'give these Rose seeds to your little girl for her
> garden.' I had a passion for sowing seeds and was very
> proud when I found out the difference between beads and
> seeds and gave up sowing the former.

And so, at this early age, the die was cast and Ellen Ann Willmott
became a gardener. Not, however, at Warley to start with, for she
seems to have got her dates mixed up, but at Heston in Middlesex,
where the Frederick Willmotts first set up house.

Nowadays, to most people, Heston means London Airport. Even
to those who have come upon Vicarage Farm Nurseries and pon-
dered how Vicarage Farm could ever have existed in such surroundings, that small remaining enclave of market garden a stone's throw
from the busy Great West Road seems an anachronism. But in 1856
things were different, and this was the year in which Ellen Fell, of
Aylesbury, married Frederick Willmott, solicitor, of Southwark, on
15 May at the new Roman Catholic Church of Holy Trinity, Brook
Green. Their witnesses were Frederick's mother, Sarah Willmott,
and two of Mrs Fell's cousins—Joseph Tasker of Middleton Hall,
Shenfield, and his daughter Helen Ann, who comes to play an
important part in this story. Helen Tasker also had a house in
Hammersmith—Kendal Villa—and it was from this house that the
wedding took place. Why Ellen Fell was not married from the family
home in Aylesbury is a mystery for which no ready explanation
offers itself. Ellen Fell's mother had been born a member of the

prominent Catholic family of Tasker, so that Ellen herself was presumably a 'cradle Catholic'. The Willmott family apparently belonged to the Church of England, but Frederick had most probably become a Catholic by the time of his marriage.

The young couple. Frederick Willmott was born on 21 November 1825 at No. 83 Borough High Street, within sight of London Bridge and in a part of the City (for as Bridge Ward Without it counted, except in certain respects concerning the election of aldermen, as part of the City) which saw and took note of all the comings and goings along this busy, lively highway into London. In Roman times travellers had used this route on their way to the Roman settlement at the foot of London Bridge, and Chaucer's pilgrims had gathered at the Tabard Inn to start on their leisurely road to Canterbury. In the early eighteenth century the row of tall houses which included the Willmotts' was just being built. There was a constant stir about the place as the hop factors moved busily to and from their business at the Hop Exchange in Borough Road; Frederick Willmott's father did not take part directly in this bustle, but he was a well-placed onlooker in his prosperous chemist's shop.

The origins of the Willmott family are obscure, but the first mention of their arrival in Southwark appears in the 1792 Rate Book for the Parish of St Saviour (now the Anglican Cathedral): here, in the fine italic hand of the period, William and James Willmott are recorded as resident at 83 High Street, Southwark. This William was Frederick Willmott's grandfather, and he has left behind him no trace of his occupation: he vanishes from this narrative now, it only remaining to relate that with him to Southwark he brought his son William, then only eighteen months old. In 1821 this second William, then aged thirty-one, made what must have been an excellent and prudent match with a girl whom he had probably known nearly all his life: Sarah Monnery, aged twenty-one, eldest daughter of William Monnery, the prosperous glover and hosier at No. 53 Borough High Street. The wedding took place at the Parish Church of St Saviour on 21 June 1821, well witnessed by a crowd of Monnery relations. There were no Willmott witnesses: presumably there were no members of the family on the spot.

Although the Willmott living-quarters were at No. 83 Borough High Street, the chemist's business is not recorded in directories until 1817, and then it was carried on at No. 317. It must therefore have been bought, or started from scratch (most likely the latter, as there is no evidence of the family having money to spare for investment) by the second William before his marriage to Sarah Monnery. In 1827, however, the surgeon and accoucheur, Robert Rowley, who had occupied the ground floor of No. 83, moved out: the chemist's shop moved in, and the Willmott family were at last in triumphant possession of the whole house. William may have served an apprenticeship in his trade, but equally he need not have done; his name does not appear in the records of the Society of Apothecaries. In the Census of 1831 he described himself, in a good firm hand, as 'Chemist and Druggist'—but in those days anyone could set up as such without formal qualification.

No. 83 Borough High Street was a tall house, with a narrow frontage but running well back from the street into the yard of the Queen's Head Inn: the house (renumbered to 103 around 1872) still stands, but the inn is no more. Here the four Willmott boys were born: William, the eldest, on 27 June 1822, followed by Charles on 21 January 1824, Frederick on 21 November 1825 and, after a gap of five years, the youngest, Edwin, on 10 November 1830. All of them were christened at St Saviour's Church.

The household was busy and lively. Two servants helped Sarah with the house and the children, and in the shop William employed two assistants, one of whom, John Hugill, became a loyal and trusted family friend. In due course young William joined his father as an apprentice: the business flourished, the name of Willmott becoming well known for patent remedies—Willmott's Antibilious or Family Pills, Willmott's Digestive Lozenges, Cough Pills, Quinine and Iron Wine, Universal Liniment, Corn & Bunion Plaisters, and Antiscorbutic Tincture—there seemed no end to them, and all were in great demand.

It is sad to record that in December 1836, at just about the time when his second son, Charles, was starting his apprenticeship, William died, aged only forty-seven. To the Willmott household this was a hard blow to sustain. It was fortunate that William before his death had asked John Hugill to stay on at Willmotts and manage the business until the boys were ready to assume responsibility. This promise was faithfully kept, and it was not until 1848, when young William was twenty-six and Charles twenty-four, that John Hugill felt free to leave them. He would, in any case, be near at hand if advice was needed. It was fortunate, too, that Sarah was a capable woman, and once the immediate shock was past she took over at least the titular management of the business. No doubt she had the Monnery family solidly behind her. Her two elder sons were safely and usefully apprenticed in the business, and it is to be hoped that the lot of an apprentice, which in those days was a hard one, was softened somewhat as it was all a family affair. Apprentices working for a master outside their own family usually lived in, working long hours, with the shop's closing time often not until eight o'clock at night. Their special task was traditionally the making of pills (large stocks of the proprietor's special pills being needed), but they also had to learn the arts of dispensing, labelling and sealing mixtures, and of spreading plaisters. It was a trade needing skill and application, and its practitioners often gained a good basic knowledge of botany and chemistry.

There was, however, the question of Sarah's third son, Frederick. It seems likely that Frederick was the brightest of the brothers, and it was decided that he should become a solicitor—not, one would imagine, without a certain amount of agonizing, because to have a solicitor in the family was an entirely new departure for the Willmotts. Moreover, the premium at that time averaged 200 guineas, with a stamp duty of £120, which must have seemed to them astronomic. It was a bold decision, and barely two months after his fifteenth birthday, Frederick left school and, under his mother's aegis, entered into five-year articles with his father's friend, Richard Carpenter Smith. Smith practised in Bridge Street, Southwark, as an Attorney of Her Majesty's Court of Queen's Bench and Common Pleas and a Solicitor of the High Court of Chancery. The articles were dated 9 January 1841. They did not run smoothly: on 29 March 1845 Richard Carpenter Smith 'did at the request of the same Frederick Willmott assign set over and transfer the services of the said Frederick Willmott for all the residue and remainder then to come and unexpired of the said term of 5 years'. With this, Frederick moved to the offices of Josiah Wilkinson at No. 6 Queen Street, Cheapside, in the City of London. Behind this act, which demonstrates a certain moral toughness, lies a remarkable story.

When Frederick's father made his will he named his friend Richard Carpenter Smith one of his executors and trustees, and as the other executor, Frederick Heath, for reasons unknown declined to act,

Smith proved the will alone. It seems, however, that he did not properly carry out the duties of a trustee as specified by the will, and with Frederick as a kind of hostage, the Willmott family must have entered into a period of acute difficulty and stress. Eventually, an inquisition was held on 8 and 9 August 1845, as a result of which Smith was declared of unsound mind—this state being deemed to have begun on 2 April, which makes one wonder what sort of precipitating incident that date had witnessed. A complicated deed survives which sets out the details of the settlement finally releasing Richard Carpenter Smith's widow, Elizabeth, from further restitution to the Willmotts. Smith's duties as trustee had required him to convert all but the personal and household effects of his friend into money which was to be invested and the income paid to Sarah Willmott for her lifetime. The extent to which this was actually carried out is unclear. Two interesting facts, however, emerge: one, that Sarah was evidently buying the chemist's business from the estate for a fixed sum covering the lease, goodwill and stock (probably £2,000), apparently using money borrowed from the trust funds, the income from which she was to enjoy for life, and with which, of course, she had to support her family until her sons came of age. The second point was that William had had the foresight to insure his life for £1,000—a very large sum for those days, but probably (and wisely) taken out against just such an eventuality.

No record remains of who drew up the deed of release, but Frederick must have been involved, if not directly then surely from the sidelines, and perhaps using the services of the firm to which he had been articled. It was a difficult exercise for a young articled clerk, and one very creditably handled. The deed is dated 26 April 1847—it had taken the Willmott family more than ten years to extract themselves from the financial and legal tangle. Now, at last, they were able to pursue their individual lives without the ever-present problem. Edwin, who had joined his brothers as an apprentice in the early 1840s, added lustre to the family record by passing two of the examinations of the Pharmaceutical Society of Great Britain, granted the Royal Charter in 1843: these were the Classical (November 1848) and the Minor (April 1849). He was thus the only one of the three brothers who held a proper qualification, for neither William, nor Charles (too busy, proud or lazy to bother with examinations), nor, it will be remembered, their father before them, had been a member of the Society of Apothecaries, the body which governed the profession before the Pharmaceutical Society was founded. Frederick, meanwhile, had completed his articles without further incident and was duly admitted as a Solicitor in the Queen's Bench on 17 November 1846. He had done well to pass the final examination in the troubled circumstances in which he had found himself; and, since he had been working for a man who was subsequently declared insane, it seems likely that his 'training' consisted of learning the hard way by helping William Weston, the clerk, to conduct the business of the office on his principal's behalf. Frederick probably continued for the first two or three years after admission in the offices of Josiah Wilkinson, thoroughly experiencing himself in his profession. Then, in 1848, he felt ready to launch out. In August he took a final long break and went on a walking holiday in the north of Scotland with his brother Charles and a friend, and on his return he set up in sole practice. He rented offices at No. 82 Borough High Street, next door to his home, apparently taking them over from Messrs Russell & McKenzie, also solicitors. Probably he acquired their goodwill: certainly, his neighbourhood connections must have brought him a great deal of work.

No. 82 is another tall house, built in the early 1700s, with four floors and premises extending well back from the street frontage. Young Frederick shared the house with Messrs Humble & Craster, hop and seed merchants, paying rent for the rooms he used, which presumably were those on the first floor. The main room on this floor made an excellent office for a solicitor—a large, light room occupying the width of the house, with three tall, graceful windows, unpolished oak panelling giving an air of richness, and a moulded ceiling and chimney-piece. And the grandstand view of everything that was happening in the Borough High Street must have given the young solicitor, when bored or at leisure, constant distraction and amusement. Also there was the roof, from which a splendid panoramic view of all London could be seen spread out below. It must have been impressive for clients.

Frederick Willmott appears to have been one of those who are born with an irresistible urge upwards. In this he was well served by his chosen profession. Attorneys and solicitors of his time were acutely sensitive about their status and reputation. Always, and latterly quite unjustly, regarded as in every way inferior to members of the Bar, solicitors were jealous of their right to describe them-selves as 'gentlemen', a right said to be implied, rather than confer-red, by the Attorneys and Solicitors Act of 1729. During the nineteenth century the profession itself, in putting its house in order in matters of conduct, discipline and qualifications, was determined to prove that attorneys were gentlemen in reality, and not only by law. Even in 1847, when as a very young solicitor he had signed the indenture of release for Elizabeth Smith (in handwriting almost identical with his daughter Ellen's), Frederick alone caused himself to be described as 'gentleman', while his brothers—William in a spidery hand, Charles writing very elegantly, and Edwin very heav-ily, with blots—were simply and accurately described as chemists and druggists. (In fact it was only the last of these three brothers to die—Charles, in 1902—and then only on his death certificate, who attained the dignity of the description of 'gentleman'.) Frederick seemed to have his sights on a different life style, and we find him in May 1856 well embarked on a promising career and on the brink of an auspicious marriage.

He had chosen to marry Ellen Fell. She had been brought up in Aylesbury and came from a family of prosperous merchants; her father, James Fell, who died when she was very young, had been a lace merchant. Her mother, born Ellen Tasker, was remarried shortly after James's death—to Thomas Fell, a relation of her late husband. Four children were born of this second mar-riage—Adelaide, Rebecca, Charles and Robert (who died in infancy). Thomas Fell was in the corn trade and perhaps it was in this way that a connection was established with Southwark, and that his step-daughter made the acquaintance of young Frederick Willmott. Another possibility is that the two may have met through one of the Fell relations, George, who was a solicitor. But however the meeting may have taken place, the auguries were good. And Frederick Will-mott had before him on marriage exactly the same choice as an up-and-coming young professional man has today: should he live centrally within easy reach of his office, so that he could spend time at home; or should he settle his family in a pleasant house with a garden, in a country district, where children could grow up in peaceful surroundings away from the grime of London? He chose the latter. Probably he had ambitions to rise in the social scale, but, more important, he may have hoped for the best of both worlds—the bustle and liveliness of the Boro' by day, and peace and quiet (and gentility) in the evenings. Again like his modern counterpart, he narrowed his choice to an area served by the railway which terminated at Waterloo Station, built in 1848, and lying not a mile from the Borough High Street office.

His search was rewarded when he found the new housing development at Spring Grove, Heston, and he and his young wife were able to move in to Vernon House, 52 The Grove, shortly after their marriage. With hindsight, it seems propitious that an early owner of Spring Grove House, built about 1756 on the site of earlier houses, was the distinguished botanist Sir Joseph Banks, who when he was in England divided his time between his London house in Soho Square and his country mansion in Heston. Spring Grove enjoyed the great advantage of nearness to Kew Gardens, which Banks had been commissioned by the King to develop as a centre for botanical activities. Perhaps Helen Tasker told her cousin of the Spring Grove development and encouraged the young couple to think of settling there, as it was so close to Hammersmith; or Frederick Willmott may have had professional dealings with Henry Davies, a lawyer and speculator who had bought and developed the estate. Either way, both Ellen and Frederick would have eagerly scanned the notice which appeared in the *Illustrated London News* in May 1855, and which read: 'This ESTATE, comprising an area of nearly 300 acres, finely wooded, has been recently laid out for Villas and commodious and handsome Detached Residences . . . with Lawns, Gardens, and Private Enclosures of half an acre, or one or two acres. . . . Every advantage has been taken of the situation on which the property stands to secure the most perfect drainage for all the houses. Each house is well supplied with gas, and water. . . . The Rents vary from £50 to £250 per annum. . . . The South-Western Railway . . . has a Station within a few minutes' walk . . . and residents have the benefit of a large reduction in the price of Season Tickets.' The estate houses soon began to be let to City businessmen, professional men (including several from the legal profession) and retired officers of the Armed Forces.

Vernon House was not one of the most imposing houses in The Grove; it was demolished in 1975 to make way for a small block of flats, but Henry Davies's plan of 1852 together with an aerial photograph taken in the 1920s record its appearance, and its yellow-brick garden wall is still standing. Double-fronted, with three storeys, a basement, and a built-in coach-house, it faced, across a tree-lined road, the wooded grounds of Spring Grove House. In front, a carriage drive from each of the corner gates curved past lozenge-shaped flower beds and met at the front door. Behind the house, a formal garden of about three-quarters of an acre, with neat flower beds, was planned by Davies. How long it stayed like that, if indeed it ever reached that point, will never be known—but it is certain that young Mrs Willmott, already a dedicated and innovative gardener, the third generation in her family, held strongly contrary views on the Victorian practices of carpet bedding and ribbon borders.

It was indeed a pleasant house to come to in 1856. Spring Grove was in fact one of the earliest estates to be purpose-built to cater for the rising class of London commuters, and it served that purpose admirably. The Willmotts settled in happily, and on 19 August 1858 their first child, a daughter, was born. Ellen Ann was named for her mother, Ellen, and her godmother, Helen Ann Tasker, and she was christened in the Shrewsbury Chapel on 4 September by the parish priest, Father Francis Weld, a member of the ancient and influential Roman Catholic family from Lulworth in Dorset. The other god-parent was John Basil Barrett, of whom nothing else is known but this one fact. Ellen was followed by Rose (born 29 September 1861) and Ada Mary (born 2 June 1864).

Little detail remains of the early days at Spring Grove, but it is known that all three girls went to school at Gumley House, a convent school run by the Sisters of the Order of the Faithful Companions of Jesus, where they were accorded the apparently extraordinary privilege of being day pupils. The school lay about a mile south of The Grove, opposite the Shrewsbury Chapel (which the family attended regularly). Presumably the girls went to and from school by coach: the school was fairly far away and it would have been thought undignified for middle-class children to go on foot to school past a number of small cottages; furthermore, to arrive at Gumley House (a very exclusive school) by any other means would certainly have lowered the children's stock in the eyes of their fellow pupils, who included the Princesses Blanche and Marguérite of Orléans. And yet . . . one wonders where Ellen picked up her habit in later life of walking everywhere. . . . It is intriguing to imagine a small child tramping home, caring little what others thought, because she was interested in what was growing in the cottage gardens. At Gumley House, the syllabus was limited and the nuns for the most part wrote their own text-books: but the subjects taught (with the obvious exception of embroidery) formed a fair basis for Ellen's later interests on which she herself—and possibly other teachers—could build. They included English with emphasis on literature, French language and literature, history, the use of the globes, botany, drawing, oil painting and embroidery. (In view of Ellen's later handling of money, the absence of arithmetic from the curriculum is to be regretted.)

Although direct evidence is scarce, some is available and from this some assumptions can safely be made. Frederick and Ellen Willmott were a lively and pleasant couple and their house was comfortable if not yet luxurious. They kept three servants: cook, housemaid and nurse; and they were young staff, the oldest not more than thirty. (The Willmotts seem, unexpectedly, to have had a source of supply in Wiltshire.) Probably a good deal of entertaining went on: certainly members of the family came to stay, for at the time of the 1871 Census, Frederick's younger brother, Edwin, was resident. There was certainly plenty going on in the neighbourhood, particularly in the 1870s, and a local magazine Our *Neighbourhood* records the existence of the Spring Grove Literary and Music Society and some of its doings. In these years too, the foundations of the magnificent library of rare books at Warley Place must have been laid. The famous music-room was certainly also taking shape, for Ellen, apparently on her sixteenth birthday, received as a present from her father a piano which had belonged to Princess Amelia, the youngest child of George III and Queen Charlotte, who died as a young adult. Birthdays must indeed have been exciting as well as profitable occasions for the young Ellen, as from an early age—seven years old, it is said—she found each year on her plate at breakfast a cheque for £1,000 from her godmother. In later years Rose too received a similar present. It is hard to appreciate the truly munificent scale of such a gift in those days—the equivalent of about £15,000 in today's terms—enough to make Ellen a very rich woman by the time she was twenty-one.

Ellen, Rose and Ada little realized how narrowly they avoided the transformation of their comfortable life into sudden indigence. Around 1870 a number of the residents of Spring Grove were concerned in an unwise piece of speculation involving investments in the Anglo-Florence Land Company, which built houses and offices in Florence, vacated when the seat of government moved to Rome. The Agra Bank of India, the head of which was Lewis Balfour, a local resident and uncle of Robert Louis Stevenson, also closed its doors at about this time. This was serious, as it held the mortgages on most of the large houses in Spring Grove: a number of residents suffered heavy financial losses and had to leave the district. Many of these larger houses remained untenanted for some years, and the area underwent a period of depression from which it only began to emerge in the late 1880s—helped by the construction of the new District Railway line from Acton to Hounslow Town in 1883, which brought in its wake a new type of resident for the area, and the building of a number of smaller villas.

But Frederick Willmott, a competent financier as well as a sound solicitor, seems to have kept out of the embroilment. His finances must have shown a sharp upturn in the early 1870s, and here we encounter the first of many persistent tales which from then onwards were to cling to the Willmott name like iron filings to a magnet. From several different sources comes the story that Frederick Willmott made a small fortune by selling land for the building of Liverpool Street Station. The relevant British Rail Property Board Lists of Deed Extracts, however, show no sign of any such transaction between the railway companies then involved and Willmott or his firm, or any recognizable nominee. So where then did the money come from? Firstly from the firm. The timing of Frederick's entry into the legal profession had been opportune. His practice expanding, he went into partnership in 1859 with Robert Shafto Hawks; and a third partner, James John Stokes, joined the practice some time after 1861. As far as can be judged from surviving deeds, the firm undertook a good deal of conveyancing work, which was profitable in itself, and the suggestion has been made that the Liverpool Street rumour may have been based on the amount of conveyancing work which could have been undertaken by Messrs Hawks, Willmott and Stokes in connection with land purchased for the station area—the fees for which could have run into a very large sum of money. Liverpool Street or no, Frederick Willmott had certainly benefited from the consequences of the railway boom of the 1830s and 40s, the joint stock company boom of the 1860s and 70s, and the general increase in conveyancing business. And over the years he amassed a considerable amount of railway stock—Argentine Railways, New York Central Railway, the Metropolitan Railway and others. Further, at that time solicitors were much more closely involved in the investment of their clients' money, and this could have been a busy and profitable part of their business. As we shall see later, Frederick had a sure hand with money.

He also began to acquire property in Southwark, to add to the property in Aylesbury which his wife had brought with her as part of her marriage settlement: warehouses in Great Guildford Street and Newcomen Street could be let without difficulty to bring in a steady income. In addition, he came into money at the death of his mother, Sarah Willmott. In 1855 she had left Borough High Street and settled in a house in Conduit Street, Paddington, with Edwin, her youngest son, who for a while carried on in practice as a chemist there, before changing over to become a salesman of medical supplies. Sarah died in 1866, and under the terms of her husband's will the capital which had provided her with an income for life now fell to be divided up between their four sons.

The resulting increased affluence of the Frederick Willmotts must have seemed in such sharp contrast to the dejected air which had come over the neighbourhood of Spring Grove in the 1870s following the departure of some of the more interesting residents, that it may well have influenced the Willmotts' thoughts towards devoting some of their capital to the purchase of a country house suitable to their social position and financial standing. They had, moreover, to consider the future of their daughters: it might well be difficult to find suitable matches for them in the immediate neighbourhood, and it would seem sensible, if a move were contemplated, to think in terms of an area where a much larger proportion of the gentry (and gentry it had to be, now) were members of the Roman Catholic Church. And Ellen Ann, at least, was showing signs of individuality as well as beauty which would need a much more powerful setting to show to advantage.

While these half-formulated thoughts were stirring there came a sudden calamity which propelled matters to a dramatic conclusion. Early in 1872 the youngest sister, Ada, complained of fever and a sore throat. She had diphtheria. This was at that time nothing out of the ordinary, and it appears that the 'perfect drainage' mentioned in the *Illustrated London News* may have proved rather less than perfect in the event. Whether this was the cause of the child's illness it is impossible to say: there were certainly other girls at Gumley House affected at the time. January and February of 1872 were mild and wet, traditionally the weather most likely to favour the spread of contagious diseases, and yet there is no mention in the local newspapers of an epidemic. Ada fought the illness staunchly for six weeks, so staunchly that in the end it was not diphtheria as such, but the onset of kidney failure, which finally defeated her. She certainly could not have been an ailing child: she must already have been a personality in her own right, with a strong hold on life, for she was remembered years afterwards by the Sisters at Gumley House. Her death on 15 February, with the long struggle leading up to it, was the first serious disaster the family had faced, and the detail that it was the nursemaid who went to register the death seems to reflect the apathy and exhaustion of the rest of the household. Ada was buried in the Sisters' cemetery. The weather cannot have helped a return to normal cheerful life: April started with thunderstorms, and May was the wettest and coldest on record, with snow falling on the 12th.

So it seems reasonable to believe that the Willmotts were ready to leave Vernon House and its mixed memories, and that Frederick Willmott's compassion for his wife's distress and his desire to help her pull out of it crystallized his determination to show a grander face to the world than the modest suburban elegance of the Spring Grove house allowed. But he was a man of sound sense, knew his own limitations, and decided that a solid country background would be preferable to a grand town house in London, especially as his daughters had both inherited their mother's passionate interest in gardens. And he himself, although town-bred, felt an urge to own stock of a kind other than financial—though the profit basis of farming would always loom large for him. So they began to look for a country house. For Frederick's work it would, of course, have been best to keep to a part of the country served by trains from Waterloo, but eventually, in 1875, it was the notice of an auction at Great Warley in Essex which caught, and held, their attention. It said:

THE RESIDENCE
is a
HANDSOME, SUBSTANTIALLY BUILT STRUCTURE

Approached by a Carriage Drive with Two Entrance Lodges, and in every way suited for the
occupation of a family of the highest respectabil-
ity . . . [and so on, at length]

All at once, things fell into place. What could possibly be a more
suitable area, near to London, close to the Tasker home at Shenfield,
in country which was familiar to Mrs Willmott from her girlhood,
and on a site avowed to be the healthiest in Essex? And further, it was
in Catholic country: the Petres of Thorndon Hall, an old Catholic
family who had never reneged on their faith through all the vicis-
situdes of previous centuries of persecution, and the presence of
Catholic missioners in their household had ensured that the surrounding population had maintained its strong Catholic element.
J. S. Lescher, a founder member of the Pharmaceutical Society, and
presumably a member of the family living at Boyles Court, near
Warley, may have encouraged the Willmotts to buy, if he did not
actually tell Frederick of the impending sale.

The auction took place on 4 November 1875. The Willmott family
enjoyed Christmas: Warley Place was theirs.

CHAPTER II

And then to Warley

Walking over his own acres at last on a fine frosty January morning, noting the weather as later he always did in his diaries, Frederick Willmott must have felt pride and satisfaction. When he stood on the crest of the land in front of the house he could see over the hedgerows, sprigged with hawthorn and elder, down through the clear air south-eastwards over the Laindon Hills and beyond them to the hills of Kent twenty miles away. Moving slowly through the garden to halt by the seven tall Spanish chestnuts, he would have seen with enormous pleasure the distant dome of St Paul's, and felt as though, far from Southwark as he was, he in some sense held the busy Borough High Street and all its activities in the hollow of his hand. With what wonder and excitement, tinged with doubt, would old William Willmott have regarded his son's rise in the world—and how great the change from 83 Borough High Street to Warley Place, Essex. It was nearly thirty years since the young and confident Frederick had caused 'gentleman' to be so firmly written after his name, and now this had proved to be a self-fulfilling prophecy—though not without a good deal of vigorous shoving from Frederick himself. His effort and industry had culminated in his ownership, while still in full vigour at fifty years old, of this entirely suitable and satisfactory property.

The Warley Place Estate, which at that time covered about thirty-three acres, once formed part of the Manor of Warley Abbess, which until the Dissolution was the property of Barking Abbey, and there-after fell to the Gonson family, the last of whom, Benjamin Gonson, was Treasurer of the Navy. The Manor was then divided between Benjamin's four daughters, and the northern part, which is said to have contained the Abbey's sanatorium and its fish ponds, was in the course of time bought by John Evelyn, the diarist. But Evelyn never lived at Warley, and after six years, in 1665, sold it because of the intolerable burden of taxes which it imposed upon him. The story persists that Evelyn planted the Spanish chestnuts, laid out the garden, sowed the early English crocus (*Crocus vernus*) in the meadow, and began writing his *Sylva* at Warley Place. There is no proof for any of this, though it is a happy idea. The house of the Willmotts' day dated from Queen Anne's time. Brick-built, with pedimented front and portico entrance, it was described in the sale catalogue as 'a Handsome and Substantially-erected Residence, Occupying an elevated position, overlooking Pleasure Grounds and Gardens of great beauty'. The pleasure grounds lay to the south of the house, running gently downhill to the South Pond and the Lodge; to the north-west stood the old walled garden, beyond it the daffodil banks and farther still the old fish ponds. Stables and out-buildings of all kinds abutted the house on its northern side, with the old orchard garden lying to the north-east and bounded by a high wall and the main road. A driveway ran through the prop-erty, guarded by a lodge at each end, north and south; the whole was encircled by meadows with names like Hoppit and Doll's Meadow.

Passing through various ownerships, Warley Place was bought, probably in the 1860s from Frederick Francis, a solicitor, by two elderly gentlemen, Antony G. Robinson, described as a ship-owner, and George Whyting, described as the manager of an insurance company. They lived at Warley Place with a small staff. No trace remains of any opinion of them, how they lived, or whether they developed the estate: so it seems a fair assumption that they achieved no changes of note at Warley, and that the garden was thereafter ripe for the attentions of Mrs Willmott and her daughters. But before the family could move in, some changes must be made—the house redecorated and in particular the drainage checked, so that there would be no repetition of the tragedy of Ada. Turning towards the empty mansion, Frederick fell to planning.

As spring came, work began on the house. Frederick and Ellen had decided that a new wing was needed—or rather, perhaps, that they wanted, and could afford, a new wing. Its extent, at least on the upper floors, can be judged by comparing the 1875 sale catalogue with the catalogue of the final sale sixty years later, making allow-ances for the differing descriptive terminology of the estate agents.

Two bedrooms, two dressing-rooms, a store-room, linen cupboard, an extra WC, and a small room later used by Ellen Ann as a dark-room, were added. To a modern eye a conspicuous omission was that Frederick Willmott did not think of adding a second bathroom: copper cans, lovingly polished and laboriously carried up from the basement and left with a neatly folded towel on top of each, were good enough for the Willmotts, and each bedroom had its washstand and basin. (The existing bathroom did, however, boast a fireplace, and if indeed a fire was ever lit there, this would have been a luxury to be envied by many a modern household.) Five bedrooms were added on the second floor: evidently a largish resident staff was envisaged. On the ground floor some rethinking must have been done, and a fittingly grandiose lay-out was produced. The original entrance hall, drawing-room, dining-room, morning-room, and gentlemen's room (presumably renamed 'study') were augmented by a library, music-room, winter garden and oratory. The kitchen, butler's rooms, servants' hall, and other domestic offices, must therefore have been moved from the west side of the house to a new position along the corridor on the north side, beyond a baize door. Again comparing the two sale catalogues, conversion rather than addition seems probable, but in this part of the house matters have been complicated by a dramatic event of the early 1900s which makes a direct comparison impossible—'the kitchen going downstairs'.

In early prints the house looks unfamiliar and stark, bare of climbing plants and with some rather ragged shrubbery and an acacia occupying the ground in front of it: the Willmotts planted climbers against the house to soften the difference between the old and the new brick, and a vine by the front door with the deeply incised leaf which appears so often in Italian decorations and embroidery. Another of the persistent rumours which clung to the Willmott family was that Frederick Willmott caused the highway to Brentwood, which used to pass immediately in front of the mansion, to be diverted to its present position, to preserve the privacy of the family; but close examination of contemporary maps and of the sale plan shows that the road was most probably moved during the period 1866–75, and certainly before the house was put up for sale. It is, however, quite possible that Frederick Willmott stopped villagers walking home by a short cut along his driveway, for privacy's sake, just as he refused a request from the village cricket team to use Doll's

Meadow once a week for cricket practice. He did not seem to mind being unpopular in what was to him a good cause!

It will not have escaped the observant reader that all these changes were directed towards achieving an establishment in which a gentleman could live with his family in considerable style, watch his estate grow in size and prosperity before his eyes, see his children and grandchildren around him and know that the dynasty he had founded would live there for ever. Fortunate indeed that no one can see ahead.

A firm line has been drawn through the name Willmott in the Heston district electoral register dated July 1876, so it seems likely that they were at Warley in time for Ellen's eighteenth birthday on 19 August 1876. Perhaps they had tea on the lawn and looked at their domain and talked excitedly of the changes they would make in the garden, beginning with the autumn planting. Both Ellen, having left school, and Rose, nearly fifteen years old, looked forward keenly to having a really large garden to work in: already Ellen's gifts lay in the direction of acquiring a solid botanical background, whereas Rose, in her sister's description of her, had that 'rare taste in effective grouping' which led her to work on the herbaceous borders at Warley Place; these stayed essentially in the pattern which she set for them until the estate was sold for the last time. But that was a long time in the future. In 1876, Mrs Willmott was still full of energy and her daughter writes that many an old favourite Essex plant, missing from the Warley Garden, had to be hunted out of other gardens all over the county. Ellen speaks of her mother's 'old home, Fitzwalters, where the gardens remained as they had been for generations'. Mrs Willmott must, evidently, have spent part of her childhood with her cousin Helen at this house where the Tasker family had lived from 1823 to 1839. Much of the work of collecting must surely have fallen to Ellen and Rose, for Mrs Willmott had a hundred and one other tasks to occupy her. There were still domestic staff to be engaged, and since she had no housekeeper to help her, she must herself have dealt with the remaining furnishings and appointments of the house. There was a formidable amount of it—Hepplewhite and Chippendale furniture in plenty, and whole services of Familie Verte, Ming, Royal Worcester and Delft. There were clocks all over the house, including one made by Webster, a pupil of the famous Tompion, and an 'Alarum Clock' by James McCabe, Royal Exchange, London,

1756, with an inscribed silver plate: 'Found in Shurfoodowlah's House, Lucknow, on the 17th March 1858.' Perhaps Frederick Willmott collected clocks, as he evidently collected snuffboxes. In the early days a great deal had to be bought to fill so much space. So Ellen and Rose went to sales at big houses in the neighbourhood, bringing home 'no end of things' with them in the pony chaise, some of which were paid for and 'given' to them by Helen Tasker. The later accumulation must have been the result of years of discriminating buying for investment as well as pleasure.

While all this activity was taking place, Frederick Willmott was grappling with the problem of his much longer and less convenient journey to work. To begin with, he commuted daily to the Borough High Street office, returning home to be met by the brougham at Brentwood Station, and falling asleep so soundly in his chair after dinner that the footman was able to remove his boots without awakening him. Exactly how he stood financially we do not know, but he must have been sufficiently wealthy to come to the decision, three years later, that he could afford to retire. Perhaps he had it at the back of his mind when the move to Warley had first been mooted, but it needed the disruption of routine to bring him finally to the point of decision. He and his partners, Robert Hawks and James John Stokes, had been joined by Ernest Frederick McKewan, probably on the latter's admission in 1877: it was thus perhaps time for one of the older partners to stand down. And in any case, although only fifty-four, Frederick had behind him a working life of nearly forty years, and may well have felt that it would henceforward be enough simply to keep in touch with the office. So for the rest of his life he spent five or six fairly leisurely days a month in London, transacting business for himself, his family, and one or two clients of long standing.

On these occasions some of his time would be spent at the Borough High Street office, giving instructions to Dixson, the clerk, who was gradually taking over the routine work on the Willmott finances; then perhaps a visit to the London Joint Stock Bank in Pall Mall 'to tear off coupons' from the sheets attached to all unregistered shares (then much more commonly held than now) to enable shareholders, on surrendering a coupon, to claim their dividends; after which he might call at Wheeler's to order claret or champagne, or at French & Muir to try on a suit of 'Cloathes' or a pair of 'Trowsers'. Lunch at the City Liberal Club (to which he was occasionally accompanied by his Monnery uncle, Edward) might be preceded by a visit to the Turkish baths and followed by a haircut and a visit to an old friend or client—George Humble perhaps, of Humble & Craster, who shared No. 82 Borough High Street when Frederick first set up in practice, or Harry Richards the stockbroker, or John Hugill of Meggeson & Co., to show him a letter from Charles or to discuss the affairs of William's brewery. Quite often his presence was required at Painters' Hall to attend a court or a dinner, and for a year he was Master of the Worshipful Company of Painters. The Grocers and Fishmongers also invited him to dine, and he took Ellie to a ball at the Fishmongers' Hall. Politically he was a firm and unswerving Liberal, recording in his diary that he voted for the Liberals in the City on 31 March 1880 and in East Surrey during April.

The Willmotts were constant and apparently indiscriminate theatregoers: everything from pantomime to Shakespeare entertained them. They saw *Aladdin* at the Gaiety, Mrs Langtry in *Ours*, Ellen Terry and Irving in *Romeo and Juliet*, *Iolanthe* at the Savoy, and also *Ici on parle français* ('H. A. T. [asker]'s treat'), *Les Cloches de Corneville* and *A Trip to the Moon* at Her Majesty's Theatre. When on his own Frederick Willmott usually gravitated towards a music hall or to the Vaudeville where he once saw *Confusion*, 'a very laughable piece', and in 1888 he went twice to see *Little Lord Fauntleroy*. Untutored as far as is known in the arts, he spent a surprising amount of time at the National Gallery, at Burlington House and at other galleries, and he bought pictures from Mr Colnaghi. Eventually he took a season ticket for Burlington House. Sometimes he went home by a late train, and sometimes slept at the Holborn Viaduct or Great Eastern Railway Hotels.

In spite of his London birth and upbringing, Frederick Willmott took easily to country pursuits. His diaries always start and finish with a methodical inventory of stock at Warley Place, and are dotted with items of country interest most oddly mixed in with news of weightier City matters—on one page 'Bank rate 3 per cent', and on the next 'set hen on eggs', 'had peaches for the first time from our own house', or 'bought 12 Mole Traps from Civil Service Stores'. The number of eggs laid by the Warley Place poultry is recorded each day. Everything was new and fascinating to Frederick: the building of the new coach-house in 1882 by Winter, a local builder; the new pigsty, and the affairs of its occupants: 'Sow Kitty brought forth 11 pigs'; the unexplained deaths of a brood of ducklings; and the occasion when he found 'a Carrion Crow playing up Old Gooseberry among my young poultry'. When foot-and-mouth disease came to Warley Place in 1883 its ravages are recorded in detail together with the precautions taken: 'Gave 3 of the Cows a dose of Salts and did all the feet with Stockholm Tar'—this treatment notwithstanding, Frederick Willmott had to send Jordan, the footman, post-haste on his bicycle to summon Henry Tunnage, who professed to be able to cure the disease, from Rainham.

The family loved dogs: Rose and her father visited the Battersea Dogs' Home, and both found it hard to resist impulse buying. Dick, a Yorkshire terrier, was bought in the Leadenhall Market, and another and more elegantly named terrier, Germano, caused acute anxiety in the Willmott household by his disappearance, eventually being retrieved from Romford on offer of a reward.

Once Warley Place was appointed to their satisfaction, carriages bought, and the indoor and outdoor staff working smoothly together, the Willmotts set out to achieve their place in county society. Here they were fortunate in having a sponsor in Helen Ann Tasker. Besides the useful-sized birthday presents which she gave to Ellen Ann and Rose (whom she treated as a second godchild), her gifts to charity were constant and she supported numerous Roman Catholic enterprises, concentrating particularly on the building of churches, orphanages and schools. In recognition of her generosity to the Church, Pope Pius XI had in 1870 created her a Countess of the Holy Roman States or Pontifical States—a signal honour and one which must have caused much satisfaction, both to her and to her Willmott cousins. Although she lived very quietly at Middleton Hall or at her town house, Kendal Villa, she was very well known in the Brentwood area, and so could ease the Willmotts' entry into local society. The family were often at Middleton Hall; they always spent Christmas there, and every Tuesday Helen Tasker drove over to Warley Place to spend the day with her cousin and godchildren. The Willmotts' close contact with the religious life of Brentwood, the parish priests and the Convent of the Sisters of Mercy there, was largely due to Helen Tasker. When the Willmott family went on holiday, it was she who paid the servants and kept an eye on how they were behaving, as well as on the house itself. Her god-daughters wrote her affectionate letters from foreign parts, telling her of the people they met, of theatres and museums, tea parties and painting lessons. She was a woman of great goodness, profoundly religious, genuinely charitable, and she exerted an immense influence on her godchildren's lives.

The Willmotts settled happily into the routine of the country: Frederick Willmott's diaries are the disingenuous record of a naturally happy man, with not much humour perhaps but not too much temperament either, and they set out the details of the comfortable and entirely unpretentious family life at Warley Place. Socially, life was exceedingly pleasant. Artlessly and with no sign of smugness and no feelings of patronage towards his Southwark friends, Frederick Willmott assumed the role of master of Warley Place, if not quite that of country gentleman. The two levels of his life came together without any difficulty: his City friends visited him at Warley, his Warley friends were invited to Livery Company dinners—though the diary records the occasion when Colonel Duberly of Warley was invited to accompany him to the Painters' Hall, but suffered an accident when his tricycle precipitated him into a ditch and was forced to decline at the last moment. It is interesting that for one garden party invitation in July 1880, there were twelve in 1882. Frederick Willmott did not force the pace. However, from the beginning, scarcely a day passed without an exchange of visits with their nearest friends—the Leschers at Boyles Court and the Inds. The other important local family, the Heseltines, hardly figures in the diaries, and the Hirsts were slow in welcoming the new owners of Warley Place. (In 1879, Frederick Willmott, raising his hat to the Hirsts when he happened to see them at Torquay, was cut—which he records in a rather hurt and puzzled fashion.)

However, social occasions were never lacking: Mrs Willmott and her daughters went to concerts at Thorndon Hall, home of the Petre family; and in the summer there were the garden parties already mentioned, some of them much disrupted by weather—there are many dismal diary entries such as: 'we went to Mrs Inds but it rained nearly all the time we were there—only about 40 came instead of about 200—the band played under the Veranda.' The Willmotts gave successful garden parties themselves—with a hundred or so guests, and ices provided by a City firm. Relations between Warley Place and the garrison at Warley Barracks were close and amiable, and succeeding Colonels of the regiments stationed there were welcome at Warley. As they were offered champagne, port and cigars on an afternoon call, it is hardly surprising that they called regularly. So did their officers: but then there were two pretty girls in the house, who must have made a welcome change from Messrs Robinson and Whyting, the previous owners. There were several balls a year at the barracks to which Ellen always, and Rose sometimes (for she seemed on the whole less eager for the social round than her sister), went escorted by her father. Hospitality was returned at Warley Place—in 1882, with a ball attended by eighty-four guests: unfortunately Frederick Willmott's diary only records the amount of alcohol consumed (8 bottles of sherry, 10 of claret, 42 champagne and 1 brandy, so the guests were not stinted) and makes no comment at all on how it all went. Especially happy were the family's relations with the 6th Foot (later the Warwickshire) Regiment, which was moved to Chatham 'much to our regret', as Mr Willmott with unwonted warmth remarks amongst his usual factual record of each day's happenings. That morning when the news came he had walked to the barracks to invite all the officers over that day to drink a farewell glass of champagne, and very many of them responded to this warm impromptu invitation, mingling with the Willmotts' tennis-guests, fifty in all. The next day the Willmotts gave the prizes for a final lawn-tennis tournament at the barracks: Ellie, coming second with Mr Clayton, was presented by her father with a white satin fan. And so the 6th departed for Chatham, but the Willmotts were invited to spend a day there with the officers of the Regiment—a day marred only by the carriage overturning on the way home, causing Frederick Willmott's wrist to be broken, for which he claimed £20 from the Railway Passengers Assurance Company. Ellen and Rose, also rather cut about and bruised, recovered quickly, but Frederick spent two days in bed.

Lawn tennis formed a very important part of social life in the district—as usual, Ellen was keen and energetic and seems even to have been rather good at it (Rose less so). In 1883 a new tennis ground was made at Warley, and it was in frequent use. The family enjoyed watching the athletic sports at the barracks, or a match on the cricket ground; and every year Frederick Willmott took his daughters to the Eton and Harrow match at Lord's. Both girls could skate, and did so almost every day in the hard January of 1880, until the ice began to soften and the Willmott parents feared for their safety. And they played badminton. They also walked. Rose in particular accompanied her father on his regular local walks, over Upminster Common and home by Brook Street or Nag's Head Lane, or to Childerditch, round by Warley Gap and home by the barracks. Ellen, bored by the daily round, eagerly undertook any longer and more venturesome expeditions which were proposed, such as nine-mile walks during holidays in the Isle of Wight, even if it meant returning ignominiously by train. The neighbourhood grew accustomed to the sight of Frederick Willmott—tall, prosperous-looking, very slightly overweight, with a good head of hair—taking his daily constitutional. Pigeon-shoots and meets at the barracks, rabbit-shooting by the officers of the 6th in the Warley Garden, visits to Castle Hedingham, to Lowestoft, 'with the Girls to see the first turf of the Tilbury Railway extension being cut'—these pleasant diversions filled their day. The Willmott parents called on the neighbours, sometimes accompanied by their daughters: on one occasion they went in their new victoria—a rare piece of showing-off and one for which they were promptly served right, for the victoria immediately afterwards needed repairs. At Christmas, carols were sung at Brentwood Grammar School, Mrs Colonel Rose organized theatricals at the barracks, and at Brentwood Town Hall Miss Rose Seaton recited Hamlet ('rather too long'). Ellie herself played her ocarina at the Warley School entertainment for the benefit of the Reading Room and Club.

Not everything, however, went so smoothly or pleasantly at Warley Place. Although the family had started well with a reliable cook, Mrs Shrimpton, whose kitchen was well under her thumb since her daughter was kitchen-maid, by 1882 this happy state of affairs was no more, and cook followed cook at three-monthly intervals. It may have been the result of London-recruited staff failing to take to country life, for every new engagement involved special trips to London by Mrs Willmott or Ellen to make their choice from a short list. And not only with cooks were they unlucky: footmen also were unpredictable—William Clarke left after only one month, and in May 1880 we find Robert Cramb 'gave notice to leave and left at once—he was either tipsy or out of his mind, no one of the Family had spoken to him'. The misguided Cramb was followed later by Macdonald, who 'was drunk and after pitching into Walter Sewell went to bed for the rest of the day'. Three months later he was

drunk again all day, and finally left in a cloud of alcohol, having been
drunk all day at one of the Willmotts' own parties. Evidently Ellen
was not yet a good judge of people, and certainly the house needed a
butler to keep these undisciplined young men in order. That day
was, however, postponed by the arrival of Jordan, a reliable footman, who stayed at Warley Place for. some years (and thirty-four
years later wrote to Ellen Willmott saying that he wished he had
never left). In the gardens, North was in charge, and won a dozen or
so prizes at the Brentwood Flower Show each July—grapes and
onions, cut flowers, outdoor nectarines, carnations and picotees—for
he seemed to specialize in everything. In the new coach-house,
Oakley was the coachman/groom and looked after the two horses
and the coaches—barouche, victoria, landau, pony chaise, brougham
and waggonette—and, later, the donkey cart which Frederick Willmott bought for his wife for 32s. (including harness) from the
Childerditch Hall sale, and the girls' new polo cart. Oakley, however, also had feet of clay, and had to be reproved by his master for
being drunk after attending a ball at Warley Barracks—perhaps, too,
Oakley's day spent with the 6th at Chatham could have induced him
to speed on the way home and so land the coach and its occupants in
the ditch.

Besides the new coach-house, other building works were undertaken. The construction of the new pigsty was also entrusted to
Winter and a new vinery and peach house were built. In February
1880 'Ellie began the erection of her Gipsy Hut near the Pond'—
whether with her own hands is not specified. In 1882 the London
firm of Cowtan repaired the roof (where there was a leak in to the
Willmott parents' own bedroom) and were then let loose on the
interior of the mansion, first on the girls' rooms and then on a plan of
rejuvenation, the details of which are not recorded in the diaries, but
which the family went abroad to Nice and into Italy to escape. When
they returned more than two months later they found Warley Place
full of workpeople and everything in confusion—Unpacked looked
about got some clean things and after waiting until ½ past 5 we all
drive to Middleton Hall on a visit.' Things have not changed much
since then, it seems, except that the number of houses which could
take in a family of four at short notice is somewhat reduced. At least
everybody had come back from holiday refreshed—health was a matter of extreme concern to the Willmotts. This was hardly surprising,

since Frederick, as a chemist's son, had always assumed that an interest in ailments was a normal pastime. Indeed, in their fifties, he and his wife had their troubles: Mrs Willmott was beginning to suffer from the serious rheumatism which within a few years was to incapacitate her; Frederick himself had lumbago and gout—he tended the latter assiduously, resting up for a day or two every time he felt it coming on. Getting his feet wet was a matter for recording in his diary. The whole family suffered recurrent colds and coughs, presumably because Warley Place was a very cold house, and exposed to bitter easterly winds. Frederick's diaries record the weather in detail, and it seems that there was a great deal of snow each year, and numerous storms with high winds, thunder and lightning in the summer.

Frederick Willmott's relations with his more distant family remained close, though he did not set out to mix family and Essex friends. His address book is filled mainly with names from his London life: unlike his daughter Ellen's from twenty years later, it contains the names of very few titled people. But he seems to have early constituted himself the family's banker, financial adviser and general decider: in 1882 he was busy with the affairs of his brother William, whose brewery in Sheffield (acquired after the sale of the family chemist's business in 1872) seems to have failed at about this time. Frederick acted as intermediary between William and Moss & Co., the London agents who were to put the brewery on the market. He paid the school fees of William's two younger daughters at the Sheffield convent, and sent a monthly allowance to the eldest daughter, Kathleen, and then to the second, Florence, until the day he died. Charles in 1881 had taken passage with his wife Agnes and young son Charlie for New Zealand, and he also required attention: a £50 loan, his half-yearly annuity paid to him, a consignment of groceries, his life-insurance premium and his bill at Meggesons (supplier of medicaments) paid. How much was reimbursed is not at all clear. It is only in a casual comment in one of Ellen Willmott's letters, dated 1916, that we learn what happened to him. 'My uncle was Charles Willmott', she says, 'he was a fair botanist and very good horticulturalist and greatly interested in plants. Many of our New Zealand plants were raised from seed sent by him to my Mother. She was growing several New Zealand plants and shrubs here long before their general introduction. . . . I believe my Uncle had a good garden but his place was totally overwhelmed when the pink and white terraces disappeared.' He had bought a farm of 150 acres at Te Puke, and so was involved in the disastrous eruption of Mount Tarawera in 1886, when the beautiful limestone terraces, delicately tinted with pink, became submerged in Lake Rotoruahama, and a heavy cloud of volcanic dust settled on the whole district.

And then there was Edwin, who since the death of Sarah Willmott in 1866 had been living in lodgings in London. In 1883 he took the decision to follow Charles to New Zealand. Frederick, hearing this, gave his brother £25, told him there would be a further £250 awaiting him on landing, and then went off to the Gaiety Theatre to forget it all. Two days later he returned to make the arrangements for Edwin to travel out by second class, and gave him another £60. Then he took Uncle Edward Monnery to lunch and, fortified, the two went to Monnery's warehouse to look over Edwin's things. Shortly after this Edwin came to Warley Place to spend the day with his family and bid them goodbye—Mrs Willmott gave him £20 and the girls, fond of their tall, good-looking uncle, £5 each. Seen from today's standpoint this seems an extraordinarily patronizing move, but perhaps in 1883 things looked different. The brothers met once more, for lunch at the City Liberal Club, and Edwin was given £10 from the Countess Tasker. They never saw each other again, for Edwin, who had set up in business in Auckland as a photographer, died in hospital there on 24 October 1888—Frederick, typically, settled the funeral expenses.

The Fells, shadowy figures of whom little is known, were seen less often, though Mrs Willmott took Ellen to spend a few days in Aylesbury now and again, and her unmarried sister, Adelaide, received generous presents from the Willmotts several times a year. That left the Monnerys, who had now left the Borough and moved into the City proper; Frederick often saw his Uncle Edward, and must have felt rather relieved that at least one elderly relative was still alive. There seem to have been two Monnery businesses in operation at that time—the original hosiery business had now added to itself an outfitting department, and there was a wine business: Frederick patronized both, especially the wine business, from which he bought a good deal of Madeira. John and Walter seem to have been the cousins in Frederick's generation, and once Frederick took the Sarah Monnery of the day in to dinner as his lady one evening at the

Painters' Hall. Mrs Willmott treated her husband's brothers with affection and indulgence, but even she was riled by the behaviour of her sister-in-law, William's wife Eliza, and two of her nieces. The draft of a letter to Kathleen, the elder niece—perhaps never sent?—in which indignation plays havoc with the spelling, survives. What had gone wrong is never stated, but evidently Eliza had caused her husband William much trouble and sorrow which had somehow rubbed off on Frederick, who had also suffered financially. With great spirit Mrs Willmott said that if she was called upon to explain the estrangement between the two families there was only one reply to be given, and that was the Truth. But she may never have been called upon to do this, for apparently some uneasy relationship subsisted between the families until Frederick's death.

Meanwhile, at least the Willmotts of Warley Place lived in harmony. One of their early footmen, writing anonymously, left this account of a family evening:

The Master was met at Brentwood Station by the coachman groom and pair horse brougham. On arrival home he was invariably met in the front hall by his two daughters, Miss Rose preceding him to the dining-room, and in her delighted capacity of butler, poured out his accustomed glass of Sherry and Angostura Bitters.

Dinner was served at 6.30 every evening. Mrs Willmot [sic] sat at the head of the table, Miss Ellen Willmot the other end, with the Master and Miss Rose Vis a Vie. There was always a very liberal table, My mistress being very particular about the dishes supplied that most Suited the Master. . . . The dinner generally lasted about an hour when the Master emsconced himself in an armchair and read till the desired after dinner nap ended his day of business. Although the young ladies retired, Mrs Willmot always consorted the Master, till I came in at 10 o'clock. . . . I could not but feel impressed and elevated by the daily recurring episodes and conversation which it became my lot to witness. The young ladies vie with each other in their vivacious efforts to amuse the Master. . . .

CHAPTER III

'The Girls'

After reading Frederick Willmott's accounts of his daughters' days, the moment has perhaps now arrived to consider what Ellen and Rose were really like. To look at, very similar, though Ellen's proud carriage, the lift of her head, gave her a more distinguished air than her sister, in spite of the fact that she was no taller than 5ft. 4in. or so. The earliest surviving portrait of Ellen is a photograph taken in France, apparently during a conversation: she still has something to say, some comment on her lips worth hearing. The dark eyes, slightly too close for beauty, are cool and appraising. The face is plump round the jaws, and very youthful, but it has a slightly judgmental air, of amusement as yet unbacked by experience. A recent visit to the hairdresser has obviously produced an unintentionally formal effect, heightened by a large hat surmounted by ostrich plumes. A charming lace collar and yoke complete the impression.

And Rose? There is only one, very informal, photograph, taken apparently in the Cardinal's Walk to the south of the mansion. It shows a young girl—not more than sixteen or seventeen—posed rather self-consciously on the stone wall for her sister's camera, with a slightly sulky face, eyes gazing downwards, plump hands and hair ruffled forward over her eyes.

Frederick's diaries, with their constant references to 'the Girls', make us forget how old they actually were during the 1880s—Ellen twenty-two in 1880, and Rose nineteen. He clearly regarded their adult pretensions with indulgence and amusement, as when in 1888 they went to town full of indignation to set right a wrong done to their father: 'The Girls . . . saw the Cardinal by appointment to complain of Father Walsh who laid claim to Primula Villas and complain of his other misconduct and they then went shopping to try on dresses etc.' But the Willmott parents were not fools: they had had plenty of experience of their daughters' ways, and understood Ellen's restless, innovative urge, her sympathies, so complete when bestowed and so impatiently withheld when not, and Rose's less academic and more practical abilities—for Rose, unlike her sister, could organize matters which did not interest her as well as those which did. In such circumstances Ellen merely turned her back. So the Willmotts wisely gave their daughters a free rein, and waited on events.

Gardening came first with both girls, and as their mother became more rheumatic and less mobile, except in Bath chair (pushed by Jordan, the footman) or donkey chaise (led by Cook, the garden boy), so they took on more responsibility. Their father also took a deep pride in the gardens, frequently fetching some officer from the barracks, or some other neighbour, to pace around on a summer's afternoon and admire the flowers; but his prime interest lay always in land and stock. He believed in investment first and enjoyment afterwards. Sometime in 1882 he invested in twenty-two acres of land on the other side of the main road to Brentwood—probably the ground which later became Warley Place Farm—and bought two hundredweight of One and All Monster seed' (presumably grass seed) to sow there. He was also interested in keeping his land and its outstanding features in good heart: he mentions buying two hundredweight of dissolved bones for the lawn and new vinery. He tells of damage done by storm to the acacia (probably *Robinia pseudacacia*) in front of the house, and mentions also the planting of trees. Haymaking, its slow progress and unpredictable results, exercised his patience to the limit. In gardening, however, his natural tastes tended towards the conventional, and he records the putting out of bedding plants and the existence of two carpet beds. (His wife and daughters hated carpet bedding, and must have given in solely to please.)

Already by 1880 Mrs Willmott was taking her daughters to the Royal Horticultural Society's Summer Show in London, and it may well have been at about this time that Ellen's botanical interest in plants was stimulated by, and began to keep pace with, her practical efforts in the Warley Garden. A list of the botanical books, both rare and standard, which were offered for sale at Sotheby's and at the sale of contents when Warley Place was finally put up for auction, make remarkable reading. It must of course be realized that these books probably formed the collection of a lifetime, but it still seems likely that Ellen was guided on to this course by her mother's deep interest in the subject and by her father's keen appreciation of a beautiful edition, an exquisite binding, and solid value in the world's markets—and that the collection was beginning to take shape. Frederick Willmott spent a good deal of money at Cawthorn & Hutt's, booksellers and librarians in Cockspur Street. And Ellen herself gave her mother gardening books: the grand-daughter of the Head of the Gardens at Warley still owns a copy of William Robinson's *The English Flower Garden* (bought at the Warley Place sale) which is inscribed by Ellen to her mother on the latter's birthday in 1884.

It has long been believed that at the age of twenty-one Ellen asked her father's permission to make an alpine garden with some of the money which she had been given on successive birthdays by her godmother. He agreed, provided that it lay out of sight of his study window. This seems rather a strange proviso, but he may well have been thinking of the noise and disturbance of the garden in the making, rather than of the results. He wrote in his diary for 1 April 1882, 'Ellie began her new Alpine Garden.' Perhaps this was the planting, rather than the excavating, for it came nearly three years after Ellen's twenty-first birthday. She chose an area just below the bowling green, to the south-west of the main drive, with the house just in sight over the rising ground behind it. Bringing in James Backhouse and Son of York to do the excavating work and supply the stone, she planned the garden to follow the natural lie of the land, creating a deep gorge which was protected from harsh winds by the higher ground above it, and divided by spurs of land running into it (though, in its early stages, it was not sheltered enough to prevent a large almond tree from being blown down in a gale). The concept was bold and imaginative: the landscape, curved and cut in wide sweeps and falls, had nothing of the modern 'rockery' about it. Huge boulders seemed to grow from the ground so that, in the upper reaches of the garden, bushy plants, cunningly placed, extended downwards the wind-break provided by the trees on the outer fringes. Deep curving stone steps traversed the garden, and smaller plants clustered near and amongst them; stepping stones carried the pathway on towards the South Pond. A stream of water ran through the little valley, keeping it temperate in hard winters, green and moist in hot dry summers. Beneath a stone bridge, the stream, its subdued murmur echoing from the rocks on either side, flowed into the South Pond, where the villagers of Great Warley are said to have drawn their water in earlier days. Below the bridge and stretching back beneath the lawn lay a cave called 'the filmy-fern grotto' where, to the sound of water, in a dim, green, cool cavern, ferns native to the British Isles and to New Zealand, as well as some from other parts of the world, clustered on the walls and over the floor.

It would have been interesting to hear the comments of Back-houses' men on Ellen Willmott as a garden designer and director of labour. But the results they achieved between them made a setting unique in garden history for a collection of plants from the mountainous regions of the whole world. (A milestone which stood until recently on the outskirts of the alpine garden and recorded the distance to York may have been the work of a homesick labourer or perhaps Backhouses' 'signature' to completed work.)

Painting was another absorbing occupation, and Ellen took some painting lessons in London, as well as the 'sketching' lessons given both to her mother and herself by a Miss Green. A number of Ellen's flower paintings survive. They are remarkably alive, showing an observant eye and a talent in some cases falling hardly short of the work of Alfred Parsons which illustrated with such delicacy her *magnum opus, The Genus Rosa*. Painting seems to have been a way of life at Warley Place. There was even a class held there for painting on china, attended by the young ladies of the district. Mrs Willmott on the whole preferred her embroidery, in which she is said to have excelled—and an entire trunk of embroidery silks and wools was said to have been found at Warley Place after her death. This, however, was as nothing compared with the extraordinary quantity of artists' materials which accumulated—easels of all sizes and qualities, from artist's mahogany adjustable to ordinary bamboo; and brushes, canvasses and paints sufficient to equip a large art class. It is puzzling to conjecture who could have used them all. Several of Ellen's paintings were offered when the contents of Warley Place were finally sold: A *Wine Jar, Continental Cathedral and Street Scenes* among others. So evidently she took her painting equipment with her when she travelled: the inevitable lady's maid must have had a hard time of it. Interestingly, the sale also contained paintings by the Countess Tasker, so perhaps she painted alongside her young god-daughter.

This thought may also lend support to a possibility which hovers tantalizingly unsubstantiated: did the cultivated atmosphere of the Willmott household derive to a large extent from the influence of the Tasker family on their younger cousin? Joseph Tasker, father of Louis and Helen Ann, had owned a fine library, and Louis, who died at the age of twenty-four, had been a considerable scholar. In such company (for as we have seen she apparently spent much time as a young woman with the Tasker family at Fitzwalters) Ellen Fell must have absorbed a good deal which was to be of value to her and to her daughters later.

Increasingly, Ellen Ann was drawn into musical circles. Her great allies in this were the Herberts, who lived near Kendal Villa, and their three children—May, Philip and Charlie—who were around her own age. She went often with them to Richter Concerts (spending the night afterwards at the Herberts' house) when the great conductor from Vienna, in the years before he became associated with the Hallé Orchestra in Manchester, was giving his annual series in London. Several times a month Ellen went up to London for music lessons—which seem to have been sometimes 'choir lessons' and sometimes violin lessons. In December 1889 she took an important step in her musical life. She went to the best of all violin-makers, W. E. Hill & Sons, and bought an Amati violin: ten days later she was being given a lesson on this instrument by a Mr Byford. Encouraged, she followed this up with the purchase of a viola and 'cello in May 1890, and finally a second violin in November of the same year, thus completing a quartet of Amati instruments. One of the violins was a beautiful instrument of 1628, which Hills later asked her to lend them for their 1904 exhibition. Whether these were among the instruments which Stradivarius had worked on while an apprentice to the Amati family, in the days when he was scarcely allowed to do more than rub down the wood, we do not know; but we do know that Ellen became a very competent violinist and one, moreover, who could appreciate and gloat over the beauty of her possessions, the gorgeous glowing colour of the varnish and the splendid singing tone for which the instruments produced by the Amatis were famous.

Frederick Willmott must have observed these purchases in a neutral frame of mind, infected but not yet invaded by doubts. He could not fault his daughter's taste (since he had brought her up to acquire it), nor could he fault the acquisition of the instruments as an investment which would appreciate as time went on. But nevertheless he must have known in his heart that she was interested mainly in owning something beautiful for its own sake and for her own use, and that the idea of investment was both purely fortuitous in this case and foreign to her nature in general (how foreign will be seen later on). Both Ellen and her father may have felt slightly guilty that the Tasker money was not going towards the founding of an orphanage or to some other worthy cause, but the guilt probably evaporated rather quickly. At some time during this period, and probably quite unawares, Ellen crossed the invisible border between fondness for music and a real commitment to an inner and outer life which took constant account of it. She seems to have been alone in her family in showing serious musical talent: her parents always enjoyed spending an evening listening to a band, both at Warley Barracks and when travelling abroad, but this did not require the same skill as mastering the complexities of an instrument or listening with concentration to a difficult piece of scoring. Ellen also attended concerts arranged by the Petres at Thorndon Hall, and for a time went regularly to the Saturday Pops (concerts of classical chamber music, with vocal and pianoforte solos, held at St James's Hall)—sometimes with the Herberts, once with Lady Doneraile, often on her own.

The nuns at Gumley House had given both girls a good grounding in French. In 1880 Ellen and Rose made a special journey to town to engage a German governess (a strange term, with Ellen already twenty-two) and in due course Fräulein Süssmilch came to Warley; she was followed by other resident French and German ladies. There is no doubt that both girls worked hard: some of Ellen's German exercise-books, full of excellent colloquial German, show that she was a good natural linguist and, as always, once her interest was captured, she really set her mind to learning. Languages were an instrument she needed to use: not only in reading botanical works, but also because the Willmott family took early to travelling abroad. The first surviving account of their travels, a letter from Ellen to her godmother, is written from Paris and dated 23 September 1875: she was just seventeen, and writing in her nightgown—it was too early to get up and too late to go to sleep again, and in any case she was much too excited to attempt it. She described the dinner of the previous evening, when a large sole was carried in, decorated with crayfish, mushrooms cut into patterns with shrimps sticking up in them, olives and truffles in patterns. . . . What a wonderful supper, a work of art, love and care, in some way symbolic of the whole enchanting city. Excitement, gaiety, enthusiasm shine through the letter—all the feelings of a young girl with beauty, intelligence and talent and the whole of life in front of her. This letter is the touchstone for everything which happened to Ellen Willmott, or which she perpetrated, later in her life.

In 1880 the family went to Brussels; besides going to the Botanical Gardens, and then to the theatre and to hear the inevitable band, there is an entry which reveals a new skill: 'Ellie rowed for a short time on the lake.' Then to Antwerp, Spa and finally to Paris again. Here, as usual, it was Ellen who accompanied her father on a four-hour trip by boat up the Seine to St Germain and back by rail, while 'Wife and Rosey' went shopping at the Bon Marché or driving in the Bois de Boulogne. They all dined at their favourite restaurant, Vefours in the Palais Royal. 1882 was the year in which Cowtans descended on Warley Place to make alterations, and drove the Willmotts away to Nice, where a certain Captain Scott from Warley Barracks joined them—and, in fact, seems to have haunted the family for a full year (eventually he tired of waiting and in 1886 married, with a handsome wedding present from the Willmotts). He was not the only young man who spent time with the Willmott family. Many young officers' names recur in Frederick Willmott's diaries: Philip Herbert, too, was attentive to the Girls, accompanying them on holiday, and a certain Mr Handley called upon the Willmotts in Rome, Naples and London. But the only name which report links closely with Ellen's is that of George Ainslie Hight, the son of a neighbour of the Countess Tasker in Hammersmith; and it is true that for a short time in the summer of 1882 the two saw each other several times. But Ainslie Hight was only on leave from the Indian Forestry Service, and soon returned to India. In 1886 he married Florence Watney, and twenty-five years later, on retirement, he went to live in Oxford, where he took a B. Litt. degree as a non-collegiate student, and became a distinguished scholar. Writing to Ellen Willmott in 1923 to urge her to attend a lecture he was giving to the Viking Society, he was still addressing her as 'Dear Miss Willmott'—and so too did his wife, with whom Ellen Willmott seemed also to be on friendly terms. So it seems not to have been a matter of great passion on either side.

Why did Ellen Willmott not marry? Perhaps, along with her considerable beauty, she already as a young woman showed signs of a wilfulness which no man wanted to encounter in a wife. She certainly had suitors. But there must have come a time when, almost without knowing it, she reached the point where she could no longer be bothered to conceal the fact that she was more knowledgeable, quick-witted and intelligent than most of the men she knew. Perhaps she simply felt that there was nobody sufficiently interesting to trouble with. And yet . . . so much depended on the person to whom she was talking, and for how long. She could be a most charming, intelligent and sympathetic companion for short periods to many people, and to the end of her life there were certain friends who provided such satisfying companionship, and who so much approved of her, that the need to assert herself simply fell away, and she behaved entirely naturally and spontaneously. The many letters which she received over the long periods of their friendship from Dr (later Sir Norman) Moore, a consulting physician with interests in Irish and classical literature, show the kind of response which she was capable of evoking, and sustaining, with a man whose thoughts and interests matched her own. Two comments recorded by close friends show how she saw her relations with others. Walking with them round the Warley Garden, she paused in front of a single pink rose and said, 'That is Cupid: I knew him not.' It was said with perfect seriousness, and it was true: for all that she sang in madrigal societies, she was not and never had been the kind of young woman to fall victim to a hail of darts. The other remark is equally revealing: 'As we grow older we find it harder to conceal our faults', she said. Her recognition that this was so, combined with her inability to grasp that the very concealing of faults might vitiate rather than cement a good relationship, was significant. Thus, in a way, she chose without choosing, electing to stay single without necessarily wanting this.

But in the early 1880s there were plenty of young men about, and no need to think of marriage at all urgently. However, as the decade progressed, the pleasant course of social life at Warley Place began to change. The Warley Garrison ceased to play such a prominent part in the Willmotts' life, and the craze for lawn tennis all but disappeared (to be replaced, later, by a more sedate predilection for croquet). Dances were very few, and in 1888 the only one offered was the

Bachelors' Ball at Chelmsford, which Ellen was not allowed to attend because her mother feared that it would exacerbate the rheumatism from which she was beginning to suffer. This marked a change indeed from the girl who only six years before had so often been dancing till three in the morning.

Bur chiefly the reason was that neither of the elder Willmotts was any longer in very good health. Heavy colds sent Frederick promptly to his bed; he took to spectacles and, like his neighbour Colonel Duberly, to a tricycle; and his wife was seriously incapacitated by rheumatism. There were days at Warley when she could neither stand nor walk, and there were days without number during holidays abroad when Frederick's diary records, 'Girls were out all day dodging in and out of churches etc.' or, 'Ellie dug up some large daisy roots which she sent home' (one can imagine her hacking energetically at the roots in full view of passers-by in the Pamphili Gardens in Rome, with an excuse in fluent Italian at the ready), and when he adds rather sadly, 'Wife would not go out.' 'Would not' one assumes, rather than 'could not' because it was too much of an effort, too painful. On good days she still went out shopping or for drives in foreign cities, and at home moved around in her Bath chair or in the donkey chaise. The result of this disability was that the family travelled more, not less, to give Mrs Willmott the chance of treatment in the spas of Europe. But Mrs Willmott, though happy to accompany her family abroad, was a chauvinist at heart and, writing from France, confided to her cousin Helen Tasker that she would be delighted to be home again. And the Swiss botanist Henri Correvon, a favourite visitor at Warley Place, teased her gently on her opinion, which she so staunchly expressed to him, that English butter, cheese and eggs were infinitely superior to those from 'abroad'. Indeed Correvon himself was an Anglophile, his comment on the Boer War being 'Bravo et Rule Britannia!'

It could well be that Mrs Willmott's condition, or at least her capacity to withstand the pain it caused her, was weakened by a shock which befell the family in January 1888: the death of the Countess Tasker. Ellen, too, felt the loss of her godmother deeply. The Countess, of a kindly but retiring disposition, not lively, not especially sociable, shown in her portrait with a plain, homely face and deprecating smile, seems at first sight to have been the least likely woman to sort well with a headstrong, outgoing personality such as

her god-daughter's. But perhaps this very opposition of tempera-
ments formed the bond between them, and certainly Ellen, almost as
if she were the older woman, treated her godmother with very great
gentleness and affection. One other factor was of prime importance
in their relationship: the Countess seems to have felt herself able to
exercise a restraining and religious hand on her young kinswoman.
No doubt it was she who persuaded Ellen to join with her in
furnishing the Lady Chapel at the Catholic church of Holy Cross and
All Saints, Warley Hill—a church later known locally as 'Miss Willmott's', which would greatly have pleased the Countess. Ellen, at the
age of twenty-six, was already Director of the Choir at the church,
and Frederick had undertaken with good grace to finance the building of a church porch.

In the Countess Tasker's will other godchildren received relatively minor recognition, and it was 'my dear god-daughter
Ellen'—and Rose, who was not officially a godchild at all—who
chiefly benefited. There were numerous bequests to the Church and
to charity, and some to relations and friends: Mrs Willmott, as
favourite cousin, received £2,000 and some of the contents of
Middleton Hall. But even after all this had been disposed of, Ellen
and Rose still received the sum of £3,000 each, Ellen 'my harp and all
my jewels and watches and "Elena Lodge", Brentwood', and the
two girls became residuary legatees. They each inherited a fortune—about £140,000 each. It was a breathtaking sum, and must
have diverted everyone's attention from the fact that, under the
terms of her father's will, the Countess had only a life interest in the
Tasker properties, which now passed to cousins. It is regrettable to
have to record that Ellen's use of the money left to her, whatever her
godmother may have striven to implant in her mind on the necessity
of being generous to the Church, was largely a selfish one. But then
Ellen possessed superabundant energy and enjoyment of this
world's goods and pleasures, which her godmother did not. For
most of that cold and foggy January Ellen and Rose sorted papers
and possessions at Middleton Hall and attended requiem masses and
memorial services all over London and Essex.

During the year, the family continued to visit spas and health
resorts, not only abroad but also at home—Ramsgate, Hastings,
and Bath (a fateful visit) in the spring. Here, they were enjoying the
usual combination of medicinal baths, walks, excursions and shop-

ping—the girls accompanied by Philip Herbert—when their friend Canon Williams introduced them to a certain 'Major and Mrs Berkeley'. A friendship quickly sprang up between the girls and the Berkeleys' daughter, Maud, and the girls were invited to spend a few days in June at the Berkeley home—Spetchley Park in Worcestershire—which they greatly enjoyed, in spite of hearing only irregularly from home. They went to look at gardens in the neighbourhood and commented with amusement and surprise on the Berkeley brothers' amiable habit of accompanying the ladies on such visits without appearing bored—so different from most men. The visit was reciprocated later in the summer, and all this culminated in Maurice Berkeley's 'proposing for Rosey' when he dined with Frederick Willmott in London one evening in August, and proposing to Rose herself the following day—' she told him she would write to him.' This is the very last we hear of the matter, and in true Victorian fashion, a week later the family were whisked off on a grand tour abroad which took in not only Aix, but also Turin, Milan, Florence, Rome, Naples, Lucerne, Mayenne and Cologne, and did not bring them back to Warley until the following June.

During this period, Frederick Willmott spent more than six weeks in bed in Rome with an unexplained complaint, the doctor visiting sometimes three times a day, and Ellie evidently acting as amanuensis for his diary. This cost him £300 in fees for Dr Young. For almost the same length of time Mrs Willmott remained indoors, so it was just as well that the Girls took full advantage of their unexpected chance to go about Rome as freely as they pleased. They visited the various catacombs, went to the English, Irish and Scots Colleges, walked around intensely interested in watching the Romans riot in the streets, with soldiers guarding the street corners. They went to a different church each day, watched processions at St Peter's and saw something of the Carnival, shopped, visited the Vatican Library with Maud Petre, were charmed by the Villa Mattei. One unexpected honour fell to the Willmott parents in Rome: they were received in audience by the Pope, who greeted them kindly and talked a good deal to them.

Throughout this sickness, and the frenzy of rushing round Rome, the gaps in the diary and the bits written by Ellen, still the daily account of egg production at Warley Place marched inexorably onwards, never faltering. (The ink is darker, the writing firmer, in the egg column—it must have been filled in later.) Poor Maurice Berkeley seems to have retired completely into the background. The family had first visited Aix-les-Bains, briefly, in December 1882, breaking their journey back home from Nice. Before long the habit was established of a yearly visit to Aix in August, September or October, the family expecting to have their accustomed rooms at the Hotel de l'Europe. In Aix the Willmotts felt at home, and settled easily to the life—baths, visits to the convents, drives by the lake, and calls on friends. And so they came to Tresserve. Here lived Lady Whalley ('les Divallets' as she is bafflingly known today, suggesting an entire French family) on whom they called nearly every day. In September 1888 Frederick Willmott recorded with an unusually sardonic air 'Captain Molyneux Seal arrived on the scene' (perhaps he had had enough in dealing with Maurice Berkeley in the previous month), but Captain Seal had no chance when competing with Lady Whalley.

Tresserve is a place of a peculiar and entrancing stillness and beauty. Neither village nor suburb, its main street straggles along the ridge of its single hill, its houses for the most part turning their backs on Aix and facing the Lac du Bourget towards which the ground falls steeply away, descending in terraces and folds of land, criss-crossed with lanes and paths and, nowadays, dotted with smaller houses. An atmosphere of dream, of trance, lies on the place, leading the visitor to speculate that a small white building on the mountain top must be a Trappist monastery, set amid eternal snow, instead of the television station which it proves to be. The lake lies still, reflecting the shapes of the mountains all around; a light mist hangs on the air, causing the shapes of distant houses to change and sway, so that all seems interpenetrated, air, lake and mountains. It is easy to understand the feelings of Queen Victoria who, trying on the advice of her doctors to free herself from the prolonged lethargy of mourning for her husband, fell so immediately victim to the spell of the place that she decided to build there. Encouraged by the presence nearby of her friend Queen Hortense, step-daughter of Napoleon, she made up her mind and moved quickly: in 1887 she embarked on negotiations with the Commune of Tresserve to purchase land for a grand house, for the building of which the main road would have to be slightly diverted. This was causing much talk while the Willmotts were at Aix in 1888, and they went, along with everyone else, to take a look at the Queen's property. Her Majesty's plans were solemnly debated and agreed by the Council of the Commune, but three years later still nothing had been accomplished because an old peasant woman, the purchase of whose land was essential to the project, stubbornly refused to sell, and no one could persuade her to change her mind. Queen Victoria, *'furieuse'*, resold the land she had originally bought, and departed, shaking the dust of ungrateful Tresserve from her feet. But in the wake of the Queen various English noblemen built at Tresserve. The most imposing of these houses is the grand villa of Lord Bellingham, which has now passed into French ownership but still carries the family name on the gatepost. A gravelled court and formal urns of flowers—a Gertrude Jekyll garden, in fact—can be seen through the wrought-iron gate. Farther along the road stands the umber-washed, be-frescoed Italianate villa which once belonged to an American Professor, Daniel Rops. Opposite the present *mairie*, La Maison du Lac, once the home of Lady Whalley, faces the road.

The place cast its spell on both Ellen and Rose; each time they approached it from Aix they marvelled afresh as, reaching the top of the hill, they came suddenly on the splendid view over the lake. Their father was well aware of this, and teased his daughters: 'home by Tresserve—where we passed the Villa d'Aimable—we got out and inspected it as Ellie is rather sweet upon it.' But it was not this house, but the Château itself which (perhaps with Queen Victoria's purchase in mind) Ellen bought in 1890 for the grand sum of 50,000 francs (£2,000)—in those days a sizable amount, but for Ellen the sum of a mere two years' birthday presents from her godmother. The purchase was made from an absentee landlord living in Paris—Madame Marie-Françoise Daudens—and over the following two or three years Ellen acquired various pieces of land from the Cachoux family to add to the Château's garden. The decision to buy must have been made when, in August and September 1889, Ellen and Rose went abroad for the first time without their parents, accompanied only by a new lady's maid, Clapton. Thus there was no cautioning hand laid upon Ellen's natural extravagance. She employed a local architect, Monsieur J-S Pin Aîné, who supervised local builders in an extensive programme of work. A terrace was built outside the house, with a graceful double staircase descending to the criss-crossing walks and pergolas which she gradually had constructed in the lower garden; and a veranda, which in turn led down to the terrace, was made leading out of the Grand Salon. Numerous small alterations and repairs were carried out in the house, and the rooms were painted. And, gradually, the garden was transformed. In front of the house and beyond the chestnut trees pergolas were made on which, as time went on, Ellen Willmott's rose collection blossomed and bloomed in profusion: pink, white and red against the blue sky, the leaves casting their graceful, dancing shadows on the ground. Flower borders of iris and poppy and canna lilies of every kind (whose successors grow there to this day) lined the walls of the terrace: and, looking over the garden into the hazy distance down to the lake, it seemed as though there were acres of blossom—*Clematis armandii*, wisteria and roses arched over the walks, interspersed with shrubs of every kind, while below the house and behind it, a mass of peach blossom met the eye. In the lower garden the indefatigable Ellen, followed around by her newly found gardener, Claude Meunier, saw that vines were planted. The best time of year at Tresserve was in May and June, when the sun was still high in the evenings, and the light streamed down on to the terrace in front of the house, and wisteria, agave and vine caught the last of the sun's rays. No wonder Ellen and Rose were captivated by the place and its somnolent beauty. A high wall, which Ellen had built, kept the garden private from passers-by along the main street.

In the early 1890s particularly, Ellen Willmott bought enormous quantities of plants, both for Tresserve and Warley, from Henri Correvon's Jardin Alpin d'Acclimatation at Geneva. In fact, since she soon grew to respect his knowledge and skill and saw eye to eye with him in appreciating the beauties of a garden well laid out, and since their families quickly reached an easy understanding with each other, she early gave him *carte blanche* to send her any plants he thought she might find interesting. So he tempted her with plants brought from the far regions of the world, but he also told her quite plainly on occasions that she was being stupidly extravagant to order from him, thus incurring freight charges, plants—particularly conifers—which were available much more cheaply in England. Here is a list of the potentillas and geraniums supplied to the Tresserve garden in Miss Willmott's October 1893 order: 'Potentilla Sibbaldia, Himalayensis, Aurea, Baldensis, Minima, arachnoidea, millegramma, splendens, subacaulis, argyrophylla, nigrescens, atrosanguinea, rupestris, Montenegrina, alpestris; Geranium lividum, Armeniacum, phacum, affine, Nepalensis, Ibericum, sp. Bosnia, albanum.' Many other species were supplied: the order for this month alone runs to four quarto-sized pages with the entries in small neat handwriting.

The furnishing of the Château took time and attention too: but while the bills for the alterations were addressed to Mesdemoiselles Willmott, the bills for furniture and decorations went straight to Ellen. They reveal excellent taste—and very considerable extravagance, the furniture being mostly of the time of Louis XV and XVI. Henri Correvon helped her here, scouring the countryside for costly *objets d'art* and harrying Jullien the bookseller to provide rare books. It is not at all clear to what extent Frederick and Ellen Willmott knew what was going on: they did visit Aix both in 1891 and 1892, but by that time the expenditure may already have been incurred.

While Ellen struggled with the builders, and performed miracles of taste and ingenuity in house and garden, the Willmott parents were, no doubt, preoccupied with matters at Warley which were also distracting Rose from giving her full attention to Tresserve. Following the debacle over Maurice Berkeley, relations with the Berkeley family had gradually returned to a normal basis, largely due to the friendship which had developed between the Willmott girls and Maud Berkeley. The three used to meet at Maud's club in London. Gradually her eldest brother, Robert, was drawn into the circle, and at some time in 1889 or 1890—unfortunately there are no diaries or letters to help pinpoint the date—he and Rose decided to marry. The prospect of this excellent match must have caused the Willmotts much satisfaction, and Ellen, devoted to her sister's interests, liked her prospective brother-in-law. It was, in many ways, a veritable lions' den into which Rose was putting her head. The Berkeleys had been Catholics for many generations, and Robert Berkeley had five brothers, one of them a priest, and six sisters, of whom Agnes Mary was a Sister of Charity in China. The family habitually had, in each generation, one or more children who entered the Church. Evidently Rose did not heed that, and the Willmott parents did not let it deter them from approving the match: the Berkeleys belonged to one of the oldest families in the land, while Rose Willmott's grandfather had kept a chemist's shop in Southwark. But Rose had the right gifts for the situation, and Robert Berkeley had chosen well. She had perseverance, and tact—and she was much loved. So Lady Catherine Berkeley (concealing as best she might the entirely natural feeling that she would much have preferred a wife of gentle birth for her son) received Rose graciously, and reflected that, in any case, her prospective daughter-in-law would not be living at Spetchley yet. It is probable that Mr and Mrs Willmott had already decided to buy Warley Lea—a house almost opposite the North Lodge of Warley Place—for the young couple to move into after their wedding, paying a nominal rent. So Rose and the Berkeley family could accustom themselves to each other gradually and, in the process, allow the Willmotts to keep Rose near to them for a little longer. Warley Lea was a pleasant house with a garden of about ten acres; just across the road there was a small gate in the estate wall of Warley Place, so that Rose and Robert could cross the road, dawdle along Solomon's Walk and wander in the gardens as they pleased.

There was much to be done in the months before the wedding, and Mrs Willmott's first care must have been for the garden. Already there were several gardeners who worked under her direction (a photograph survives showing thirteen of them, in caps and bowlers, standing somewhat awkwardly in three rows gazing fixedly at the camera in what must have been one of Ellen's early photographic attempts), but with the wedding preparations to be made, and with the attention of one of the garden planners distracted by approaching marriage, and of the other by general excitement, it was time to appoint a Head of the Gardens who would take all in hand. The garden needed no further major changes, in Mrs Willmott's eyes, but it did need to be in perfect order, since Rose's wedding was planned for August, and the reception was to be held at Warley Place. The Berkeleys, accustomed to the centuries-old gardens at Spetchley Park, would certainly have a critical eye open for those of Warley Place, even if they did contain John Evelyn's chestnut trees; and the Willmotts, if they had no deer, at least could arrange to have no weeds either. So inquiries were put in hand, and a short list made: the job finally went to James Preece, who with his wife had up till then worked for the Wernhers at Luton Hoo. James Preece lived in lodgings at the start of his time at Warley Place, and his wife, coming to visit him, was taken aback to find her hitherto clean-shaven husband suddenly sporting a beard. He told her, as he met her on the station platform, that he had grown the beard to make himself look older and so get the job: now he had got it, he would have to stay bearded. A little later the Preeces moved into North Lodge in time for the birth of their eldest child, Charles, in 1890. James Preece's first job was simple: on 20 August the garden must look its best, and there must be flowers in abundance for the house. James Preece was a chrysanthemum man and his eyes must have glistened as he proudly sat in his new home when tea was over and scanned the catalogues for early chrysanths, while his wife put Charlie to bed.

Meanwhile, plans were going forward in the house too, and the services of an excellent butler to supervise the arrangements were fortunately secured (perhaps Mrs Willmott had started the search as soon as the faintest possibility of an imminent engagement had been sensed). Among the carefully written applications Mrs Willmott received was one in a neat hand—not unlike her daughter Ellen's, and the writer about the same age, she noticed. The name was James Riches Robinson, and the letter was written from Alnwick Castle, Why should he want to leave the service of the Duke of Northumberland, she wondered. Reading on, she learned that James Robinson had for three years been engaged to be married to the cook-housekeeper to Lady Algernon Percy, and expected to be married in about four years' time (she must inwardly have breathed a sigh of relief that Rose had been spared such a long-drawn-out engagement), and so he wished to take up a permanent post which would ultimately offer a family cottage and which was nearer to the Robinson home at Thornham in Suffolk. The letter left a favourable impression which the interview confirmed. Very soon afterwards, probably early in 1890, James Robinson was installed in the butler's rooms at Warley Place.

The surviving photographs of Robinson show a man only moderately tall, with a pleasant, open face: there is a look of humour there, but humour kept well under control by its owner's quiet, serious manner. Robinson was an excellent organizer, adept at handling his employers, loyal and trustworthy, and feeling an especial bond (which was to be sorely tested in later years) with their beautiful and temperamental elder daughter. Perhaps Robinson was the only man beside her father with whom Ellen Willmott felt really free to speak her mind. In spite of the responsibility which he was shouldering, and which he was never again to lay down, Robinson could be a lively man: he owned a fiddle which he played with gusto, and having learned tap-dancing while he was in the north, he loved to demonstrate his skill. Cricket was his sport, but he never had time to take part in village matches—his job was to organize cricket teas, not carry a bat himself. So he put up a large framed photograph of W. G. Grace in the butler's pantry and left it at that. He and the house-keeper, Mrs McCullum (who probably joined the household at about the same time), had plenty to supervise. The house had to be springcleaned from top to bottom, the servants smartened up and drilled, and (since there is no mention of caterers in the newspaper account of the wedding) a wedding breakfast planned for the 'large circle of relatives and friends' who were to attend.

At last the day arrived. Characteristically, Rose had chosen as her wedding day the 20 August, the day after her sister's thirty-third birthday, so as not to overshadow it. (Indeed, it is strange that, in various years, this period in August saw so many important happen-ings in the Willmott family.) August 1891 was a very wet month—rain fell on twenty-two days—and though, presumably, this was good for the appearance of the garden, it must have kept the family on tenterhooks. The warmest day was 14 August and the wettest the 27th; Rose's wedding day was apparently not remarkable for any extremes of weather. The wedding was held at the small and simple Roman Catholic church at Warley, Holy Cross and All Saints, which was, however, invaded and taken over by a priestly contingent from London. The ceremony was performed by the Willmott family's old friend, now Monsignor Francis Weld, who had christened all three Willmott daughters in their Spring Grove days. He was assisted by the parish priest, Father Moncrieff Smyth, and the nuptial mass was sung by Father White, of Holy Trinity, Brook Green—the church in which Ellen Fell and Frederick Will-mott had been married—and Robert Berkeley's Benedictine brother, Father Oswald Berkeley. The local choir had been supplanted, one hopes not too tactlessly, by the choir of Brompton Oratory, Lon-don. The church was full and the dresses of the bride and her eight bridesmaids delightful: ivory satin and brocade with a court train for the bride, trimmed with rare Venetian point lace (surely an heirloom from the Fell family lace merchants, and probably among the items lent by Mrs Willmott for exhibitions at Nottingham) and worn with a tulle veil; cream bengaline trimmed with gold, and cream crinoline hats with shaded roses, for the bridesmaids. Rose carried a posy of white flowers with orange blossoms and showers of white ribbons; and each of the bridesmaids wore the badge of the Berkeley family, made in gold, enclosing the initials of the bride and bridegroom and a diamond, and carried posies of shaded roses with showers of green ribbons, the gifts of the bridegroom. Ellen, naturally, was the chief bridesmaid, accompanied by three of Robert's sisters, three Berkeley relations, and Miss Ann Somers-Cocks, an old friend of the bride and her sister, in some measure to counteract the preponderance of Berkeleys. Two of Robert's brothers were present besides Oswald: one of them, who was a captain in the Black Watch, acted as groomsman; the other, Wolstan, not quite twenty-one, was presumably just allowed to enjoy himself. Absent were the two remaining brothers, one of whom was Maurice, who had earlier proposed to Rose, and who may still have felt too deeply for her to wish to attend the wedding.

The guest list was long and distinguished, and heavily Berkeley- and clerical-oriented. It is sad that not a single Willmott name appears: but Uncle William Willmott had died in 1885, Edwin in 1888, and Charles was far away in New Zealand. But surely *someone* could have been invited, to make a link with Southwark—a Monnery cousin, perhaps? Other notable absentees were representatives of the Tasker and Fell families. The list of wedding presents, set out in detail in *The Tablet's* account of the occasion, is formidable: it included a diamond necklace, tiara and spray from the Willmott parents and Ellen; a number of expensive items from various titled families; and humbler presents, such as a painted handkerchief sachet from the Faithful Companions of Jesus at Gumley House. And—a reminder of the 6th Foot—a silver scent-bottle from Colonel Colthurst. The reporter of the wedding, with little humour (and reflecting a certain lack of tact on the part of the givers) recorded the gifts by Mr and Miss Green (who, it will be remembered, used to visit Warley Place to give sketching lessons) respectively of a portrait of Rose's St Bernard dog, Czar, and a portrait of Mrs Willmott. The omission of Mr Willmott seems unfortunate.

In spite of these vexing thoughts, it must have been a beautiful wedding. As young Mr and Mrs Berkeley were waved off on their journey to the Continent, Rose wearing a fawn cloth suit and a satin and lace waistcoat, with a hat trimmed with pink roses, what did the Willmotts feel? Frederick and his wife, satisfaction that their well-loved daughter was so happily and successfully married, and pleasure that the marriage cemented their own place in society; and

Ellen, who was fundamentally sweet-natured when nothing was happening, as it so frequently did, to disturb this, chiefly happy on Rose's behalf. But she would not have been human had she not glanced back, perhaps to Ainslie Hight in India, perhaps to one of the officers of the 6th. As the reception came to an end she realized that she was still carrying a sprig of orange blossom which Rose had given her from the wedding bouquet; standing irresolute a moment, she suddenly moved quickly to the conservatory, found a tub, the occupant of which she unceremoniously removed, and set the cutting, which survived to appear in later photographs. There was a sense of anti-climax. It was all over: she was the only daughter left at Warley Place.

1. *The indoor staff are grouped at the south front of Warley Place: Robinson stands to the immediate left of the seated group and Mrs McCullum to the right.*

2. *The gardener's annual photograph. Some of the Warley Place garden staff, wearing their uniforms, are posed for Ellen Willmott's camera by the front entrance to the mansion: James Preece, with a neat beard, is seated fifth from the left.*

3. *Every year, when the frosts were over, agave in pots were taken in a small cart from Headley garden greenhouse to be set at intervals along the drive and at other strategic spots. In this photograph the ritual is just beginning: Mr Adams from the Warley Place farm holds the bridle of the shire horse, and little Mr Fuller stands solemnly at attention in the rear. To the right of the group of gardeners, clutching the tow-rope of the cart, Maurice Preece—youngest son of the Head of the Gardens—faces the camera.*

CHAPTER IV

'Dear Lady Warley'

On 22 August 1892—barely a year after his daughter's wedding, as though fulfilling some ancient contract—Frederick Willmott died. It was sad that he did not survive to see his first grandchild, Eleanor Mary Frederica Augusta, born on 26 August—and named with a sidelong glance at her maternal aunt (for there could not be another Ellen in the family, it would be too confusing), at her grandfather Frederick himself, and at two deceased paternal aunts, Augusta and Mary. Frederick's death was quite unexpected: he had been ill for only a fortnight with phlebitis when septicaemia set in, and within a few days he was dead. For a man who was constantly taking long walks he suffered much trouble with his legs: rheumatism, strains and pains continually beset him, his toes turned septic and he was ever vigilant against the first signs of gout and quick to send for the doctor at their approach. Perhaps his doctor thought that he was crying wolf again, but the last entry in Frederick's cash book, made on 30 July, shows how ill he must have been feeling: there is a dramatic change from his normal steady handwriting to a shaky and almost unintelligible entry, the words tailing off into a scrawl. He was sixty-six; no age at all by today's standards, but not a man in the prime of life by the standards of the Victorians.

His death was reported with regret, but with less attention than had been given to his daughter's wedding in the previous year, by the *Essex Weekly News*. A good Catholic and a good neighbour, he contributed generously to local causes where his help was sought (the Warley Workmen's Club, Lady Petre's Night Refuge, the Aged Poor Society and the Catholic Union were some of those who had cause to thank him), but it does not appear that he went looking for honorary tasks in the district: the centre of his interests still lay in London, and obviously he preferred to be Master of the Worshipful

Company of Painters than a member of the Brentwood Urban District Council. As a young man he had obviously felt his own gift and made his way in a profession which suited his abilities: foresight, the weighing of alternatives, decisiveness where necessary, tactical withdrawal where not—these were the qualities needed for his upward movement in society. He was a wise and sound financier, possessing both flair and timing with investments. But he wisely avoided the temptation—if indeed he ever felt it—to become a fashionable lawyer, and stayed to practise where he belonged, among merchants and businessmen where long experience and native wit were shrewdly valued at their true worth.

He was also, however, the architect of a life style totally different from that of his own youth: far from the liveliness and stir of the Queen's Head yard, on which as a boy he had stared fascinated from the windows of No. 83 Borough High Street, he chose to settle his family in ample and beautiful surroundings. And he had to contrive that the financial support would always be there to sustain, replenish and prolong that way of living. At the time of his death Frederick Willmott might well have thought that his daughter Ellen would marry to live at Warley all her days, and it would have been a reasonable guess that one or other daughter would provide a grandchild—the fifth generation of gardeners in the family—to develop the Warley Garden still further. The influence of his example on his daughters, and particularly on Ellen, was profound; but the indications of this are subtle and indirect, and in discovering them one feels always that Frederick Willmott has just left, by another door, the room which one has entered. Perhaps the text which appears on the notice of death: 'I have fought a good fight, I have finished my course, I have kept the faith: as to the rest there is laid up for me a crown of justice which the Lord, the just Judge, will render to me in that day . . .' is the most apposite comment on his life.

The marriage had lasted for thirty-six years; Mrs Willmott bore her loss with fortitude and dignity and, a robust character, supported by her daughters and son-in-law, luckily so close at hand, she was well able to take over the complete direction of the house, in spite of her infirmities. Frederick Willmott's will recognizes this, as well as his debt of affection to his wife, in leaving the whole of his estate 'unto my dear wife Ellen'.

It was fortunate that the young Ellen had many occupations to

distract her mind from the grief she felt on her father's death. One of
these must have caused some of her mother's friends to look askance,
for in March 1891 she had bought herself a lathe for turning wood
and ivory—not just any lathe, but one of the very expensive, numbered lathes made by Messrs Holtzapffel—a London firm founded in
1792 by a tool-maker from Alsace. Ellen's lathe was No. 2287. At
least, however, her parents must have been relieved to find that it
was secondhand—even so, it cost £425.

The lathe was a delicate-looking instrument rather like a treadle
sewing-machine and quite elegant enough, one would have thought,
for the drawing-room, especially as it produced only a gentle noise,
purring away like a sewing-machine or a spinning-wheel. But
perhaps Mrs Willmott had misgivings about bits and pieces of
machinery on the drawing-room tables ruining their surfaces, or
perhaps Ellen herself preferred to work in comfort in a room where
she could do as she liked, keep everything where she pleased, and
above all concentrate without visitors peering over her shoulder as
she worked: for it was indeed work which demanded a sure, deft
hand and the worker's full attention. So the work-room came into
being, and it was always kept locked. Mrs Willmott perhaps reconciled herself to the presence of this machine, and the frequency with
which her daughter shut herself up in the work-room, by reading the
list of distinguished female turners: as these included Lady Emily
Fitzmaurice, Margaret Lady Amherst, the Marchioness of
Ormonde, and Baroness Burdett-Coutts, to say nothing of many
titled owners going back to Marchioness Townshend who was the
first of the long line in 1798, then perhaps Ellen could have chosen a
worse occupation. Mrs Willmott must also have closed her eyes to
the cost of further apparatus ordered by Ellen in December 1892 (or
perhaps she had simply given up trying to curb her daughter's
extravagance). The description of the Rose Chuck, Rose Engine and
Rose Cutting Frames and Patent Automatic Driving Gear and Seg-
ment Stop Apparatus (£90) plus packing case and packing (7s 6d)
occupied six full pages of Messrs Holtzapffel's ledger, and kept Ellen
happy until 1897, when she again launched forth, this time into the
purchase of a new pattern balanced Eccentric cutting frame and a
further Rosette for use with the Rose Chuck, at a cost of £21 5s.

With this apparatus she produced some extremely attractive turnery, and is said to have made rings out of coins and performed other

party tricks, besides the more serious and accomplished work which she produced in ivory and rare hard woods. The delicate ivory boxes she made were much sought after as wedding presents. She seems to have been extremely neat-fingered and to have possessed an unusually well-developed aptitude for handling machinery. Perhaps her naturally inquiring mind directed her fingers. The only job she allotted to others was a boring (and potentially dangerous) one, requiring a great deal of patience: the sharpening of the hundreds of cutting tool-bits that she used. One of Holtzapffel's skilled workers Our Man Brown' attended at Warley Place for two stints of four and six days to tutor one of the gardeners in the job, though which of them was detailed for this, and whether as volunteer or pressed man, is not revealed. As the visits took place in 1895 and again in 1897, perhaps two gardeners had to be indoctrinated (possibly even the first left to go and do some real gardening elsewhere). The job of sharpening tool-bits was amazingly complex and demanded skill in at least six different techniques, depending on the type of tool. Some required sharpening on the oilstone, after which their edges were polished; some were sharpened by means of small straight metal grinders charged with fine flour emery; while in the case of convex and rectilinear-edged tools 'the restoration of their edges is effected by small slips of oilstone delicately applied with the fingers'. Not all gardeners, accustomed to heavy manual work, can have had the right touch or a liking for metal, and the book of instruction comments 'considerable practice is however required to sharpen the small ornamental drills and cutters of mixed forms, without losing the necessary accuracy of shape'. No mention is made of how often the tool-bits need sharpening: for the gardener's sake, one hopes that it was no more than a twice-yearly operation.

For Ellen Willmott, as usual, practical skill was backed up by a thirst for theoretical knowledge, and she acquired some valuable books on the subject, including the first book in any language devoted solely to the art of turning, *L'Art de tourner*, written by a monk, Charles Plumier, and published in Lyons in 1701. It is worth mentioning, also, that besides her very large collection of turnery tools, she assembled over the years a formidable collection of carpenter's tools, amongst which pincers (large Persian design); plane, diminutive; plane, circular rabbit, dated 1738; plane, long trying, dated 1702, particularly catch the eye. She even had a set of farrier's tools. She collected from all over the world: Oberammergau, Shiraz, Aosta, Sigmaringen, Askerabad, Annecy, Ipswich, Worcester.

Near the work-room was 'a small photographic dark-room' as a later sale catalogue describes it. Ellen's photographic interest seems to have developed alongside her talent for painting. The first surviving photograph believed to be hers is the early gardeners' photograph already described, and there are many others taken in the 1890s or 1900s which show a very good feel for people and atmosphere. Mr Potter, one of the gardeners, appears with his mongoose in one photograph, and Mr Preece, Head of the Gardens, unbending amongst his hollyhocks, in another. The first of the long series of annual photographs of gardeners must belong to 1898 or thereabouts: there they are, grouped round the sundial in front of the mansion, formal in general intention with their uniform boaters and aprons, but humanized by the sets of large boots confronting the camera from the front row, and also by the addition of several small boys who may or may not have been on the pay-roll, wearing gardeners' boaters and sitting cross-legged in the middle of the picture. There are also groups of the indoor staff, taken rather less often, but none the less interesting for that, and especially because of the strange mixture of staff who managed to be included. One such memorable photograph includes Jacob Maurer (alpine-garden foreman at that time) looking particularly mournful, Thomas Candler (herbaceous foreman—a strange title, conjuring up a strange picture) and James Preece with two of his children—Nellie, sitting bolt upright and unsmiling on the housekeeper's knee, a large hat perched on her head and her small legs dangling, and Sid, aged about two, clad in a marvellously complicated white infant's outfit and wearing on his head a halo-like confection, held tightly by the lady's maid. Apart from the children, this group somehow contrives to look like the particularly intelligent staff of a professional office. But at the same time Ellen Willmott was already prowling the garden with her camera, experimenting with views taken in all seasons, many of which she gave to her gardeners and which have come in turn to their children. Gradually she became more and more proficient and ultimately the best of her garden pictures were published by Quaritch in 1909 in a book of photographs, dedicated to her sister Rose, called *Warley Garden in Spring and Summer*. The introduction of the Kodak Box Camera in 1891, with roll-film more or less as in the present day, must have given great impetus to her photography in Warley Garden, though for group work she continued to use plates, which William, the footman, was detailed to carry to and fro for her: William would certainly rather have been up on the box of the brougham than dancing attendance on Miss Ellen, which involved hanging around downstairs with one ear cocked for the noise of distant thuds from the dark-room which would betoken the imminent ringing of a handbell.

Ellen Willmott's notebooks indicate that she had a real grasp of the technicalities of photography: they are full of notes about such matters as the ratio of exposures using spectrum plates. She also produced some coloured photographs of the garden, using the Sanger-Shepherd process. Nor did her interest stop there: she produced plates and slides for giving magic-lantern shows—a great favourite with the children of friends and an occasional treat for the estate children. The Russell children, who lived at Stubbers, near Romford, and whose parents, Champion and Isabel Russell, were close friends of the Willmotts, had such faith in her capacity to turn her hand to anything that they were quite ready to credit her with having personally photographed Vesuvius in eruption for a thrilling moving picture—and in this they were probably right, for during the Willmott family's long tour of 1888–9 they were at Naples during a 'grand irruption of Vesuvius part of the cone tumbled in and the lava rushed down the side opposite our rooms all night'. A week before this event the intrepid Ellen and Rose had made an excursion up Vesuvius, leaving Naples at eight in the morning and not getting back until six. No doubt the camera came into play on both occasions. When the contents of Warley Place were finally auctioned, no fewer than three magic lanterns appeared in the catalogue.

She owned a microscope (presumably kept in her work-room) and also a telescope, which was kept out of doors, and she was teased by Isabel Russell about the observation of Martian canals. For some reason her mentor on the use of both these instruments in the mid-1890s was Mr Green, father of the Miss Green who gave the Willmotts sketching lessons.

These occupations, however, were only diversions: Ellen's absorbing interest in gardens was developing and broadening, and it dominated everything else. In 1894 she joined the Royal Horticultural Society. She was then thirty-five years old, and had been interested in gardens all her life: why did she wait so long to join, and who persuaded her to do so (if indeed she needed persuasion)? The whole thing seems very mysterious, the more so since she was elected to the Narcissus Committee (later the Narcissus and Tulip Committee) in 1897, the three years between the two events being by RHS standards an unusually, indeed an incredibly, short interval, arguing the operation of some force outside the usual zeal of a new member. The most likely explanation seems to be that her earliest fame was as a daffodil grower and hybridizer—certainly according to the evidence of numerous small notebooks with multi-coloured shiny covers which survive and which record seedling development—and assuming that the period from seed-gathering to flowering was five years, daffodil hybridizing at Warley Place must have begun in the early 1890s. This timing tallies with the interest aroused by the second of the two Daffodil Conferences which took place under the auspices of the RHS in 1890 (the first having been held in 1884) to consider the daffodil in all its aspects: for after a long period of obscurity, this flower was regaining its lost popularity with gardeners. Some time after this conference Ellen Willmott became a member of a syndicate which bought much of the stock of that great raiser of new daffodils, the Revd G. H. Engleheart of Appleshaw, Andover. This would have carried her into the midst of the daffodil fraternity, and almost certainly also into the RHS, securing her a committee membership after only a token period of 'probationary' membership.

The committee in 1897 was chaired by Professor (later Sir Michael) Foster, with whose work on Iris Ellen Willmott became deeply involved. Vice-chairmen of this committee were the two daffodil specialists, the Revd Charles Wolley-Dod and the Revd G. H. Engleheart, and J. G. Baker of Kew, who later cooperated with Ellen Willmott in her work on Rosa. Committee members included five nurserymen—Walter Ware of Inglescombe, Peter Barr, Amos Perry, Henry de Vilmorin of Paris and Max Leichtlin of Baden-Baden. Her fellow-members were intrigued by the enthusiasm, knowledge and intelligence shown by Ellen Willmott, and gladly introduced her to other specialists: so began the growing network of contact which brought her so much satisfaction as time went on.

Just enough of her correspondence from this period survives to show, too, how she became so widely known among the numerous talented garden owners of the era, for it indicates that Lady Falmouth of Tregothnan, Lord and Lady Henry Grosvenor, and Countess Grey (born Alice Holford, of Westonbirt with its splendid Arboretum), all good gardeners, were foremost among those who spread the fame of Warley Garden and its charming and purposeful owner; and that it was certainly Lady Falmouth who introduced her to Dean Hole, so late in that great rosarian's career that he expressed the most lively regrets at having been so long deprived of such a rewarding acquaintanceship. There was no one knowledgeable about horticulture who failed to find the Warley Garden enchanting. 'It seems to me that your garden is the happiest combination of alpine, herbaceous and florist flowers, I have ever seen', wrote George Wilson of Wisley to Ellen Willmott. As a visitor, showing the most sensitive appreciation, she excelled too. 'I told a gardening friend', wrote Wilson in the same letter, 'that I never had a visitor who seemed so thoroughly to enter into what I had been driving at.'

As it fortunately transpired, her experiments at Warley continually fed her work of judging new cultivars at the RHS. Since earliest times the fields and banks at Warley had been covered with the bloom of the English lent lily (*Narcissus pseudonarcissus*) and Ellen had set eagerly to work to enhance this ancient beauty with several artistic schemes of her own. *Narcissus incomparabilis*, with the Pyrenean narcissus—*N. pallidus* (now *pallidiflorus*)—and *N. campernelli* mingled together and, spreading into drifts, began to infiltrate the North Bank and fields. In the borders and sheltered spots the diminutive *N. cyclamineus, bulbocodium* and *minimus* established themselves. Part of the secret of the entirely natural appearance of these carefully planted slopes was the manner of their planting: the gardeners' children were persuaded, without much difficulty, to throw handfuls of bulbs from a wheelbarrow over the ground—where they fell, there they were planted and there they multiplied. In the same way she encouraged the early English crocus to spread and cover the lawns and fields in front of the house, and she also laid seed beneath the turf. Once started, the bulbs scattered through the grounds in early spring had only to multiply naturally, and each year the emphasis and appearance of the grounds would shift and the colour spectrum change. Ellen Willmott also began to buy large quantities of bulbs—one order is said to have consisted of

10,000 camassias for naturalizing—and she bought from 'J. D. F. W. & Co.' (Wholesale Bulb and Seed Merchants at Co Covent Garden) crocus bulbs, white, yellow and purple, by the thousand; fritillaria and muscari; and tulips, 600 of 'Rose Queen', 600 of 'Rose Gris de Lin', 400 'La Merveille', and from 12 to 300 of many other varieties.

Her notebooks record, year by year, daffodil planting all over Warley Garden—the Wild Bed, the Fuchsia Bed, the Strawberry Square, the Sycamore Bed—in the main garden, the walled garden, the Headley garden, and the fruit garden (the old orchard). Every variety grown from the main divisions cultivated at Warley of Incomparabilis, Ajax, Burbidgei, Leedsii, (all now included in Divisions I, II and III) and Poeticus, is numbered, and the hybrids are numbered also, and many described in detail. Obviously, as she walked round the garden she mapped in her mind the treatment and fate of each new variety, stopping to prop her notebook against a tree to scrawl a reminder to herself in untidy pencilled writing. Some of the hybrids were considered to have passed the test and were destined to have a new row made of them in some suitable spot; others merited a further trial: 'might put 3 rows between chrysants by Winberry' and some found no favour: 'I bicolour deformed', and were cast at once on to the rubbish heap. Certain areas of the vinery border were used for rogues. The successful new varieties were given a name, and were then multiplied by offsets and used in their turn for further hybridization. The effect of this constant surveying of the daffodils in their season was the development of an artist's view in even the smallest areas of planting—a feel not only for the blend of colour in space, but also in time, as early blooms gave way to their later fellows. And it meant too that Ellen Willmott knew her garden to the last bulb in the smallest bed. Her notes to herself show all this: 'Mrs Bowley makes bed too crowded put her where there is a space—I think Lucifers ought to be re-planted and not so thick only the largest bulbs—The rest on this bed need not be lifted.' 'Corydon may come Snowdrop end of Moonstone group Moonstone must come next to Moon Ray instead of putting Ada and Betty between Moonstone and Moon Ray.' Other items which struck her as needing attention also went down, interspersed with the daffodil notes: to cut lime boughs away by the sweetbriar, to look to a lily clump between bay and rhodos and trim the rhodos . . . to put a bed of arum in the old place.

Many of the seedlings which she grew were entered for RHS awards, and judged by the very committee of which she was a member. Some of these were her own hybrids, but most were seedlings bought by the syndicate of which she had been a member and grown by her to great perfection. She was a good all-round grower, and did not seem to favour—at least not numerically—one division of daffodils over another. The impression nevertheless remains that she had a weakness for Triandrus hybrids: 'Mrs Berkeley' and 'Robert Berkeley' were both crosses of Triandrus and 'Minnie Hume' and both gained First Class Certificates, while the daffodil rather sadly named 'Ada' for the youngest Willmott sister was a Triandrus hybrid and also gained a First Class Certificate. 'Rev. Charles Digby', 'Count Visconti' and 'Countess Visconti', all of which gained Awards of Merit, came into this category too. In the period 1900 to 1906 Ellen Willmott took a formidable number of Awards of Merit for daffodils of various classes, including 'Eleanor Berkeley' (1900); 'Dorothy Wemyss' (1901); 'Warley Magna', 'Incognita' and 'Betty Berkeley' (1902); 'Moonstone', 'Lilian' and 'Strongbow' (1903); and 'Helen Countess of Radnor' (1905). Then for four glorious years, 1904–7, she was awarded the Gold Medal of the RHS for various groups of fine and rare daffodils. Each citation gives evidence that the group changed from year to year, and perhaps the most interesting is that given in 1906: 'Exceptionally fine group of rare Daffodils. This display gave ample evidence of the great advances made in the raising of new Daffodils during recent years, while in arrangement and from a cultural point of view it was of unusual excellence.'

The daffodil bulbs were now beginning to get into the trade. Ellen Willmott carried on business with a very large number of nurserymen and growers and the huge orders which she placed no doubt both subsidized the trade and encouraged nurserymen to step up their work on trials and to find hardy and enterprising individuals prepared to undertake the hazardous expeditions abroad necessary to make available a constant supply of new plants and bulbs. It is perhaps not understood what respect, indeed almost reverence, was accorded to Ellen Willmott by nurserymen all over the world. She was thought to be unrivalled as a cultivator of difficult subjects, searching out their requirements with great intelligence, patience and care. This comes through with particular clarity when reading straight through a series of letters from John Hoog of van Tubergens or from Henri Correvon, who always entrusted to her their rarest and most precious plants, confident that she could bring them to the point at which they could be shown more quickly, and better, than anyone else could have done. She was, however, quite capable of writing in the most stinging and icy tone when she considered the service poor. To one unfortunate nurseryman she wrote methodically listing the bulbs received from him and the results obtained down to the last bulb—a lamentable record of non-flowering and in many cases of not even being the type ordered. She ends, 'the above by no means completes the list of inferiority and error'.

Walter Ware of Inglescombe acted as her agent from 1908 to 1911, taking bulbs of Ellen Willmott's and growing them on in different conditions at Inglescombe or at Woodborough in Wiltshire. Ware took his commitments seriously, and after careful trials offered the bulbs on her behalf within the trade. There were sometimes difficulties in doing this: Hogg & Robertson of Dublin, one of the firms thus supplied, on one occasion complained that the bulbs they had received were single-nose and badly shaped, and proposed that they should pay less for them than the other seven or eight houses who had bought the bulbs, which were listed at ten guineas each, but Ware refused. However, he did not always let Ellen Willmott off lightly either, for he plainly told her that the bulbs of 'Great Warley' with which she had supplied him were rather flat-sided and that, at five guineas each, this was apt to make purchasers grumble. He suggested that she should supply him (or van Tubergen in Haarlem, if she preferred) with some big splits to plant on sandy soil to produce good round clean bulbs. In general the system worked well: the initial hybridizing and raising done at Warley, the showing at the RHS, followed by a period of growing and trials by Ware or other nurserymen, and then a gradual taking up by the trade. Sometimes the process was reversed, and in 1904 Barrs were tempting Ellen Willmott with an offer of six 'Apricot Phoenix', a double daffodil which they had exhibited at Birmingham in 1903 and which they had tried to purchase from a grower but balked (as well they might) at his price of £100 per bulb. Now they were offering Ellen Willmott all of the grower's saleable stock in that year, six bulbs at £30 each, so that she and the grower alone would possess the whole stock.

She often met and talked with nurserymen at the various shows in

London, Birmingham and other cities, or at the Narcissus Committee of the RHS (though this only convened over the period March to
May each year). These included Barr of Covent Garden, Hogg &
Robertson of Dublin, Ware, Kingsmill of Harrow, James Douglas of
Great Bookham, van Tubergen of Haarlem (with whom, in the
person of John Hoog, she exchanged many letters, not only on bulbs,
but also on shrubs and herbaceous plants), Miss Currey, who owned
a flourishing nursery at Lismore in Ireland, and a pleasantly diffident
man, Christopher Bourne, who was gradually building up a nursery
specializing in daffodils. There was considerable controversy at the
time about the price of bulbs, and indeed by the standards of the day
the cost seemed huge: for example, Miss Currey's list for 1902
quotes new daffodils being sent out by James Douglas at costs
ranging from one guinea for 'Golden Bell', a large, rich yellow
trumpet daffodil, to £20 for 'White Queen', a large flower of 'Sir
Watkin'-like outline, of uniform ivory-white when fully out. It
took, in all, a period of about twelve to sixteen years from the initial
hybridization of a daffodil to its being fully taken up by the trade.
Thus Ellen Willmott's work of the 1890s was producing results in
the new daffodils shown at the RHS in the early 1900s, reaching its
peak of achievement in her Gold Medal groups of 1904–7, and in the
Award of Merit gained by 'Great Warley' in 1904, described as 'the
finest Incomparabilis yet raised'; for its presentation at the Show the
Revd G. H. Engleheart gave her the most strict and detailed instructions. By about 1909 the daffodils which Ellen Willmott had
been showing in the early 1900s had passed into the trade, and she
then gradually ceased to exhibit at RHS Shows, and very possibly
ceased also her daffodil hybridizing activities, reflecting the changing
focus of her attention, which was beginning to turn to bulbs and
seeds from China.

The last major award for a new daffodil—the Award of Merit for
Narcissus 'Warleyensis' (an Ajax daffodil)—came to her in 1906, and
the last Gold Medal for a group of daffodils in 1907, the same year as
Walter Ware gained an Award of Merit for the splendid Poeticus
'Miss Willmott'. Thereafter, though she was assiduous in her attendance at Narcissus Committee meetings, there were no further
awards for new daffodils grown at Warley Place—though she was
still supplying the trade with quite large quantities of bulbs, as letters
written to her by Barr in 1912 indicate: how many of the 500

'Cresset' bulbs for which a customer has asked can Miss Willmott supply? They would like to take up the supplies of' Scarlet Eye' and 'White Queen' for which they had asked. This seems to argue a high production, if less experimental work, at Warley.

It seems hardly possible that chicanery could find its way into such seemingly blameless surroundings, but it did. The Revd G. H. Engleheart disputed hotly with Barr over their use of the daffodil name 'Mars', which he claimed was his. And Ellen Willmott believed that she had bought the whole stock of 'Incognita', a beautiful Incomparabilis with a glowing crown, but a bulb was intercepted and in 1904 one or two bulbs were being offered for sale at seven guineas a bulb. 'It is well worth it', she said, 'but I am sad about its thus having got into the trade.'

The alpine garden also needed her attention, and she was finding that even with help from her sister, and from the Warley Place gardeners, expert advice was going to be essential for the propagation of alpine plants and the gradual planting of the slopes she had fashioned with a harmonious gathering of rarities.

It happened that in Tresserve Ellen Willmott was well placed for making a foray from time to time to the Jardin d'Acclimatation of the Swiss horticulturist Henri Correvon, at Geneva. Here, while viewing Monsieur Correvon's garden, her observant eye fell on a young Swiss boy, then no more than seventeen, who seemed to have a way of handling plants, and an air of being entirely absorbed in his work and undistracted by the charming but purposeful visitor, which recommended themselves to her. And so there took place the first of many pieces of poaching from other people's garden staffs, some triumphant and some successfully repelled by indignant employers or refused by loyal gardeners. The young Swiss was Jacob Maurer, who came from Herrliberg on the lake of Zurich. He had been apprenticed to a market gardener at Steefa, also on the lake of Zurich, and then after two short-term jobs had come to Monsieur Correvon. Ellen Willmott (who could be extremely persuasive when in pursuit of something she really wanted) promised him a house of his own and a pension of £1 a week after his retirement, and so he agreed to come to Warley Place in 1894. Correvon was perhaps less affected by this than might have been expected, for he had often referred in correspondence to his wish to help her find a good gardener who could properly tend the rare and delicate plants which he sent her—often when some traveller returned from Persia, Bosnia, Turkestan or other distant places bearing only a strictly limited number of plants Correvon allowed only one of them to leave his nursery, and that one would be consigned to Warley. Jacob Maurer was known to be trustworthy and a good propagator, and could almost be treated as a kind of out-station of the Correvon garden.

Maurer was nineteen, and alone in a strange country, but he was adaptable, and his employer spoke good German. The sight of the alpine garden, and the chance it gave him to use his knowledge and skill must have rejoiced his heart. Here were conditions in which every mountain plant in the world could flourish: sheltered, exposed, dry or moist conditions, sun or shade, and small areas where the composition of the soil could be altered to suit the foibles of some exigent newcomer. The first surviving photographs of the alpine garden were made after Jacob Maurer had lavished ten years of the most devoted and unremitting attention upon it—there it is, recorded in *Warley Garden in Spring and Summer*: *Primula sikkimensis* and *sinensis* cascading down between lichen-covered rocks; great spreading clumps of tiny *Dianthus gracilis* and *plumasius* (among twenty-four species and varieties grown at Warley); iris; geranium; *Campanula pusilla (cochlearifolia)* from the Rhône Glacier; *Gentiana verna* in many shades of colour and *G. acaulis*; *Aethionema persicum* and *graecum*; and countless varieties of *Sempervivum* brought from Tresserve. In a sunny spot *Daphne odora* filled the air with scent, and helianthemum in every shade of red, pink, yellow and cream coloured the sunny slopes. *Trillium*, *Cistus* and *Erodium* diverted the eye, the murmur of the stream and the movement of countless butterflies making the alpine garden an entrancing and hypnotic place to wander in.

Correvon, however, was not entirely satisfied, and did not hesitate to voice a counsel of perfection in his strange English: 'You will, I am sure, quite agree with me when I say that Mahonias have nothing to do there in an alpine garden and even that Cotoneasters must be put away. Those plants, of a foreign and exotic temper and aspect, must be avoided in the composition of such a garden as they are not at all "dans l'esprit de la chose"—You can replace them by small & dwarf conifers/Juniperus Sabina and nana, Pinus Pumilis etc. Mr Preece was quite of my opinion, I am glad to say. And double flowers have too nothing to do there: put them away. For the others [*sic*] things all

[78]

is right. . . .' No one else would have dared so harangue Miss Willmott of Warley Place.

Such a huge area could not rely on seeding and spreading alone, so behind South Lodge, into which Jacob Maurer moved with his young Swiss wife in about 1905, there was installed a circular alpine propagating house which supplied the garden.

Quietly, from about 1890 onwards, the Willmotts had added to their estate some twenty-two acres of land on the eastern side of the main road to Brentwood. Warley Lea, bought for Robert and Rose Berkeley, accounted for just over ten acres, and also included were the Headley garden, headquarters of the vegetable and fruit growing for the estate, splendid with peach houses, vines and an orangery (and which may have been part of the project of launching James Preece); the Bothy (which actually consisted of two semi-detached houses, now called The Croft and The Glen) in which the single gardeners lived and were looked after by Mr and Mrs Saywood; and groups of cottages, thatched or slate-roofed, some of them near the Headley garden and some almost opposite the south gate of Warley Place, in which the foremen and some of the more favoured of the other gardeners lived with their families. There was also a considerable acreage of land behind the gardeners' cottages, a wild area near to them, and behind that the Well Mead garden which held Miss Willmott's prized and rare rose collection. We must not, however, in talking of Miss Willmott's collections, lose sight of the fact that her mother was, in her prime, a most energetic and enterprising gardener, and it may have been she who started the rose collection with seed which she obtained from friends travelling in distant parts of the world (perhaps including the kind friend of her husband who set Ellen Ann's feet on her destined path many years before). One of these may have been *Rosa fedtschenkoana*, collected in the Turkestan and Koram regions of Central Asia in the 1870s by Madame Olga Fedtschenko (who later spent some time working at Kew). The rose reached Warley via the Botanic Garden of St Petersburg and flowered there for the first time in England. So, imperceptibly, the garden moved from being a country gentleman's garden of considerable beauty and artistry to an estate with a complex organization, managed with an originality and inventiveness which the gentle Essex countryside had rarely seen.

During this period, James Preece must have made his first tentative efforts at showing his chrysanthemums and other plants reared in the hothouses in the Headley garden. At the start, his efforts were confined to the immediate neighbourhood, and his family still possess a cup presented to him by Mrs Willmott in 1897 for a group of chrysanthemums, and a medal won at the Crystal Palace National Chrysanthemum Show for eighteen Japanese blooms.

Another enterprise was set on foot in about 1902. Miss Willmott's purchases from Messrs Holtzapffel had not stopped at the lathe and its adjuncts: printing, it seemed, tempted her as much as turnery and so she invested in a printing press—or rather, in two of them. On 26 January 1897, Holtzapffel's ledger records the sale of a best Cowper's Parlour Printing Press, with a small mahogany type case with brass lock and key and brass handles, and drawers containing about 2,500 types and a proportionate supply of leads and brass rules etc.—price £8 plus 6s packing case and packing. Its performance, however, cannot have given satisfaction, for on 9 March in the same year we find her purchasing Holtzapffel's Monotype Printing Press complete, plus a hand chase in painted case with cushion, ink roller and inking tray, price £3 15s complete. Ellen Willmott probably used this machine to turn out her own lists of seeds gathered at Warley Place and to be made available both to her friends and to botanical gardens all over the world in exchange for seed from their gardens. In some years (the exact dates are not known) lists of *Bulbophyllum* (a genus of the orchid family) were also sent out.

The seed lists were formidable affairs—six or seven pages of foolscap, printed in Pica type fount, nicely lined up except for the occasional lurch, and without mistakes. Page 1 was embellished with two pieces of Latin, which Ellen Willmott took trouble to check with H. E. Luxmoore at Eton and with the Revd G. H. Engleheart of daffodil fame. In the first of these, which appeared at the head of the first page, she confined herself to commenting that there followed a list of seeds available from Warley Place for exchange: but in the second, at the foot, she was unable to resist a tart admonition to the recipient not to mess up the list with pencil marks, since space had been left at the bottom of the page for comments. She forgot, it seems, that her gardeners were unlikely to understand Latin prose, however accustomed they might be to Latin names of flowers, and a list surviving from 1912 has been heavily annotated in James Preece's handwriting. In other ways, though, the use of Latin had distinct practical advantages. Ellen Willmott's seed lists were distributed world wide, and it was certainly easier for the botanical gardens in Latvia and Tashkent, for example, to send their lists of desiderata with comments in Latin than to attempt communication in their native languages. The operation was a time-consuming business: Ellen Willmott kept a book for each year's 'harvest', recording dispatches, and also recording the arrival of similar lists from other establishments, which she scanned avidly and from which she acquired seeds that provided her with many interesting plants. The Warley seed list makes fascinating reading, showing the great variety of almost everything cultivated there—twelve kinds of Mecanopsis, twenty-four of *Delphinium*, forty of *Campanula*, thirty-five of *Crocus*, forty-five of *Saxifraga*, and twenty-five of *Primula*, amongst many other sizable groups. The lists must have been popular, as they were repeated annually, and certainly printing became one of Ellen Willmott's very useful minor skills. It is also evidence of the amount of trouble which she could expend—or cause to be expended (she with the printing press, every foreman she employed with the finicky task of seed-gathering, and hours of paperwork for James Preece in sorting out and supplying the incoming demands)—on the effort to share with others the riches of Warley Garden. Views of her attitude towards giving things away vary enormously, from the Linnaean Society's obituary which talked of 'the treasures from her garden, which were always at the disposal of her friends', to the rather more realistic comment of the Russells, who had known her and her gardening ways for many years: 'As gardeners go she was not considered generous, and one looked carefully at gift plants for fear they might be fearful spreaders.'

The list of the RHS Narcissus Committee members in 1897 contains a remarkable number of people who became important to Ellen Willmott in later life, including the French nurseryman Henry de Vilmorin, brother of Maurice de Vilmorin who subsequently was to suffer from her tongue and pen—perhaps the result of a prolonged visit to Warley Place in 1906, when the whole de Vilmorin family stayed with her for four weeks, which she found to be quite long enough. Her contact with F. W., later Sir Frederick, Moore led to her long association with the Glasnevin (now National) Botanic Gardens at Dublin, where there are still some of her photographs in the library, and for a long personal correspondence with him.

A Vice-Chairman of the Committee was the Revd C. Wolley-Dod, and sometime about 1897 he must have invited Ellen, possibly also with Rose, to stay at Edge Hall in Cheshire. During this visit, and as a result of some brisk discussion on the subject of daffodils, with varying opinions held by the company, it was suggested that Ellen should go and visit Canon Ellacombe and see his famous garden at Bitton Vicarage. Her account of this first visit is interesting, and typical.

> On my first visit to Bitton I went from Paddington by the nine o'clock express, having ordered a good pair of horses to meet me at Bath to take me out to Bitton. Just as I was getting into the victoria at Bath, a voice said: 'I am sure you are Miss Willmott, and coming to see my Vicarage Garden? You are very welcome, and your visit is one to which I have been looking forward.
>
> 'I travelled down by the same train and looked out for you at Paddington, but expecting to see one of more mature years, I missed you.'

There is no doubt that such comments fed Ellen's natural vanity—the vanity which made her, to the end of her life, when asked for a photograph of herself, send a copy of the pastel of a much younger Ellen Willmott. Besides this natural pleasure in a flattering remark, Ellen was obviously pleased that her visit to Bitton was a success, and she in her turn greatly and genuinely admired both her host and his garden. It is, of course, always doubly pleasant when one is received into the elite while others are excluded, and Ellen Willmott clearly conveys this in her description of the treatment meted out to those visitors who did not altogether please the Canon—' I admired the neat, but unmistakable way in which the intimation was conveyed to the visitor.' (Ellen herself was to develop a very similar skill in her later years.) Not only at Bitton, but at other interesting gardens she was a welcome, but not always an uncritical guest. She went to stay with Lord and Lady Falmouth at Tregothnan, and commented to Sir William Thiselton-Dyer, Director of the Royal Botanic Gardens at Kew, that the Cornish knew all about New Zealand and Australian trees but absolutely nothing about herbaceous plants, bulbs and alpines.

She carried on a lively if sporadic correspondence with a wry and imperious Irishman, W. E. Gumbleton, who gardened at Belgrove in County Cork, and who was the possessor of a notable botanic library. In these letters they discussed the whole range of their interests, which coincided in a remarkable fashion: botanical works, performances at the Saturday Pops (to which Gumbleton was addicted, travelling from Ireland to attend some of them), the sets of photographs taken at Warley and at Tresserve which Ellen Willmott sent to him and what the best professional photographer in Cork thought of them, and so on. Gumbleton was not a patient man, and frequently took her to task for the gaps in her correspondence. A typical letter ran as follows:

> Dear Lady Warley
> Although I do not know *where* you now are having last heard of the Meteor as temporarily abiding at *Vienna* I suppose these lines will reach you on your return home or elsewhere. . . . *You promised* in your last hurried line to write to me at greater length from Tresserve but did *not* do so.

Nor did he spare others, for he went on to say:

> I am sure you will agree with me in *regretting* the lowering of the price of *The Garden* to one penny from the commencement of the New Year. When the Editor told me of it yesterday I said to him at once 'it will be *Cheap* and *Nasty*'. . . .

The Garden was not then, as now, a publication of the Royal Horticultural Society, but a weekly journal started by the indefatigable William Robinson in 1871. Robinson, who had started work as a gardener's boy in Ireland, and had later moved into the field of writing about gardens, was the most senior of the three—the other two being Gertrude Jekyll and Ellen Willmott—who at the end of the Victorian era pressed the cause of natural and artistic gardening and carried it against the restrictions of Victorian garden planning, which aimed for mass effects in the summer months only. Indeed, it must have been about this time that the gardening friendship which lasted for the rest of their lives began between Ellen Willmott and Gertrude Jekyll. The latter made the garden at Munstead Wood and many other famous gardens, most of them designed to complement houses planned by that rising architect Ned Lutyens, whom Ellen Willmott herself commissioned to make some alterations at Warley Lea for the Berkeleys. Gertrude Jekyll was a completely different character from

Ellen Willmott: sturdier, more equable, and yet quite as capable of administering devastating rebuke when deserved; but she had similar ideas on the development of a garden as an artistic whole, and was generous with her praise, for it was she who in her book *Children and Gardens* gave Ellen Willmott the accolade of calling her 'the greatest of living women-gardeners'. She also wrote to Ellen Willmott saying that she was having great pleasure in translating Henri Correvon's description of Warley for *The Garden* (of which she was then the editor), in doing which she had asked the botanist to '*modérer ses transports*' for otherwise he might pile up the language so that the translation had to be done twice—first into moderation and then into English! (Not his fault, for French expression is naturally more exuberant and flowery.)

And so Ellen's contacts and friendships in the gardening world multiplied and her opinion became respected and sought after. The gardens she planned did not quite match the scale of Miss Jekyll's, but her advice was often sought and willingly given. The Royal Horticultural Society demonstrated its view of her worth by including her among the first sixty recipients of the Victoria Medal of Honour, inaugurated in 1897 as a mark of homage for the Queen's Diamond Jubilee. It was fitting, and a matter of pleasure to them both, that she and Gertrude Jekyll were the only two women who were honoured in this way. A strange feature of the occasion, though, is that Ellen Willmott (along with several other recipients, it should be said) was not present to receive her honour. The date was 26 October, and this was the time of year which she normally spent at Tresserve. All the same, for this unique occasion, and one where the award bestowed must surely have flattered her self-esteem, it is very odd that she apparently made no effort to attend the ceremony. Gertrude Jekyll, who did manage to get there, received the acclamation due to both of them, as well as the President's very pointed reference to the 'one lady present'. Dean Hole, the rosarian Dean of Rochester and first President of the National Rose Society, responding to the Loyal Toast on behalf of the medallists, went so far as to remark that although only one lady was present, no other could have represented the fair sex so appropriately, so regally, at this Jubilee meeting, because they all acknowledged Miss Jekyll as the 'Queen of Spades'.

With Kew, as with the RHS, her contacts were developing fast, and in the grand manner she wrote to Thiselton-Dyer in January 1897: 'I should be glad to have the accompanying tree named.' It seems a pity that no description remains of the arrival at Kew of the postman bearing this request.

She was not falsely modest: she also wrote, rather grimly, to Sir William saying, 'Persons who ought to know better have stood me out that I was wrong', but as she was talking about the importance of the library at Kew, which she felt to be too little understood, he probably forgave her.

Life, however, was not all turnery, photography, printing and gardens. The family claimed her attention too. The presence of Rose and Robert Berkeley with their small daughter at Warley Lea must have given both sisters enormous satisfaction, particularly as Rose was also engaged in making a garden—a much smaller one, it is true—for the new house, and needed advice, and plants, from Warley Place. Then in the late summer of 1893 Rose's second child—a daughter, Rosamund—had been born in London, and died of meningitis in March of the following year. There was nothing to soften the blow—only work in the garden, the presence of her family near her, and young Eleanor, now nearly two years old. Three years later, when Rose was again pregnant, the pleasant life of the young Berkeleys at Warley Lea came to an end, for in September 1897 old Mr Berkeley died at Spetchley and it was Robert's turn to assume the care of the estate and to live at Spetchley Park. Both to Rose and to her family the move must have been a matter of great sadness, and though Warley Lea remained for the Berkeleys to use as a holiday house, it could never have been quite the same. Worcester was a long way away across country, and the sisters had never been separated for any length of time before. Life at Spetchley Park was obviously going to be a good deal less cosy than life at Warley Lea: Robert would be very much absorbed in the affairs of the estate, and since Lady Catherine Berkeley survived her husband, and two of her unmarried daughters, Maud and Constance, were still living at Spetchley, the arrival of Rose would mean that adjustments would have to be made on all sides. Rose, however, distracted the energies and attention of the family and thus smoothed a potentially difficult situation by producing a son, Robert George Wilmot, in April 1898. (Wilmot happened to be the name of a relation on Lady Catherine's side, and thus was a compliment to her rather than a perpetuation of

Rose's maiden name.) In fact, Lady Catherine and her daughters moved away from Spetchley, and Rose set to work on an orgy of redecorating in the house, and in the garden swiftly set her own imprint.

Meanwhile, at Warley Place, the health of Mrs Willmott had over a long period been slowly deteriorating. Her crippling rheumatism had for long prevented her from undertaking in the garden the energetic work to which she had once been accustomed, and her determination to see what was going on from her donkey chaise gradually faltered. In the winter of 1897–8 she was ill enough for Ellen to be summoned back from Tresserve to look after her. She survived to see her new grandson, and died some six weeks after his birth, on 31 May 1898, of heart disease. Jacob Maurer wrote to Henri Correvon to tell of the sad loss that had befallen them all—at least, he said, Mrs Willmott had been out in the garden in her Bath chair only a few hours before her death, so that she had enjoyed her flowers almost until the end. Only a simple notice of death appeared in the *Essex Weekly News*, but 'mamma' was greatly mourned and missed —as Correvon had said earlier: 'Madame Willmott . . . has such a large and good heart.' Ellen herself, who was so rarely ill, took to her bed immediately after the funeral, presumably succumbing to the strain.

Sensible and energetic in life, Mrs Willmott, well knowing the characters of her daughters, disposed her will accordingly. At that time many ladies of her years would have taken advice and then left the whole business to solicitors, but in this case, although it is quite clear that Mrs Willmott had sought the opinion of her late husband's firm—now Messrs Hawks, Stokes and McKewan—her will yet bears the stamp of a robust, individual approach. Made in the year of her husband's death, the will was witnessed by the solicitor's clerk, Henry Dixson (who had acted as her business adviser) and also, setting the seal of approval on its provisions, by the family's old friend, Monsignor Francis Weld. The will left a small annuity to her unmarried sister Adelaide (also included by Frederick Willmott in his will as a contingency item, and thus obviously considered by his wife as a fair use of his money). Of the rest, everything in and around Warley Place was to go to Ellen (for Rose now had a far grander house and possessions of her own). Everything else was to be converted into money and, aware of Ellen's careless attitude and perhaps fearing (as it happens, with some justification) that Rose might be tempted to overspend in her new life, Mrs Willmott prudently put all the proceeds into a residuary trust, half for Ellen absolutely, and half for Rose, with suitable provision for the Berkeley children after Rose's death.

On 21 June 1898—during another recurrent period of importance (Uncle William's birth and death, Ada's christening)—probate was granted to Ellen and Rose. A new era was beginning at Warley Place.

CHAPTER V

The Silver-headed Key

It must have been an awesome feeling to be at last alone, the only Willmott in the house. Though no one could have described Ellen Willmott as a biddable woman, at least if anyone could protect her from the worst of the mistakes her impulsiveness drove her to make, it was her parents. And now they were both dead. She was nearly forty, with no ties of marriage. Perhaps she would have liked them, but she was a forceful woman in early middle age and it seems that the time for ties had passed. The days of Ainslie Hight, of Captain Scott and of Mr Handley, seemed far away.

The realization gradually dawned on her that she was free, at last, to do exactly as she pleased. As the thought settled and penetrated, and the natural grief at her mother's death lifted a little, her spirits suddenly rose and a wave of energy pulsed through her. Now she would no longer be trammelled by the inherited sense of thrift of her parents, but could live in a style as grand as that of some of her friends, and make Warley Garden the envy of the civilized world. She could move in circles brilliant and distinguished, concentrating on matters of large interest, or on the kind of detail which, planned with careful attention, could influence the course of events. Other people could deal with trivia which she considered too tedious to merit her time and energy.

Her resources must have seemed enormous: she was mistress of Warley Place and of everything in and around it, and she had also inherited from her mother some £70,000; from the Countess Tasker her inheritance had been in the region of £140,000, and there was also the residue (after the alpine garden had been made) of the £1,000 which she had received every birthday. Most of this money had been invested for her by her father. So by any standards she was a very wealthy woman, and since not even Ellen Willmott could spend money as quickly as all that, and since she had her father's firm to advise her, she must have received a considerable income. But money in itself was of no interest to her: she cared for it only in its creative capacity. And one disservice which Frederick had rendered his daughters was to give them the impression that they would never need to soil their hands with financial management. Presumably he thought that they would both marry, and that their husbands would carry the responsibility. It was a very shortsighted attitude. Ellen seems to have been aware only of the income, and thought little of the outgoings. As an outward sign of her new status, she changed her signature, writing simply 'Ellen Willmott', rather than signing her full name, as she had done when her mother was alive. And one other thing: she had built for her new possessions a second safe, and for this she had made a special key with a silver head carrying her initials. She had become the head of the family.

A necessity of Ellen Willmott's existence was that she must have the best, and have it without stint, and without needing to count the cost. So, after the death of her mother, her first task was to review the household arrangements. Here Mrs Willmott had been firmly in charge for many years: she had received £50 a month for housekeeping when the family first arrived at Warley, and this was doubled in 1891. Though there had been some difficulties with servants, she had in general been an excellent mistress of the house: fair, calm, pleasant—and extremely particular. As she had had the invaluable Robinson working with her, there was, on the change of ownership, little which needed more than the small modifications which Robinson himself could deal with. Robinson was now firmly installed in the Red House, a pleasant little double-fronted Victorian house set between the post office and the village store/tearooms. Ironically, whereas Rose Willmott had been married at the local Catholic church, Robinson had been accorded a very grand wedding at St George's, Hanover Square. This was because his wife had been cook-housekeeper to Lady Algernon Percy, the daughter-in-law of the Duke of Northumberland, for so long, and was in the nature of a parting present. Lord Algernon Percy, who had been MP for the Hanover Square constituency for several years previously, had a house in the district and it was from there that the wedding took place in the early spring of 1894.

Moving into the Red House, however, brought the Robinsons

down to earth with a bump, for the house was sketchily divided into two with curtains; the back part was occupied by one of Miss Willmott's elderly gardeners, and no proper kitchen or washing arrangements were available. Neither Robinson nor his wife was accustomed to such frugality. They used the laundry-room at the back of the house, but it was very inconvenient. Still, they were together and they had a house, and in the early summer of 1895 their son, James Robert—called Jim—was born. The print of W. G. Grace was put up on the kitchen wall, and they made the best of things. Robinson enjoyed his job: he had liked and respected the elder Willmotts, and sincerely mourned their deaths; and now he felt real responsibility towards the wayward and talented Ellen. She, for her part, respected his qualities. It seems unlikely that she told him so, for such was not her way, but she showed her reliance by the demands which she made upon him and the expectations which she clearly felt.

The recruiting of good house staff does not seem to have given Robinson and the housekeeper, Mrs McCullum, much trouble; and staff stayed, for although standards were high the company in the servants' hall was good, and there were always gardeners at work near the house to negotiate or gossip with, according to who you were and what you wanted. Furthermore, the mistress of the house was often away and when she was in residence she was usually busy in the garden and had no time for, or interest in, prowling round the house checking for dust. Robinson, while keeping everyone well up to the mark, was no tyrant in the servants' hall and so, on the whole, only marriage or some pressing family concern caused staff to leave. Besides Robinson and Mrs McCullum, the indoor staff at full strength seem to have consisted of three footmen, three housemaids, a lady's maid, kitchen-maid and scullery-maid—but it varied at different stages in the household's history. Robinson was not pretentious enough to take his meals separately in his sitting-room, so all the staff ate together in the servants' hall. Occasionally there were French staff, brought from Tresserve, and one of these, Jean Perroux, acted for two years as a kind of travelling footman; but until the early 1900s there was no one else who spoke French at Warley Place except Miss Willmott herself, and she was much too occupied to concern herself with giving English lessons or talking to foreign staff.

Out of doors, there were changes to be made after Mrs Willmott's death. Oakley and his successor King had both been described as 'coachman/groom', but Ellen Willmott now engaged an experienced coachman, Henry Hurcombe, who moved with his young family of two boys and a girl from Hampstead to Apple Tree Cottage, a white-painted cottage covered with white clematis in early summer and set in a large garden almost opposite Warley Lea. Hurcombe had plenty to do. The coach-house, a little distance from the mansion, was, as later sale particulars describe it, 'a red-brick, roughcast, part weatherboard and tiled range surmounted by a clock turret and fox weathervane' and had six stalls and a harness room, with four loose boxes. Three horses were kept, and one of the stalls housed the Warley Place watch-dog's kennel, until he was eventually given a little railed-off enclosure rather like a Victorian tomb, in front of which he appears proudly waving his tail in one of Miss Willmott's prints of the estate. Every night a watchman patrolled the grounds with the dog. Next to the stalls and loose boxes came the coach-house itself, and on the first floor, reached by an outside staircase, were several rooms where the groom and stable-boy lived, together with two or three of the gardeners. There was nowhere for them to eat in these quarters, and they could not use the servants' hall, so they probably joined the gardeners in the Bothy, about five minutes' walk away on the other side of the road.

The stable pond on the north side of the stable yard was not strictly speaking in Hurcombe's province, and the four-foot wall bordering it meant that in any case the horses could not drink there. It belonged to the garden rather than to the stable and was used, together with the large underground tank which collected rainwater from the eaves of the house, for the prodigious amounts of watering which had to be done—hand-watering normally, with the immediate supply taken from a small zinc tub on wheels. The Warley habit was for one of the gardeners to check the borders first and then flag with a red-topped post those plants, newly set or otherwise, which were in dire need of water. It was a system which worked well. The stable pond was kept filled by Mr Thomas, the water engineer, who pumped well-water from the pump house, either on demand, or more likely at a regular time each day. The lengths of suction pipe which were kept in the outbuildings must have been used to draw supplies from this pond. There was another pond in the old orchard, and one in the nursery area, both presumably kept filled in the same way. The pump house lay on the other side of the road, through a white gate near the smithy, and down the path leading to the Well Mead garden; it was surrounded by bushes and the wells which served it. This must have been a most inconvenient arrangement, for what happened if the stable pond overflowed? Even a gardener running at full tilt would take some minutes to bring this intelligence to the pump house. But most likely the safe maximum of pumping had been early established, and thereafter the life of the water engineer, who doubled as shop-and-tearooms proprietor (though his wife and daughter did most of the work), must have been a pleasant one. It is typical of Ellen Willmott that the care of the garden loomed so large that she should appoint a water engineer for such a relatively small estate.

To return, however, to the stable yard. If the groom wanted to wash down the horses, there was a tap at hand. With such a variety of carriages for Miss Willmott to choose from, all had to be kept in first-class trim, but as often as not her choice fell on the brougham, especially if she was alone or with one companion. She liked the good view ahead, the protection from the weather, and the fact that the groom or footman and the coachman could travel together on the box, driving to only one horse. It was a light and handy method of transport.

But the coaches were not used as much as they might have been, for Ellen Willmott was an energetic woman who favoured walking and so, where possible, she carried out her local business on foot. Some of the carriages were never used; some were used only for picking up visitors or parcels, or when the lady's maid had some piece of business to transact. When she did use a coach, the turn-out looked very smart with the coachman and footman in fawn livery with black top hats and cockades, wearing dark blue mackintoshes when it rained. Sometimes she went calling in the afternoons, but when alone at Warley did not normally go out in the evenings. As a rule, therefore, Hurcombe's evenings were not disturbed, except for feeding the horses. On Sundays she was driven to the Warley Catholic church in the brougham for early mass; Hurcombe then drove back to his cottage for a cup of tea, returning later to collect her. The arrival of her coach on those occasions when she travelled from Brentwood Station, the groom springing down from the box to let the step down for her and the station master bustling out to greet her, is still remembered by people who lived on Warley Hill.

From the coach-house to the garden. With James Preece now firmly established and in control, and several excellent foremen working under him—Jacob Maurer for alpines, Thomas Candler for herbaceous plants, Messrs Haynes, Gooch and Horton for vegetables and fruit, Goodwin for roses and Dyer for chrysanthemums—everything was poised for development. For there was more, much more, that Ellen Willmott intended to do with the garden, and that which was already satisfactory must now be perfect. Most important of all was the serious work which she herself undertook in the growing of plants, testing them in every variety of soil and conditions. This care and skill ranged all the way from the single plants which she grew for showing, to her work on roses, which was in its early stages and which ultimately was to test to the limit all her intellectual and practical abilities. Experiment fascinated her above all else and in one year, for example, every known variety of potato was cultivated in the vegetable garden, to find out which was best suited to the Warley soil.

For all this she needed a vastly increased staff, and Preece must have been hard at work recruiting. Many years later Robinson told the last of Ellen Willmott's housekeepers that in the heyday of Warley Place there were 104 gardeners, and there was certainly work for that number, since no weed was allowed to show its head in path, border or bed, and the usual operations of digging, manuring, spraying and mowing were increased a hundredfold in a garden of that size kept to that standard. (One wonders if Ellen Willmott kept to old-fashioned methods of insect-killing and plant-feeding or whether she indulged in some of the new products which had been coming on the market since the late 1870s—' Feedmright' and 'Killm-right', for instance.) There were countless jobs to be done in the Warley Garden: clearing the streams, lifting and planting thousands of bulbs, gathering seeds on an almost commercial scale, swaying perilously out to the middle of the lake in a punt to cut the overhanging branches of the trees, garden jobs, greenhouse jobs, jobs with the cold frames, in the stoke-holes, up trees, clipping hedges—the list is unending. Miss Willmott devised a uniform for the gardeners, consisting of boaters (which presumably were taken off while working) in green and natural straw with a green band round them, knitted green silk ties, and navy blue aprons (which they had to remove, fold up and tuck under their arms when they went home or even when they crossed the road to get to the other part of the garden). The uniform looked very smart and may have made young gardeners feel they were entering a very grand establishment, but it could hardly have been fun to wear.

Some of the gardeners taken on were apprentices—among them, at a slightly later stage, was Preece's eldest son, Charlie, who worked for a time with Jacob Maurer and then with Tom Candler; when he left in 1911 to work for James Veitch & Sons Ltd he received testimonials from all three. His notebooks, kept in a neat, round hand, record propagating notes for plants, and jobs he had been engaged in, such as budding roses. Then there were improvers, foreign gardeners brought over from France, Holland or Germany because they possessed special skills, or because their employers wanted them to gain further experience, and finally good experienced gardeners looking for a change and to better themselves.

Accommodation for all these extra workers was a problem, but somehow they were fitted in. Some lived in Great Warley anyhow and others within walking distance, while there were about twenty cottages in the village belonging to the estate in which gardeners who had come from farther afield could live, as well as rooms above the coach-house. The Bothy was probably drawn into use for gardeners at the turn of the century: two houses together, with no interconnecting doors, it had large rooms and could have taken as many as forty men if they had shared rooms, which many of the younger ones must have liked doing for company (it was one thing to be glad to leave home, if home meant sharing a small room with four brothers, but quite another to be happy entirely alone—different qualities were required). To some, coming from large families, it must have seemed the height of luxury to be thus housed, well fed and looked after by the Saywoods, while enjoying each other's company when work was over. Not that there was very much time left, for they worked from 6 a.m. to 6 p.m. (4 p.m. on Saturdays). Sundays were free. Yet they did apparently enjoy entertaining themselves, and sometimes organized musical evenings, when one of them played the mandolin. Their wages were 18s. a week—18s. 6d. for the foremen—and a rise was apparently never contemplated by Miss Willmott. That was the agreed wage, and no more.

Preece had a great deal of organizing to do, and also a great deal of paperwork—which he may not have liked, although clearly he was the possessor of a good, firm hand. There were frequent emergencies to deal with: Miss Willmott could be impulsive and generous, and often large quantities of plants had to be packed and shipped here and there at short notice. Correspondence at Kew contains a very long saga concerning a box of herbarium specimens which was packed but never collected from Warley; naturally, the packers from Kew who came to collect the boxes from Warley were blamed, and had not the Director of Kew quietly but firmly closed the subject it could have developed into one of those complicated battles in which Ellen Willmott specialized. Then there were the plants to be packed for shows in London, Birmingham, Colchester, and so on; and finally the seed lists to be checked and distributed, seeds to be packaged and sent out to friends, and seeds coming in to be carefully sown and watched as they grew. No wonder Preece sometimes stayed working in his little office behind the mansion until after his men had gone.

When the Willmotts first bought Warley Place it was described as having 'early and late Vineries, greenhouse and Cold Pits', and the outbuildings at the side of the house included provision for cows, pigs and poultry. After Frederick Willmott's death, however, this had to give place to the needs of the garden, and was converted into the office of the Head of the Gardens, and various potting and working sheds. In later years the estate carpenters' shed moved over here also. Here all the packing for dispatch was done and the winter jobs carried out—sawing logs, sifting and making up different types of soil, potting and re-potting of plants, checking stores, sharpening tools, and so on. A good deal of work on the estate trees was needed during the winter before the sap began to rise, and the hothouses needed attention all the year round. So there was no need for anyone to sit in idleness. It seems likely that the greenhouse mentioned in the 1875 sale catalogue was the large building set against the coach-house which became known as the palm house, where the Preece children, standing outside, were awed to see the tops of the palms grazing the glass roof within. The heating system for this must therefore have been installed before 1875. The orchid house, the hot frames producing cucumbers and melons, the fern house, and the other greenhouses which lay to the north and east of the house, were probably built in the last decade of the century, when experienced hands would give them daily attention. Evidently some of this work was done in 1899, when Ellen Willmott wrote to John Hoog of van Tubergens to report that she had made a bed for tender bulbs which was warmed by a hot water pipe. Today, there are still signs of the extensive underground piping which carried hot water a considerable distance from the boiler to maintain an even temperature in the hothouses and frames. The boiler had to be stoked morning and evening, and there was a stoke-hole in the yard near the estate office and another in the nursery area of the garden, between the glasshouses and frames, a glistening pile of silver sand beside it. How the system was installed is a matter for conjecture: it must have followed closely on the construction of the greenhouses, but it may have been completed all in one enormously messy and disruptive operation, or the greater part of the piping may have been installed to begin with and connected to the existing boiler, which does not seem to have been changed or augmented, and the new stoke-hole with the remaining pipes added piecemeal as new frames or glasshouses were built. A separate system with its own stoke-hole operated in the Headley garden across the road.

It is quite interesting to ponder on how the water and heating systems for the estate were managed. There were springs at the pump house, and also probably above the old fish ponds which date from the time of the Barking Abbey ownership, and in the South Pond below the alpine garden: these normally kept going even in the hottest weather. It is said, too, that land pipes were laid which drained rainwater into the fish ponds. Nowadays there is no sign of a spring in the South Pond, while only a group of Himalayan balsam (a plant normally associated with marshy hollows) growing uncharacteristically on the steep slope above the fish ponds betrays where the spring may once have been. The stream running through the alpine garden, however, most probably drew its supply from the pump house; and in the fernery, which is thought to have contained a device for controlling the water level, there was probably also some means of pumping the water back up the slope to cascade again down it. Where the water for the Headley garden came from is not known, but whatever it got it could conserve, for there was a pond in the middle of the garden; and past the gardeners' cottages lining the road, on the other side of the Headley Arms public house, there was the large Headley Pond, indicating that there may well have been a spring there, too. On the other side of the estate, in the Well Mead

4a. Jacob Maurer, in his prime.

b. Mr Potter with his pet mongoose, about to set to work on the Warley Place rats.

c. James Preece, Head of the Gardens, casts a critical eye over his hollyhocks.

d. Mr Potter shows off some fine foliage plants by the front entrance of Warley Place.

5. *Portrait of Ellen Willmott as a young woman, taken at Aix-les-Bains by Numa Blanc fils: calm and self-possessed, she appears to be winning a point with the photographer.*

6. *1924: the royal party– Queen Alexandra the Queen Mother (centre) with her daughter Princess Victoria (left) and her sister the dowager Empress Marie of Russia—accompanied by Miss Willmott and an unidentified member of the royal household, advance upon the National Rose Society's Show.*

garden, there was another pond, which seems likely to have drawn its supply from the nearby pump house. It was all rather complex, but it worked; and as back-up there was the Company water laid on to the house.

Perhaps the most ambitious of Ellen Willmott's plans, however, concerned the building of Warley Place Farm. It is possible that Frederick Willmott had intended to do this, as an investment and as a more commodious home for his livestock, and then died before he could do so. Ellen, in turn, had found at Tresserve, where she made the farm that formed part of her estate, that it was very convenient to have a source of supply for meat and dairy produce under her control—possibly, also, the farm at Spetchley Park may have encouraged her in the idea that this was a necessary feature of a country house. In any event a farm, with its twenty-four acres of land used for pasture, was made. It was just under the brow of the hill below Warley Lea, and boasted a large model dairy on the ground floor, and extensive farm buildings, consisting of cow houses, calf pens, poultry houses, tiled piggeries with paved yards and a lambing shed. Access to the farm was down a lane next to Warley Lea. A couple of small farm cottages were built alongside the main farm building, and a small wood protected the buildings from the easterly wind. It was Ellen Willmott's aim to be able to drive in horse and trap right through her estate down to the Well Mead garden without once needing to use the main road, but for some reason the necessary paths were never opened up.

Building must have started around the turn of the century, and Mr Browne, the farm bailiff during this period, with his wife and young daughter, Elsie, lived in South Lodge. The farmhouse was completed about 1904 and the Brownes moved in, leaving the lodge to Jacob Maurer. The farm was devoted to livestock—cattle, sheep, poultry and pigs—and certainly, to a limited extent, justified its existence financially by providing the mansion with its entire consumption of dairy produce. The savings here did not, of course, go very far towards offsetting the costs of running the farm, but Ellen Willmott was pleased with it, and that was all she cared about. Unlike her father, she did not concern herself with the minutiae of egg production for the year—she had other matters on her mind. The farm cattle consisted mainly of Scotch bullocks, with large horns and lowering expressions, bought from the Scottish farmer brothers of

Mrs McCullum the housekeeper. Hurcombe's daughter, whose first job was to help in the Great Warley Post Office but whose home lay at the other end of the estate, was very relieved when Miss Willmott was away and she could take the route between the two lodges, which passed in front of the mansion, to get home, avoiding possible fracas. This would never have been permitted had Miss Willmott (who had something in common with that nobleman who sacked any member of his indoor staff below footman level whom at any time he actually saw performing his or her duties around the house) been in residence.

Ellen Willmott was regarded warily by her staff. She was thought to be fair, but by no means generous. As far as money was concerned, the gardeners were paid an average wage, but there were, from time to time, incidents worth noting. On her staff was a gardener who stoutly maintained that he was entitled to be called Sir John Peacock: the proof had been lost in a fire, he asserted, and so he could not claim the money which was rightfully his. A stocky, elderly figure, he is to be seen in several of the gardeners' annual photographs, but the time arrived when he became due for the old-age pension, which in those days was 5s. a week. He opted to go on working; Ellen Willmott promptly docked 5s. a week from his pay. This was thought by the rest of the gardeners to be exceedingly mean, but no doubt she did it *pour encourager les autres*. She was often very kind to her gardeners, especially if their work pleased her, and more especially if they wanted to learn: stupidity coupled with interest could call out amazing reserves of patience, but stupidity with sluggishness would earn its owner the sack. She is said to have had favourites, which endears no one to her staff. The main problem as the gardeners saw it, however, was that Miss Willmott worked among them, and no one ever quite knew where she was going to appear next. So the safest thing, if you wanted to keep your job, was to put in a good day's work—and, mostly, they did.

But what was all this effort directed towards? Ellen Willmott, after all, was a single woman living alone. Nevertheless, she was a single woman with ideas of very considerable grandeur, and she knew exactly what was due to her in the way of a setting for her personality and talents. She saw her path clear ahead of her. Into her beautiful house, filled with furniture, pictures, silver and china in exquisite taste and of high value, she invited the great and good to visit her.

The summit was reached when she came to be introduced to royalty—when or through whom this happened we do not know, but later in life she was able, with confidence in its reception, to dedicate the culmination of all her work, the book *The Genus Rosa*, to Queen Alexandra. The Queen's second daughter, Princess Victoria, and later her daughter-in-law, Queen Mary, often visited Warley Place. And Ellen Willmott liked to boast that Edward, Prince of Wales (later Edward VIII), had broken one of the instruments in her music-room, though whether as an adult or on the date, 4 July 1909, that his signature appears in the Warley Place visitors' book, along with the equally childish signatures 'Albert' and 'Mary', we do not know.

For the grand-daughter of a Southwark chemist this was a long way to have come.

CHAPTER VI

On the Pinnacle

In the early years of the new century, Ellen Willmott was honoured not only by the friendship of royalty, but also by various awards which were made to her. In 1903, Sir Thomas Hanbury, a distinguished patron of horticulture, gave a site of sixty acres which he had bought at Wisley in Surrey to the Royal Horticultural Society, and the Society's garden was moved from its then much too small site at Chiswick. Ellen Willmott, it appears, was instrumental in persuading Sir Thomas to buy the land and present it to the Society (despite strong objections from the Director of Kew, Sir William Thiselton-Dyer, to the RHS having it—one of the items which Sir Thomas, on a postcard to Ellen Willmott, says he intends to amuse her with when he and Lady Hanbury come to Warley). How did she come to know the Hanburys? Very likely through the Willmott family's pharmaceutical connections, since the group responsible for the founding of the Pharmaceutical Society in 1843 included Daniel Hanbury, and the name has become famous in Allen and Hanburys, makers of baby food; as early as 1882 an entry prophetic of later years appears in Frederick Willmott's diary: 'Cecil Hanbury came to spend the day with us.' The administration of the new garden was vested in three trustees: Cecil Hanbury, to represent the family interest; John Bennett-Pöe, well known to Ellen Willmott from the RHS Narcissus and Tulip Committee; and Ellen herself. The setting-up of the new garden must have imposed a considerable burden of work upon the trustees, but also gave Ellen Willmott further opportunity to prove her worth before the public eye.

The work there had been in progress for about a year when, in company with ten other distinguished lady botanists, she became a Fellow of the Linnaean Society. This group made up the first women Fellows of the Society, and was the result of a campaign by a most determined and energetic personage, H. J. Elwes—landowner, traveller, naturalist and horticulturist specializing in nerines. The move was not without opposition, and so unprepared were the Society's administrative staff for the occasion (perhaps they could not bring themselves to believe that it would ever happen) that the form of recommendation which was read aloud at the Society's general meeting on 17 November 1904 was the form normally used for a gentleman, suitably altered in pen and ink. Some well-known names were among the seven Fellows who supported Miss Willmott's candidature—Lord Avebury, Frank (later Sir Frank) Crisp (a city solicitor with extensive horticultural interests, who was Treasurer of the Linnaean Society from 1881 to 1905), Otto Stapf of Kew and H. J. Elwes—and indeed six months earlier she had been unashamedly lobbying Sir William Thiselton-Dyer for his vote in her favour. The ballot took place on 15 December and Ellen Willmott, being successful, was formally admitted to the Society on 19 January 1905. For the occasion a group portrait was commissioned of the lady Fellows, who are shown disposed round the room in rather stiff and uncomfortable-looking attitudes completing the formalities of entry, while some of the more settled and faintly condescending gentleman Fellows stand about watching. Sheila Pim's biography of Dr Augustine Henry, the plant-hunter for whom *Lilium henryi* and *Clematis henryi* were named, and collaborator with H. J. Elwes in the writing of *The Trees of Great Britain and Ireland*, recounts the rather humorous circumstances of the first meeting following the election: well known as a supporter of greater freedom for women, Henry had been asked to speak, with the idea of leavening the rather dry proceedings, but his time was pre-empted by a speaker who discoursed on Crustacea for thirty-five minutes longer than he should have done, and thus filibustered Henry's much more amusing material. Nevertheless, Henry's much reduced talk found favour with Ellen Willmott, and she invited him to Warley, where his name appears several times in the visitors' book.

A notable visit made by Ellen Willmott in 1904 was to Munich where, helped by an introduction from Sir William Thiselton-Dyer, she was well received at the Botanic Garden. This was followed up later in the year (again with the support of Sir William) by a visit to Vienna, where she was charmed to find so many of the types which Nicolaus von Jacquin, Professor of Botany and Chemistry at

Vienna, and Director of the Botanic Garden at Schönbrunn, had figured in the *Hortus Vindobonensis*, still in perfect health. Writing to Sir William afterwards, she added, more tactfully than was sometimes her custom, that her letters of introduction had stood her in good stead: Kew was a great power all the world over—it was the standard, and everything was compared to it.

At Warley Place, the gardens were taking on the richness and splendour which endless care and attention could give, and were moving towards the high point at which it was estimated that 100,000 species and varieties of tree, plant and shrub were grown there. The latest addition to the grounds was the water garden. With great skill and artistry, but leaving no impression of artificiality, the ponds which were said to have been the fish ponds of Barking Abbey, centuries before, were gradually converted into a water garden, with many British water plants naturalized on their borders, and rare trees and bushes surrounding them. To complete the setting, Miss Willmott engaged in another remarkable and extremely expensive exercise: she had brought from Bourg St Pierre an alpine hut—complete with mountain furniture and herdsman's gear—in which Napoleon was said to have spent a night while crossing the Alps in May 1800 on his way over into Milan. She had this hut erected beside the ponds, and a landing stage built for the boat to serve it. Dr Stearn, in his brief biographical sketch of Ellen Willmott, tells how on visiting Warley Place shortly after her death he was astounded to find a sizeable collection of books about Napoleon, whom she evidently regarded with unstinted admiration. Certainly in 1906 she was spending £150 (a considerable sum in those days) on the purchase of Ashton's *Caricature and Satire on Napoleon I*. Her enthusiasm provided a pleasing, if costly, adjunct to the sheltered, sunny water. Here Ellen and the Berkeley family organized fishing parties (Ellen herself was photographed fishing in a businesslike and concentrated fashion, back to the camera, and wearing the usual large hat), and here Rob Berkeley and Jim Robinson sometimes went fishing together. When parties were held, tea was carried down from the house by Robinson and the housemaids, either slipping and sliding perilously down the grass bank, or crunching along the Nut Walk carefully carrying the spirit burner and the kettle. Fortunately for everyone, a table was kept in the hut.

One day, however, the pleasant feeling of privacy enjoyed by the family was shattered by the unbelievable sight of ground being cleared for building on the other side of Dark Lane, which bounded the Warley estate and whence the future inhabitants of the cottages which were obviously planned would command a clear view of the lake and the surrounding garden. Ellen Willmott set a very high value on privacy, and at this invasion of it she flew into a rage and rushed off to upbraid her neighbour Count Lescher, whose land fronted the other side of Dark Lane and who had clearly arranged it all. She used every argument to get him to build elsewhere, but this he obstinately refused to do, and so enraged did they both become that he threatened to shoot her at sight. This was different indeed from earlier and sunnier times when harmonious relations prevailed between the families. Next time she visited Stubbers Ellen Willmott regaled the Russell family with the tale, and her version carried so much conviction that two of the Russell daughters remembered it all their long lives. Having met with no success with Count Lescher, Ellen Willmott next set vigorously to work to protect her privacy by other means. She caused Coe the blacksmith to build a huge iron framework, apparently constructed of old railway sleepers, which was dragged into place on that part of her own property which bordered on Dark Lane opposite the detestable cottages. Within this framework, earth was piled almost up to the lowest branches of the elms which lined the hedge. The story goes that Ellen Willmott invited the local cavalry regiment to trample the earth and firm it, but as Warley Barracks did not house cavalry, if the story is true she must have persuaded the 16th Lancers over from Colchester to do the job. And the gardeners were left with the task of planting several hundred ivy plants of various kinds to cover the mound and soften the bare earth. Tempers subsided, the ivy grew, the fishing parties continued without being overlooked, and no one attacked Ellen Willmott with a sawn-off shotgun.

While balls were no longer held at Warley Place, Ellen Willmott's friends still came to stay, and innumerable visitors wrote asking to see the Warley Garden, with and without introductions. Energetic as ever, she visited her friends all over the country: the whole of the winter of 1901 was spent with friends near Torquay, and letters survive written from addresses in Northumberland, Rutland, Ireland, Scotland. Three or four times a year she went to stay with the Gascoigne family who spent some months each year in Argyll. The children looked forward to her visits because, to them, she was exactly the right sort of visitor—ready for anything, full of enjoyment, wit and enthusiasm, a ready joiner in games and never minding a wetting in a small boat, where the usual large hat was exchanged for a beret. There could rarely have been a woman whose ways changed so completely when in the company of congenial people (and to her, children were people, whom she liked or disliked in exactly the same way as she liked or disliked adults, treating their conversation with courtesy and attention), where she could talk freely and feel herself easily understood. Hauteur, rudeness, maliciousness, all were dissolved and disappeared in a tide of mirth and enjoyment. On these occasions she was enormous fun to be with. Her rapid speech, words tumbling over each other, her completely natural manner, the laughter, the enthusiasm—all these made her a friend to be cherished, a visitor worth having.

But this is a long way from Warley Garden. The re-ordering of the fish ponds was the last of the major structural changes which took place in the estate, which now assumed the form in which it was best remembered by the scores of visitors who came there. The faultless maintenance of the garden, its smooth, perfectly kept lawns, its borders without a weed to be seen, and the artless and uncontrived abundance everywhere made it a sight to beguile the eyes of the most inartistic visitor—and, to those who were well versed in botany and horticulture, evidenced its owner's remarkable gift for settling plants of great horticultural interest and divers origins in this most English of settings. A panoramic print gives a bird's eye view of the estate, from the sheep grazing in the daffodil field to the last gardener working on the farthest flower bed of the nursery, rake in hand. Miss Willmott herself is shown on the walk below the south front of the house, with her trug and trowel, and wearing a large hat; while two tiny gardeners, looking vaguely oriental, are about to cross the bridge in the alpine garden—which seems, strangely, to be entirely filled with water. Another print consists of an estate map, surrounded by a series of small drawings of its main features and surmounted by a coat of arms and a motto, 'Garde ta Foy', and described as 'A Plan of Miss Willmott's House and Gardens at Great Warley, lying in the County of Essex, England—1904'. These arms were granted to one Edward Wilmott [*sic*] in 1628 and there is nothing to prove that Miss Willmott was a descendant of this family. The print was made by William M. Walker.

Satisfied now with the shape of the whole garden, Ellen Willmott's attentions shifted to concentrate on stocking the vast flowering area she had created. She had, with her two sunken hothouses and at least four others, an enormous potential for raising bedding plants, but her preference was always for herbaceous plants and shrubs, many of them half-hardy, and she certainly used her hothouses for raising seeds and growing on cuttings and small plants sent to her from all over the world. 'I have a man collecting Pelargonium for me out on the Cape', she remarks nonchalantly in passing in a letter written in 1908. This was Gerald Davidson, who wrote to her of the short trips he was making into the Cape country, bringing back these plants from which he would set cuttings for her. The Arnold Arboretum at Harvard sent her numerous plants, including a collection of *Crataegus* under number before they had been named—a very unusual consignment; she was invoiced for some of these plants, but many she received as an exchange or a gift. It is said that she used to walk for considerable distances to visit gardens, often in the intervals of other activities, and would then return home late, a knapsack bulging with plants over her shoulder. Wherever possible she acquired, along with each plant, as much as she could carry, or dared ask, of the soil in which it flourished. In the gardens she visited she is said to have scattered pinches of seed here and there to remind the owner—in a way which may not always have been entirely welcome—of her visit. Her favourite plant for this purpose, was *Eryngium giganteum*, which came to be known as 'Miss Willmott's ghost': and indeed the tall grey-white stems stand out at dusk against the deepening shadows, branching out into great candelabras of grey-green flower heads, sometimes thirty or forty to a plant, spectral and strange in the twilight. Graham Thomas, writing of this in the *Gardeners Chronicle* (31 August 1966), asked if any reader could confirm the origin of the name: but apparently no one could.

Ellen Willmott was in constant touch with Mr John Hoog, a Director of van Tubergens' Zwanenburg Nurseries at Haarlem. She was much interested in the bulbs discovered by his collectors in Asiatic Russia—Bokhara, Turkestan, and other countries—and one of these importations was named *Iris willmottiana*. This has now died out of cultivation, but *Iris willmottiana alba*, a dwarf Juno iris with large pure white flowers, survives. *Iris warleyensis* has also died out, but survives in *Iris* 'Warlsind', a hybrid of *I. warleyensis and I. sindjarensis*. Not only iris, but also tulip species, came from these regions: *Tulipa willmottiae* was found in the eastern Armenian mountains; *Tulipa praestans*, one of the Revd Engleheart's seedlings, was shown by Ellen Willmott at the Royal Horticultural Society in 1903 and awarded a First Class Certificate and *Tulipa fosteriana*, shown in 1905, gained her by unanimous consent an Award of Merit. Around 1897 Ellen Willmott began to contribute to these expeditions, supporting van Tubergens' two excellent collectors, Kronenburg and Sintenis, as they ranged over the wild and dangerous country of Persia, Armenia and Turkestan. Starting with a modest £25, she ended by receiving a proposal from John Hoog that Sintenis, who had been very successful in the mountains of Persia, should be engaged for a period of three to four years searching the North Persian range up to Afghanistan for novelties. This would cost van Tubergens £150 a year, and Ellen Willmott £200. It is not clear whether she accepted, but it indicates the extent of her interest and commitment. Without any doubt, however, the most fascinating sources of new material at that time were China and South-east Asia.

Ellen Willmott's friendship with Sir Thomas Hanbury was growing, and she often went to visit the Hanburys at the beautiful pink-washed Palazzo Orengo at La Mortola, between Menton and Ventimiglia, surrounded by the garden of tropical plants descending in terraced splendour to the sea. Pacing the garden with his guest, Sir Thomas, drawing on the experience of his twenty years as a merchant in China, told her of the flowers growing in the wild valleys of western China, of the lilies and roses, and of the rare blue tree paeony. Ellen Willmott drank all this in, and Lady Hanbury, writing to her nostalgically years later, mentioned with gratitude the pleasure which this interest and enthusiasm gave to Sir Thomas.

Ellen Willmott's interest took a practical form in the support which she gave to the expeditions of E. H. ('Chinese') Wilson. It was in 1899 that Wilson first went to China, and this trip, with his second in 1903, was made on behalf of the nurserymen James Veitch & Sons. In 1906 it was again mooted that he should go to China, this time under the aegis of the Arnold Arboretum; the trip was to be organized by Professor Sargent of the Arnold Arboretum, and Ellen

Willmott was pressed into service to persuade Wilson, who was hovering in agonizing indecision. Wilson himself found the idea extremely enticing, but his young wife, understandably, did not want to be left on her own for a full two years, and so tried to influence him to stay. Miss Willmott had no time at all for these manoeuvres, and in her letters to Sargent roundly denounced Mrs Wilson as a tiresome, ignorant woman, and short-sighted into the bargain, since she was unable to see the possibilities of this pioneering journey. She arranged 'someone to entertain the wife, whilst I turn my attention to Wilson'. In the end, Wilson went: he was in fact much excited by the prospect of the expedition, but someone was needed to keep up the pressure on him lest, having agreed to go, he should change his mind in the face of his wife's pleadings. Ellen Willmott, besides this major effort of persuasion, which she herself likened to pushing a stone uphill and keeping it there, made other very practical contributions to the expedition: £200 in cash (although it took several reminders before she actually paid it over), and certainly advice on photography, possibly even some tuition. She suggested others who might contribute: M. de Vilmorin, the French nurseryman, and Lord Kesteven, a good gardener and a great traveller; carefully paving the way, she even led Sir Thomas Hanbury to take a share.

By late 1907 Wilson had sent Ellen Willmott numerous seeds of herbaceous plants, and she also received 116 packets of seeds of shrubs and trees via the Arnold Arboretum: these she promised to try in varying conditions in each of her gardens in England and abroad. Along with Kew, and with the Hon. Vicary Gibbs, a son of Baron Aldenham, who gardened at Aldenham House in Hertfordshire and who had a reputation as a careful cultivator, she shared the seeds of the new cherries which Wilson was discovering. She was also lucky in that cases of lily bulbs (5,000 in one consignment), shrubs and herbaceous plants reached her direct from Wilson in good, or at least in plantable, condition, while those which he sent to the Arnold Arboretum were quite dead on arrival. Wilson had been obstinately certain that his method of packing was an improvement on that advised by the Arboretum, and had to learn the hard way that he was wrong. During the following years seeds continued to arrive sporadically at Warley, and then early in 1909 came a quantity of rhododendron and rose seeds, followed by the seeds of *Paeonia delavayi*. Ellen Willmott evidently sold her share of Wilson's rhododendron seeds (as she had a perfect right to do) to Gauntletts' nursery at Chiddingfold, who circulated a note about them to their customers which was worded in such a way as to bring a protest from Professor Sargent, since it seemed to indicate that Gauntletts had acquired the whole stock of Wilson's seeds: whereas these had been distributed among about twenty-five people in all.

The next year some of Wilson's roses were flourishing at War- ley—Ellen Willmott rather smugly commented in a letter to Profes- sor Sargent that she did not think any of Wilson's roses had bloomed yet at Kew, but in *her* garden at Warley they had been a mass of flower, and that she never saw anything so beautiful as the fruit. These roses may well have included three roses collected by E. H. Wilson in south-west China on his third Chinese expedition in 1907: *Rosa caudata, Rosa banksiopsis* and *Rosa saturata*, all of which are known to have flowered at Warley. Later in the year Miss Willmott wrote again to Sargent reporting that, in general, Wilson's seeds had done very well at Warley; she looked forward to receiving their names. But the Arnold Arboretum refused to be hurried, saying that they did not want to name any of Wilson's plants until the different groups had been worked up, and for this Ellen Willmott had to wait until the spring of the following year. However, she had the satisfac- tion of being the only gardener to have succeeded in raising certain varieties of Wilson's *Helwingia* and *Sabia*, and Sargent begged her to have cuttings propagated, adding that unless she had a skilful propa- gator it might be a good idea to ask Mr Veitch (one of the family of nurserymen) and also Mr Bean at Kew to put in a few cuttings. (William Jackson Bean, who had started work at Kew in 1881 as a student-gardener, busying himself in his spare time with the writing of his *Trees and Shrubs Hardy in the British Isles*, rose to become Curator in 1922.) This goad was immediately effective, and the cuttings were set at Warley. Wilson, who had apparently just visited Warley Place, gave his verdict to the Arboretum staff in August 1911 on his return from a second trip to China on their behalf, in which Ellen Willmott does not seem to have been involved at all: she had been wonderfully successful with the seeds, he said, and had plants which no one else had managed to raise. Before he left England he also wrote to Ellen Willmott herself; a charming letter in which he said, 'That I accepted the work on behalf of the Arnold Arboretum was due more largely to your influence than possibly you and others are aware of.' So it had all been worth while.

To read the correspondence between Ellen Willmott and Professor Sargent is to become sharply aware of the immense amount of activity at Warley. Careful, intensive organization was required. First came the sheer problems of allocating space; then, decisions had to be taken on the conditions in which seeds were to be sown and cuttings set; and finally, the young plants needed not only careful tending but also skilled observation of their progress and quick first aid when necessary. Much of the labour required could be unskilled, but many of the decisions and tasks needed skill and experience, and it was quite evident that Ellen Willmott herself was firmly in charge of the enterprise.

The traffic with Kew, by letter and visit, was constant. Ellen Willmott grew plants with which they had no success, patiently trying them in innumerable different situations until she found the one which suited them best. Kew, on the other hand, was able to help her a good deal with identifying plants. She took a great deal of trouble with the preparation of soil for her plants: she writes of making ready a special bed for half-hardy and tender plants, and a specially prepared deeply trenched site for the Arboretum's *Crataegus*, which she left open to the elements for a month or two while she was in France; the *Crataegus* she shared with her sister Rose, who, she reported to Sargent, was also making 'a very good plantation for them where they would look fine' (they survive to this day, looking rather ragged). Her hybridizing experiments had been in progress for years. In 1909 she commented to Sargent 'I have had a very beautiful series of *Primula viscosa* hybrids, I have been working at them for 10 years crossing and re-crossing them with every Primrose I could get in flower at the same time. I gave sets of some 60 different ones to Kew, Edinburgh and Dublin. . . .' Strange that, although Kew noted this, the well-documented receipt books at Edinburgh and Glasnevin show no sign of any such arrival. In the mid-1920s she was still at work on *Primula*, producing one day for the amazement and delight of the last of her housekeepers a beautiful blue primrose—a plant which, to the housekeeper's chagrin, was collected almost at once by a young man from Kew. She was for a time in correspondence with Miller Christy, who was interested in the instability of colouring in the primrose and cowslip, having evidence that a change from low to high manuring, or from growth at high to low altitudes, could change flower colours from yellow to red. She was able to help in this, for she had grown red cowslip and oxlip from the Urals. *Primula* was a genus on which Rose Berkeley had also worked for many years, producing many beautiful varieties at Spetchley Park, one of which was known as the Spetchley prim-rose—'results that entirely satisfy the most fastidious taste', as her sister Ellen was to describe her work.

Undoubtedly, however, the most important contribution which Ellen Willmott made to horticulture was her work on *Rosa*. Many years of research went into her monograph *The Genus Rosa*, the first part of which was published on 15 September 1910. The suggestion for this work seems to have been made originally by Canon Ellacombe, and in the preface she pays graceful tribute to the Canon and to Lt-Col (later Sir David) Prain, who in 1905 had taken over from Sir William Thiselton-Dyer as Director of Kew: 'But for the first I should never have undertaken the book at all; but for the last it might never have reached the stage of publication.' Much of her work, however, was based on practical experience in the crossing of roses. She was steeped in the work of Linnaeus, Thory, Lindley and others, and had read extensively in older botanical and historical works; but although she was aware of the work of Gregor Mendel on the laws of heredity she had certainly begun her work before his famous paper was rediscovered in 1900, and her collection of wild and species roses, both at Tresserve and in the Well Mead garden at Warley, must have been started well before the turn of the century. Had Ellen Willmott undergone formal scientific training, she would have understood more clearly why it was that the results both of her own crosses, and of the plantings she made of rose seeds brought back from China by Wilson, were so infuriatingly impossible to classify—for each time she seemed about to succeed, some puzzling result overturned the whole painstaking structure. It was not so much in the main classification of species—for here she seems only to have erred in putting the dog rose with the Musk Roses instead of with the Caninae, and in this she may have been partly influenced by Wolley-Dod's monograph in the *Journal of Botany* in 1910—but rather in the detailed working out of varieties, and the strange and unexpected breeding behaviour they showed. Writing many years later to Dr C. C. Hurst, whose work on genetics had put him in the forefront of the field, she revealed her puzzlement, and the extent to which she had been swamped, until she could work no further on it, by the mass of material which was continually coming in from the plant hunters: 'I have worked upon roses all my life and the difficulties are insurmountable. I have over and over again felt I was nearing some satisfactory classification and then fresh material has set me astray again.' Her inability to grasp the whole picture of the genetical basis of rose systematics betrays itself in her two short letters to Hurst, for in them she did not attempt to grapple with the content of his paper or to challenge any of its conclusions. In someone like Ellen Willmott, this was unusual to the point which arouses surprise, even perturbation, in the reader.

In spite of her lack of scientific training, there seems little doubt that with her good brain and sure grasp of botanical principle and horticultural detail, she should have been equal to understanding enough of the genetical work in progress to have commented acutely and perceptively on Hurst's work. History was against her in two ways: first, the firm intention of the Willmott family to be recognized had led their parents to concentrate on the education of Ellen and Rose as socially acceptable young women, well-bred and intelligent; but they had quite failed to think in terms of giving their daughters the sort of education which they might have given to sons. And secondly, the timing was just wrong: Girton College opened its doors in 1869, Newnham not until 1871, and the first of the women's colleges at Oxford—Lady Margaret Hall—not until 1878. The Willmott family seems to have been Oxford-oriented anyhow: and it would have taken very modern parents indeed (which the Willmotts were not) to make a decision so early in the history of the new women's colleges that their two daughters should be given a university education. So, in the period when Ellen Willmott was really wrestling with *The Genus Rosa*—say 1904 to 1909—she was probably in no position to realize the full significance of the current work on genetics, and its application to Rosa. In consequence, the great monograph, in spite of its wealth of botanical and historical detail, belongs to an earlier tradition: to that of Thory's *Les Roses* and Lindley's *Rosarum Monographia*, rather than to modern scientific work. The book's dedication to Queen Alexandra seems to emphasize the status rather than the nature of the work, and betrays what she herself regarded as its true lodestar:

Most Gracious Lady
Herewith I lay at Your Majesty's feet a Book of Roses, wherein I
have striven to set down, with such poor skill and diligence as has
been vouchsafed me, all that I have learned of that most Royal
Family of the Kingdom of Flowers. . . . Wherefore, most Royal
Lady, it remains only for me to dedicate, according to Your
Majesty's gracious permission, my Roses to our own peerless
Rose, my Queen of Flowers to the Queen of our English hearts.

She consulted Sir Dighton Probyn, Queen Alexandra's Comptroller,
about making a present to the Queen of a set of parts bound in
white vellum. Sir Dighton, while deprecating the expense, thought
this an excellent idea, and approved the writing she proposed to put
in the book, with the small (but significant) alteration that he felt she
should not put, as she had suggested, 'devoted servant', but '*humble*
and devoted servant'.

In the light of this it becomes understandable that in 1924, the date
of her correspondence with Hurst, to immerse herself in the work
described in his paper might have seemed to her tantamount to
denying the value of her own contribution to the continuing work
on *Rosa*, though she recognized clearly enough the value of the
work which he had sent her.

But to return to the composition of the work: for this, Ellen
Willmott had secured the services of John Gilbert Baker, the Kew
botanist, who wrote the Latin and English descriptions of the species
concerned. Though she, like her mother, was a skilled painter of
flowers, she did not feel confident enough to undertake the series of
plates which would be needed for her book, and so the work was
entrusted to Alfred Parsons R A, whose delicate work fully justified
her choice. She herself produced the historical and literary material
which followed.

Perhaps Ellen Willmott was not very good at working in cooperation with others. At any rate she had problems with Mr Baker, who
(she said) told her something different each time she asked him a
question about roses; and with Mr Parsons, who was careless about
the blooms he selected to paint from a given rose bush while, in 1908,
he added to his crimes by finding some new patrons and having no
time to take any further interest in her book.

There is no doubt that she felt very much weighed down by the production of this work. She complained to Professor Sargent: 'This Rose book has cost me so much in time and money that I am anxious not to leave any stone unturned in order to improve it', and again, 'I have no experience in such matters and I have many difficulties in struggling alone through my undertaking.'

This comment is hardly fair to her publishers, Messrs John Murray. In the course of the twenty years or so during which she had dealings with them, she wielded the full range of her formidable armoury from anxious submission to imperious domination. John Murray showed persistent steadiness under fire; but Ellen Willmott, sailing in with relish to a fight and being particularly good at prolonging battle to its ultimate limit, succeeded at the end in drawing blood.

Correspondence on the production of the book goes back as far as October 1901. It was clearly a slow business, and it was not until 21 January 1910 that agreement was finally reached and committed to paper: 1,000 copies of *The Genus Rosa* were to be printed and issued in twenty parts at the cost of one guinea each. A very substantial yield—£13,860, less publisher's commission—was expected. The question of finance had already ruffled the feelings of both sides: John Murray, as firmly as he could, urged progress on the text, which was not keeping pace with the well-advanced work on the plates, but in February he agreed to settle further costs, to be recouped from sales, with commission increased. Murrays had early suggested that Ellen Willmott might find it convenient to employ a managing editor. These tactics were entirely justified, but they did not work, for they presented her with full scope for expressing a sense of injury; she had, she said, sent her man of business, Dixson, over to them to talk about money, and nothing had been mentioned on the subject. As to the question of an editor, she wrote from the Villa Bonaventura at Cadenabbia: 'I should be only too glad if I could get some help, but as I wish nothing spared which can contribute to the perfection of the book I must do it myself.' With this she must have felt that she had manoeuvred herself into a position from which she could afford to take a lofty attitude. Everything was, of course, all the fault of the Murrays, father and son, and they had compounded their error by hastening the text, when she had been expressly counselled by knowledgeable friends that haste was the enemy of the scholarly and accurate work which she aimed to produce. And to be fair, it is clear from her correspondence with Professor Sargent that she was meeting with real difficulties. She had to weigh the sometimes contradictory opinions of various experts in the field, to attempt to classify disputed cases without benefit of cytogenetic background, and she had an immense amount of information to absorb, distil, put into words and then check. The Murrays, therefore, must wait, and if waiting cost them money then this was a cross which a publisher should expect to have to bear for the privilege of producing a high-class work. For them to expect money from her (largely to pay Griggs, who was making the plates) at this point was, in her view, carrying things a little too far. But she was ready to pay, and over the period 1905 to 1907, the Murrays were reimbursed for their outgoings to a total of £2,000. So far so good.

John Murray, on his side, was learning the hard way some of the risks attendant on dealings with Ellen Willmott. Having told him to progress a particular matter she would then vanish for several weeks abroad, and on her return it would be days before she could deal with her accumulated correspondence. She did not employ a secretary. Her imminent arrival at the Murrays' office was usually signalled by telegram and frequently took no account of office hours—having been incommunicado for weeks, she would then expect one of the Murrays to be available to receive her at 5.30 or 6 p.m. (at which, wisely, they put their feet down). And anything which went wrong was always somebody else's fault. 'It seems impossible to make my gardener in Savoy understand which parcel he ought to return. . . . My gardener is not a scholar and anything apart from actual gardening I find very difficult with him.' 'It was my butler's fault in picking the parcel off the table to pack up and I have been hunting everywhere for it.' The scenes at Tresserve and Warley are easy to imagine, and the Murrays must have thought that their eccentric author was employing a bunch of incompetents, instead of the knowledgeable Claude Meunier and the meticulous Robinson.

Meanwhile, the Murrays moved ahead with as much speed as possible, though they had other problems on their hands besides the personal vagaries of Ellen Willmott. Hatchards in 1905 jumped the gun in circulating a draft note of the work with their usual monthly circular: an apology and withdrawal had to be sought, and in June 1910 Sotherans issued a misleading prospectus, causing further trouble. Meanwhile, a whole tide of small queries and problems ebbed and flowed from printer to publisher to author and back again—slowly. In May 1910, in a letter to Canon Ellacombe, John Murray permitted himself one heartfelt comment which broke through his normal urbanity: 'I cannot tell you how relieved I am to see daylight at last in this great project. It has given an incredible amount of trouble and anxiety.' But he spoke too soon. A fundamental weakness in the whole project was beginning to reveal itself: its publication in parts rather than in volumes. For there were some people who on principle would rather wait till the series was complete before subscribing; others who would default in the payment which they undertook; and the whole arrangement for overseeing the placing of orders was rather uncertain, so that at any given moment it seemed impossible to find out where the enterprise stood financially. Obviously it was a wise move to issue the work, which had cost so much, in a form in which some early returns on the heavy outlay could be expected. But Ellen Willmott's enthusiasm rather got in the way and Henry Dixson, who seemed to be acting as a receiver of orders from her friends, came in for much contumely on this score. Luckily, and by means undisclosed, she was able to obtain the services of the Duke of Wellington's secretary, Mr Gordon 'to straighten out Mr Dixson's muddles'. After that, things moved with military precision. But it all took time, and with hindsight it seems so obvious that a system which would have worked could and should have been thought out beforehand. Murrays were made to suffer for this. On 20 October 1910 a telegram in Ellen Willmott's usual peremptory tone requested a rough statement of account to be sent to her at her solicitors' office by 3 p.m. that afternoon. They had to bestir themselves to provide it in time. Later it turned out that this was simply a convenient picking-up point for the information which she needed before going to Tresserve. She whisked the letter away without her solicitors being aware of its existence.

Another problem connected with the issuing of the work in parts concerned the reviewing. There seemed to be no particular point at which a crop of reviews could be expected. The book had, of course, been long in preparation, and Hatchards' premature circular of 1905 had not helped. There were notices of its appearance in the *Gardeners Chronicle* and in other journals. So it hardly burst upon the world as a brilliant surprise. Ellen Willmott's blistering comment to John Murray shows the kind of review she expected. 'I am afraid I know who has been arranged to review *The Genus Rosa* someone who has never lived in the country and does not know a Tea Rose from a Cabbage Rose and who has help from several incompetent hands for each review.' The National Rose Society (now the Royal National Rose Society) for some reason—perhaps because it was not so much interested in wild and species roses—did not notice the book until 1916, well after its completion. In the face of all this, it is gratifying to hear at last a note of sanity in the happily phrased, genuine and authoritative tribute published by Gertrude Jekyll in the *Quarterly Review* in October 1914, and it is typical of her that she also thought of the publishers and wrote to John Murray: 'May I be allowed to offer my sincere congratulations on the whole get-up of this most important and beautiful book.' How glad he must have been to allow her to do so after all he had suffered.

It must be said of Ellen Willmott that she was indefatigable in her efforts to obtain subscribers and was constantly sending to Murrays the names of those whom she believed to be interested. Unfortunately she did not always check that interest shown was going to translate itself into hard cash. A friend of hers living near Lake Maggiore was embarrassed to have to return a part of the work because he could not afford to subscribe. Ellen Willmott arranged for the Rose Society to give her a stand for the display of material relating to her book at their show in the summer of 1910, and with Lord Blyth for some of the paintings to be exhibited at 30 Curzon Street. She constantly chivvied Murrays to send a second display copy to the Army and Navy Stores, who were taking orders but who would, she alleged, take more if they were not forced to keep their only display copy locked up in the manager's office for fear it should become dog-eared. (When John Murray mildly replied that it would surely be better for the Army and Navy to have one copy only, and let that get thoroughly handled by the public, than take up two from a limited edition, she was not very pleased.) She kept hammering away at the question of the American market, which had been much in her mind from the start of negotiations on the book. Even Professor Sargent, however, had been consistently discouraging here, but he finally suggested Macmillans, with its Canadian connections, as being the best firm to handle this, and that she should see the firm about it in London. There was no indication that this was ever done, but some copies did find their way over to the States, and in 1912

Sargent himself, perhaps feeling that he had been a little harsh on the subject, went out of his way to mention that he knew of two amateurs in Boston who had her book (not perhaps a very tactful comment) and that no doubt there were others. He also inquired whether an effort had been made to sell copies to the Department of Agriculture in Washington, the New York Botanic Gardens, the St Louis Botanic Garden and the Lloyd Library in Cincinnati? Doubtless it had not. Ellen Willmott clearly regretted that she had not accepted an earlier offer from Sir Thomas Hanbury to finance *The Genus Rosa*, and it was sad also that his death in 1907 had deprived her of his promise to take up twenty-five copies and give them to various botanic gardens. Eventually, she left Murrays to make the best deal they could with the Americans. And she hoped (though this hope turned out to be vain) to get Hachettes to agree to sell the book. And finally, various raffles for charity disposed, admittedly only at trade prices, of more sets complete to the time of raffling. These efforts created a lot of disturbance but did not sell a lot of extra copies.

The last part of *The Genus Rosa* was published in 1914. Its sales lurched on, recorded (apart from the work of the Duke of Wellington's secretary) in secretary) haphazard fashion. Various attempts were made to interest an American publisher, but they all baulked at taking on the responsibility of marketing such a costly work. Countess Grey, wife of the Governor General of Canada, was notified as a subscriber and was thought to be able to dispose of some copies in Canada.

From about 1912, Miss Willmott had been employing a typist, Mrs Slater, who had been struggling as best she might, and in general reasonably satisfactorily, with the material and instructions left with her in Ellen Willmott's frequent absences. But unfortunately she made a mistake in the text with some inverted commas, bringing down on her head recriminations which one would have thought were well beyond the nature of her transgression. 'I am very vexed at Mrs Slater's mistake,' wrote Ellen Willmott to John Murray, 'she is hopelessly careless and has made endless muddles and given me such an unnecessary amount of trouble all through. . . . I am very long-suffering and put up with a great deal otherwise I should have looked out for another typist long ago. . . . Mrs Slater wants to throw part of the blame on the printers . . . but your printers and readers are so extraordinarily good and careful that too much ought not to have been made of almost the first mistake that has occurred.' In such a

back-handed and casual fashion did Ellen Willmott issue the first
word of praise to be committed to paper on the first-class handling
which her work had received. She also, however, in passing, and not
for the first time, lambasted John Murray for dealing direct with Mrs
Slater. But that gallant man had had enough; it emerged that Ellen
Willmott had, also not for the first time, vanished from sight for a
longish period, and so he turned tough: only after his son wrote
twice and telegraphed once and received no answer, said John Murray, was he compelled to go to Mrs Slater. After this Ellen Willmott
temporarily ceased to complain.

The unsold parts of *The Genus Rosa* languished at the printers, and
the war killed sales stone dead. The costs of the book, both to John
Murray and to Ellen Willmott, were so heavy that the profits hardly
served to recoup them. Ellen Willmott was not entirely to blame: her
standards were high, and she was right to press them. And she had
taken on a task of enormous complexity on which no two botanical
experts could agree, without at that stage any cytogenetic
advice—and with little experience in book production. That her
publisher did not understand her difficulty is very plain. 'As regards
the names on the plates,' said John Murray 'I had no idea names of
roses were fluctuating as they seem to be. I always supposed that in
this, as in other scientific matters, the names at least were pretty well
fixed.' But Ellen Willmott's manner was guaranteed to enrage and
disrupt, and she utterly lacked the capacity to enlist sympathy and
support when in this frame of mind; instead she marched round to
Murrays' offices and, as one of the staff comments in an office note
'grumbled a little as usual on a variety of matters'.

One piece of considered and valuable praise which Ellen Willmott
did not live to see, and which would have pleased her greatly, came
in C. C. Hurst's words in the obituary he wrote for *Nature*. 'It is
evident that the whole conception of the work, and the welding
together of the artistic and scientific elements into a realistic whole
with a universal appeal, were due entirely to the genius of Ellen
Willmott, and her monograph on roses stands as a lasting monument
to her artistic and scientific sensibilities.'

These were generous words, but there was another tribute which
Dr Hurst paid to Ellen Willmott: in his book *The Mechanism of
Creative Evolution*, published two years before she died, he echoed
the words she had used in her letter to him written nearly ten years

previously, and in his altered version of them offered her the solution to her puzzlement: 'Many difficulties which appeared almost insurmountable with taxonomic analyses alone are found to be quite simply explained when investigated genetically and cytologically.'

The Genus Rosa was not the only book produced by Ellen Willmott: it had been preceded in 1909 by *Warley Garden in Spring and Summer*, the book which, with the finest of her photographs, stands as a record of Warley Garden at the height of its beauty. 'Brava! Brava! our greatest gardener,' wrote Gertrude Jekyll, going on to point out how much more effective than sepia was the black and white used for photographs in the book, for it could depict light and shade where sepia could only present a confused blur. The book achieved a very respectable success and its technical and artistic merits were much admired, but it made only £7 1s 8d for its author, and the absence of an accompanying text seems to account for this. Besides this, Ellen Willmott had been working in cooperation with Sir Michael Foster on a monograph of the genus Iris. His sudden death in 1907 when the book was about to go to press (or so she said) came as a severe shock to her. Mr W. R. Dykes, of Charterhouse, who was to succeed William Wilks as Secretary of the Royal Horticultural Society in 1920, now entered the field, and Ellen Willmott had more than a passing comment on this. 'Everyone too knows that the work of Sir Michael Foster's lifetime will be in the book', she wrote to John Murray; and again later (stepping up the tone): 'He [Dykes] now says that you and also I were absolutely mistaken in thinking that he was going to claim anything more than a minor part of it. He seems to forget that we have his letters to refer to even if he repudiates what he has said to us.' What was behind all this? Whatever it was, stimulated Dykes to come to Murrays in 1910 with a letter from Otto Stapf of Kew saying that he (Stapf) had examined Sir Michael Foster's notes and that in present conditions it was no use attempting to get them into shape and moreover they had all been used in published works of his. In this interview Dykes seems to have made his peace, and his *Iris* book was published in 1913; in the preface he states: 'I can never cease to regret that he himself [Sir Michael] found it impossible to give us a monograph on the Genus Iris, but he was unwilling to take any steps towards this end. . . . At his death, there passed into the hands of Miss Willmott of Warley Place, about a dozen rough notebooks, containing accounts of some of the Iris that flowered in his garden. . . . These notebooks have been most kindly lent by Miss Willmott and I owe much to the insight into Foster's methods which I have derived from the perusal of them.' There is plenty of acknowledgement of Foster's work, therefore, but the impression is nevertheless left with the reader that Sir Michael was rather a muddler, and that Ellen Willmott's part in the work was perhaps not as extensive as she had claimed.

And finally, there was Pritzel, and this again proved a protracted undertaking with a disappointing outcome. Miss Willmott had apparently been engaged for some time in preparing a continuation for her own use and that of her friends of the *Iconum Botanicarum* of Pritzel, which provided a bibliography of illustrated botanical works. This evidently had proved extremely useful—so useful that Professor Sargent used it constantly, and the botanist de Candolle set his whole staff at the Boissier Herbarium, Geneva, to copy it. Late in 1904 Ellen Willmott was approached by Sir William Thiselton-Dyer to ask if she could help them with their wish to print a supplement to Pritzel—a suggestion which greatly pleased her. Discussion ebbed and flowed on the project. Professor Sargent took up the idea with his usual enthusiasm, and wrote in 1907 rallying Miss Willmott to produce a list of references accepted for the new Pritzel. Until she did this, he said, he could do nothing towards sending her new titles to be included. A month later, a representative of Wesley the bookseller was over in America and talked to Sargent about Ellen Willmott's work, telling him that everything was satisfactorily arranged; Sargent hoped that nothing was going to interfere with the speedy completion of the work—an empty hope. The next year he was writing again, this time about the difficulties of the gigantic task, and urging Miss Willmott on to use all her resources of patience, industry and enthusiasm on the work. It appears that Mr Hemsley, recently retired from the post of Keeper of the Herbarium and Library at Kew, had been persuaded to help, and his botanical knowledge and good relations with Kew were expected to be extremely useful. A few months later, however, news reached Professor Sargent that a German in Berlin was working on a new *Iconum*, and he commented with surprising casualness that, under these circumstances, he supposed it would not make very much difference who did the work, the Germans being pretty sure to do things well. Six months later the subject was raised again: this time Professor Sargent was approaching the botanical representative of the Carnegie Institute for support on the project, but was not entirely sanguine about the outcome and so suggested examining the possible alternative of financing the new Pritzel by private subscription. Four months later the business was still hanging fire, and was to be discussed with Lt-Col Prain on his next visit to the Arboretum.

Meanwhile, the Royal Horticultural Society's Council came also to the view that a revision of Pritzel's work was necessary, but it was not until 1912 that they were able to take action and set some money aside for the purpose, contributions from other sources being added later. In 1917 two committees were set up to deal with the project and an honorary editor was appointed. Work began in July 1918 at Kew, where a room was provided for Otto Stapf, the editor, to work, with all the resources of Kew at his disposal. Very soon a provisional list of titles was circulated to botanic gardens at home and abroad, and many additions made. The first of the six projected volumes, published as the *Index Londinensis*, appeared in 1929. There was no acknowledgement of help from Ellen Willmott. Presumably they thought the job was too big for a part-time amateur, even a gifted and knowledgeable one, to take on. But it must have been a galling experience for her to be thus excluded.

Ellen Willmott also contributed some very delightful photographs to other people's books: some of these appeared in Gertrude Jekyll's *Children and Gardens*, published in 1908; and there are some charming pictures of a Mediterranean garden—very probably La Mortola—in a pleasantly conversational book published in 1903, *Riviera Nature Notes*, which was written at the behest of Sir Thomas Hanbury, and very fulsomely dedicated to him, by 'C.C.'—the Revd Charles Casey. Sir Thomas Hanbury contributed some pithy footnotes which give the book an added attraction.

The decade from 1900 to 1910 saw almost the whole of Ellen Willmott's output as an author. (When in 1922 the publisher Edward Arnold wrote to suggest that she should write a book about the Warley Garden his offer was not taken up.) She spoke, evidently, nothing but the truth when she wrote to Professor Sargent in 1906: ' . . . as you know, my plants and my gardens come before anything in life for me, and all my time is given up to working in one garden or another, and when it is too dark to see the plants themselves I read or write about them.'

Seen over the enormous gap of seventy years of startlingly rapid development and the overwhelming catastrophe of two world wars, her life seems one full of interest and change against a moneyed and leisured background. But Ellen Willmott's self-image had two sides, and she enjoyed embroidering on the dark one: in spite of her dearly loved family, her numerous friends and her passionate interest in so many subjects, she undoubtedly felt herself to be deeply alone. 'I wish you were here this spring', she wrote to Professor Sargent from Aix in 1908, 'I am quite alone with nothing to think about but plants and gardening.' Her friendship with Sargent was not her only friendship with an intelligent man—indeed she had many—but it is unique in being so well documented in their exchange of letters over a period of six years. Nor was it one-sided: for Sargent himself comments that the year 1906 is marked with a white stone in his memory as being the year in which he made her acquaintance; he hopes that the new year will bring him the opportunity of securing her friendship. And it is quite obvious that Ellen Willmott valued above all things companionship with a man of intellect and stature who shared her own interests. As far as other women were concerned, if they were educated, cultured and sympathetic, or alternatively if they were warm-hearted, partisan and admiring, they could be admitted at once to her circle of friends, but if they were in any way opinionated and pretentious—and as such she clearly classified young Mrs Wilson, whom she regarded as a lower middle-class woman with 'defective education, which is far worse than none'—then they were to be regarded with contempt, as being unfitted, indeed unable, to appreciate the finer things of life. Another type of woman, by no means uneducated in the strict sense but rather chilly and rigid in attitude, also earned Ellen Willmott's abiding scorn, and to the end of her days she referred witheringly to an acquaintance who fell into that category as 'that Alice'. Even poor Mrs Sargent rates only one dutiful and unenthusiastic comment: 'I hope that Mrs Sargent is pleased at the plans you have made to bring her to Aix next year'—these, evidently, were Sargent's plans and not Ellen Willmott's.

Nothing pleased her more than being in on everything: 'I am behind a good many scenes and know a good deal about what goes on and as I never repeat anything I get told all manner of details.' It is plain to see, behind much of what she says, the intelligent little girl, accustomed to her father's companionship and also to his rebukes; for, where she would argue with her own contemporaries and despise them, she was quite unreasoningly meek under the impact of the very plain speaking which she received from Sargent, who remarked: 'I have devoted three weeks continuously to your manuscript and I am about ready to retire into a sanatorium for the remainder of my life as a result of this effort. . . . The principal fault that I find with your work is that under the species you quote many plates of Redouté, Laurence [*sic*] and Andrews which represent varieties of the species and not the species or type.' These were stirring words, but Ellen Willmott reacted with anxiety rather than indignation. Did he really feel there were many inaccuracies? . . . She had really worked so hard and so incessantly over these references, and in going over them she had hardly ever found any inaccuracy. She was obviously feeling stale and tired; she felt an amateur, not entirely sure of her ground, and from Sargent she wanted not only advice, but also reassurance and appreciation. She got plenty of the former but, alas for her other demands, Sargent's letters were bracing rather than sympathetic. Ellen Willmott was making a painful discovery: those who have elected to be treated as intellectual equals cannot suddenly decide to show weakness and expect immediately to be taken seriously. She was undoubtedly extremely nervous about *The Genus Rosa*: 'I hope I have done nothing outrageously wrong', she wrote. But like many others in her situation she just had to wait until, in the normal course of events, she felt better.

There appears also the disquieting sign of a tendency to divide and rule: she could apparently make a two-against-one situation out of anything involving three parties: 'this is quite between ourselves', she writes; and, 'this is all private naturally'—the attempt to create a cosy relationship in this way was not only quite enough to send any unattached man running swiftly in the opposite direction (E. A. Bowles, plant-hunter and crocus specialist, who gardened at Myddelton Hall in Enfield, which he later inherited from his parents, reacted in this way when he received letters from Ellen Willmott written in such vein), but also somehow seemed to need enmity and opposition on which to thrive. It is a pity that there is no record describing Ellen's paternal grandmother in detail: it seems possible that some of Sarah's drive, and her heavy involvement in human relationships, may have reappeared in her grand-daughter. But although Ellen may well have been her father's favourite daughter, she was so much attached to her sister Rose and to her mother that there seems little reason to suppose that the habit of engineering an unpleasant three-some lay in some unresolved childhood situation.

And so Ellen Willmott was advancing into middle age in possession of a character designed to wear patchily rather than well. When her interest was aroused, her intellectual grasp and breadth of knowledge were remarkable; she could rise to brilliance, and her wit and gusto, her infectious sense of enjoyment, captivated her circle; she could be sweet-tempered when things were going well, a loyal and responsive friend, a just employer. But against that she had to struggle with innumerable faults: she was a staunch hater, an implacable enemy—wayward and temperamental, accustomed to having her own way, and a snob (with a peculiarly persistent brand of snobbery fuelled by the knowledge that she herself had her origins in 'trade'). Such drive, and such brilliance, were only easy to take when her audiences were capable of response at the same level, or uniformly admiring. The key to her behaviour seems to lie in the fact that she was a personality much larger than life. Dull people bored her; dull conversations bored her, so that she sought to enliven them with malicious and entertaining stories, or to toss in conversational balls at random, regardless of whether they were exaggerated or untrue, simply to see what happened and so to enliven the proceedings. As a raconteuse she excelled. She never had time in her life to accomplish half of what she intended, and she felt bitterly the fact that circumstances, and the need to attend to them, had so distracted her from her main work.

Looking back to the girl who wrote her first letter from Paris, it seems that the promise of that youthful enthusiasm has soured a little, matured a lot, developed in some directions, been frustrated in others: in fact, the whole human progress, but on a larger scale than many human beings come within sight of, and thus much more forgivable.

CHAPTER VII

The Leaf-mould Pit and Other Concerns

The village of Great Warley, nominally in the hot dry summer of
1906, but let it stand for the summer of any year around the turn of
the century:

'Can we have a piece more jam tart, please?'
'Well help yourself then, but don't come back asking for any
more.'

Clatter clatter of black boots along the passage, shoving, pushing
and whispering in the larder, and then all nine of them streaming out
of the house again, the hungry ones cramming the hunks of juicy,
sticky tart (for Mrs Hurcombe was a generous baker) into their
mouths, the provident ones carrying their slices carefully to protect
them. The Lady was away, so out they rushed into the field behind
North Lodge. The daffodils which covered this field in interweaving
patches of subtly different colour had long since died down, the grass
was higher than waist-level in the field; Essex Blue butterflies were
fluttering over the wild flowers—vetch and clover and harebell—and
it was almost time for cutting the hay: a busy time, for the fields all
round the mansion, as well as over by the farm, were allowed to
grow on for hay. So the children were well screened. On they went,
the Hurcombes and the Preeces, two girls and seven boys, more or
less identically clad, the girls in pleated skirts and jap silk blouses,
with pinafores over, long legs in black stockings and boots, and the
boys in sailor suits. At least the girls were allowed to discard their
hats. (Presumably their mothers were reconciled to a lot of washing,
for no one had yet devised hardwearing play-clothes for children,
and they wore the same things for school, in the house, up trees: the
only difference was between everyday and Sunday best, and the
latter were a good deal more carefully looked after.)

The children's destination was the leaf-mould pit, a lush, dank, rich-smelling place well away from the cottages and at this time of year well trodden down, with somewhere to sit along the sides. They crowded in. The girls carefully took out the things they had been carrying bundled in their pinafores. May Hurcombe bought loaves two at a time in Brentwood, thus saving a ha'penny, which she pocketed, and this eventually mounted up so that the children, hiding behind the hawthorn hedge near North Lodge, could catch Gutteridge the baker and buy a fine crusty loaf from him for tuppence ha'penny. Any other pennies which came their way were usually spent at the shop—where money went a long way, since a bar of chocolate only cost a farthing—and by dint of hanging around they could usually contrive to get served by Mr Thomas's daughter Lizzie, who used to plunge her hand into the jar and trickle the sweets straight into a paper poke, usually overdoing it in favour of the fortunate child who was buying. Then there were pieces of bread and dripping to be saved from tea and smuggled out. Mrs Hurcombe baked and cooked energetically and unceasingly: she made eighty pounds of gooseberry jam each year, and everything else was done on the same scale, so there was usually something to be wheedled out of the Hurcombe kitchen besides jam tart. It all added up to quite a feast. Fred, the third Preece brother, had a knife which he drew from his pocket with a flourish, and used this for cutting and spreading.

In the warm summer evening, the sweetish smell of the leaf-mould all around them, the last of the sunlight falling in slanting rays over the field, they savoured the feast, the more exciting because meals at home were strictly affairs for eating only, and even in a relatively indulgent household children were not expected to talk. Here in their secret hide-out they could giggle and chatter to their hearts' content, until it was time to go home and, brushing the crumbs into the leaf-mould, they straggled across the field, the Preece children into the Lodge and the Hurcombes to Apple Tree Cottage. Preece and Hurcombe were pleased to have been allowed peace in which to have their tea, and indeed the children may have met Hurcombe strolling over to give the horses their last feed of the day. Bedtime now, in the low-ceilinged attic rooms, where they fell asleep to the distant noise of bullfrogs croaking by the lake, and perhaps the tinkle of cowbells worn by any of Lescher's herd left out at night in the fields on the far side of Dark Lane.

The gardeners' families were up early, for work started in the Warley Garden at 6 a.m. James Preece kept these hours too, for he felt it unfair to expect his men to start so early if he were not there to work alongside them. The children had a more leisurely start, even in term time, when they left about 8.30 to start school at 9 o' clock at Christ Church National School, down the hill towards Brentwood. Before they actually left their homes, however, there was time for various minor crimes to be committed: the boys went off to take eggs from nests, and one day the two oldest Preece boys dared each other to set off the trip wires which fired air guns protecting Miss Willmott's daffodils in the fields from the hand of the thief. Luckily they were too close to the guns to do themselves any harm, but it was the last time that anything of the sort happened.

In the summer holidays, however, the day was theirs. In the Preece household it began when Fuller, a diminutive, cheerful gardener, to whom the children were much attached and whom they knew as Budler, arrived at the back door with a wicker basket full of splendid fruit and vegetables—nectarines, grapes, peaches, vegetables of every kind—for the Preeces lived off the fat of the land. The children called the contents of this basket indiscriminately 'plums' and thought nothing of it. Nellie Preece sometimes helped her mother with various jobs; and now, nearly eighty years later, she can recall a day when together they made a set of lace covers to protect some of Preece's favourite apples, which he was cosseting to put into a show, from the competitive attentions of the birds. When eventually the covers were taken off, the delicate pattern of the lacework was faithfully reproduced on the fruit. As soon as jobs in the house were done, the children set off to see what was afoot in the village, while Mrs Preece got to work in the house.

At ten o'clock the gardeners were hungry again after four hours' hard work, and Preece was partial to a cold lamb chop—a bit of best end of neck, with some bread and butter, set him up again till dinner time—and there must have been many others who needed a substantial something at that time too. Again, Preece was usually able to have his break in peace, while the children wandered off. Turning first down towards Brentwood, and crossing the road when they had rounded the curve, they then made for the Headley garden, an endless source of fascination to them, for there was always something going on there. Behind the gardeners' thatched cottages which bordered the road, and just before they came to the entrance gates to the Garden, stood the carpenters' work-shop. Long and narrow, it resounded to the noise of sawing and planing, and was full of the resinous, heady smell of freshly cut wood. The carpenters, Mr Tanner and Mr Norfolk, stopped work for a few minutes to talk to the children and let them play around for a while, tuck the long ribbony shavings under their hats for curls and laugh prodigiously at their own wit and humour. But this skylarking could not go on for too long, because there was work to be done: the carpenters made all the fences and gates and undertook repairs throughout the estate, and there was plenty to keep them busy. The children knew the moment had come when Mr Tanner picked up one of his enormously long nails, which they called 'Tanner's tintacks', cleared his throat, and prepared to give his whole attention to the wood under his hands. But the carpenters did find time to make hay forks for all the children to use in the summer, when they came to the farm to toss the hay for Farmer Browne.

So off they went, to edge round the gate into the Headley garden, with its neat rows of vegetables and chrysanthemums in very early leaf (some outdoor and some greenhouse varieties, including a pale pink one named 'Nellie Preece'); backing on to the wall behind the carpenters' work-shop were the peach and grape houses, and fig trees too. In the centre was the pond. Perhaps there was nothing much going on in the garden, but a sense of activity just out of sight. Quickly, the children doubled on their tracks and rushed round to the other gates, near the Headley Arms, in time to see a cart, which could drive right through the gates into the garden, being loaded with vegetables to go up to Covent Garden, or with flowers to be sent off to a show. The latter were neatly and carefully packed in large green purpose-built boxes (probably made in the carpenters' shop) where the blooms were held in place in individual containers lodged in a tray. Once the loading was over, the children lost interest and straggled back along the road, perhaps passing Polly Longstock-ings from the cottages, who stopped in her tracks to make grimaces, or Towry Jack, out to beg a drop of hot water at the door of North Lodge. At this hour housewives were mostly busy indoors and those who went to work were also out of the way.

Occasionally, a carriage or trap, or a rider, would trot smartly past with a wave of the whip and a clatter and whinny, but for the most part the village belonged to the children. The only hazard was that they might suddenly be confronted either by Mrs Murray Ind (who had married into the brewing family of Ind and who lived at Coombe Lodge) a formidable figure who stalked along with head thrust forward and arms clasped behind her, a cane thrust under them, *en route* for her mother-in-law's imposing house near Warley Barracks, or, indeed, by the Lady herself, always in a hurry and moving swiftly and gracefully about her business, whether walking to Brentwood Station or just crossing the road to visit her sister if she happened to be in residence at Warley Lea. If either of these emergencies occurred, the girls had to curtsey and the boys touch their caps. But with luck they passed North Lodge and Apple Tree Cottage on their right without untoward incident. It was a pretty road, with hawthorn hedges green and fresh in spring, and verges full of flowers. Next, down a lane to the left which skirted the edge of Warley Lea garden, came the farm, which exercised an irresistible pull: it seemed impossible to pass the path to it without going down to investigate. The girls were friendly with Elsie, daughter of Farmer Browne, and if they caught sight of her they might well be able to spend the rest of the morning on the farm, riding the donkey or helping with some task or other.

If the children decided to go up to the shop, there was of course the dreaded obstacle of the Scotch bullocks to pass. Standing at the edge of their field almost level with the road, and only hindered from leaping down by what seemed to the children a most inadequately low fence and shallow ditch, the cattle regarded passers-by with a threatening shake of their enormous horns. Indeed, they did sometimes get down into the road, which was then closed until they could be rounded up. Still, there was safety in numbers, and once the danger was past there was all the rest of the village to explore. Past the cattle field came a row of haystacks on the left, followed by a cluster of gardeners' cottages, all with gardens full of flowers, vying with each other for colour and scent and sheer mass of bloom. On the right the children came to the South Lodge, where in the late summer of 1996 there was a new baby in the house: this was Max, the oldest of Jacob and Rosina Maurer's family, which was eventually to consist of nine children (first four boys, and then five girls, in an orderly Swiss fashion). There is a photograph showing Max on the day of his christening: his mother is gazing down at the child in her arms, but Jacob looks unusually menacing, turning sharply to one side with one hand slightly raised, as if to hit anyone who had a word to say against his son.

Three roads met at the village green, opposite the Thatchers' Arms: the road from Brentwood, along which the children had come; the road to Childerditch and thence to Ockendon, running off at an angle to the left; and the road to Upminster Common, which bore to the right past the post office. The children at this end of the village went to the village school, and did not often come into contact with the families living at the north end. The only exception to this was Jim, son of Robinson the butler, who at Miss Willmott's behest started his school career at the Catholic school on Warley Hill. Jim's mother, however, was equal to this ploy: a staunch member of the Church of England, she was not going to let the Catholics get hold of her son, and somehow, without offending the Lady, she managed things so that, before many years were past, Jim had joined his friends at the Great Warley School. This allowed him to cadge lifts home on the cart which had been delivering coal for the steam engine at the waterworks: he arrived home in a terrible mess and was roundly scolded by his mother. The boy was a favourite with Miss Willmott, and was always summoned to play with her nephew, Rob Berkeley (who was just a little younger), when the Berkeleys came to Warley. Because Robinson worked such long hours in the house, often being on duty in the evenings and at week-ends, and sometimes abroad or at Spetchley Park, he used to make a point of doing as much as he could with his son on those occasions when a little free time came his way. Jim Robinson can still remember going with his father to the bank in Brentwood to collect the wages, and standing fascinated while the clerk tipped sovereigns expertly into a leather bag with a little brass shovel. And once he went with his father to Covent Garden, to buy fish for one of the ponds—very likely the Japanese carp which one of Ellen Willmott's friends had suggested she should obtain from Greens.

So it was probable that the children from the other end of Great Warley decided against going in to see the Robinson family, and unless they had money to spend in the shop they turned their attention to the road down to Childerditch. Here, past one or two larger houses, there was the smithy, which was well worth a visit, and before that a sortie could be made down the lane to the pump house, whence the noise of Mr Thomas at work might be heard. There was a glimpse to be had from this lane of the Well Mead garden, with its roses, grapes, figs and vegetables, and of the wild garden, where all the wild flora of Essex flourished and hybridized with wild flowers from all the countries of Europe, planted amidst the English grasses and left to acclimatize themselves. The noise of the smithy was to be heard as the children approached: peering inside, they could see Mr Coe at work in his leather apron, hammering the shoes for one of Mr Heseltine's hunters perhaps, or for the shire horses at the farm. The rhythmic clanging, the hissing of the red-hot forge, the sparks from the blacksmith's hammer, all held the children spellbound. But when they asked Mr Coe what the time was, he told them it was getting on time for their dinner and they'd best be off home. So they did not bother to carry on down the road; in any case the excitement over the new church had died down since the church itself—St. Mary the Virgin, but always known as 'Heseltine's'—was completed about 1904, in the nick of time to avoid a Roman Catholic church being erected by Miss Willmott, so said local rumour. Nor were the children interested in the village school or the main Essex pumping station farther down the road, so it seemed wisest to follow Coe's advice and hurry home, particularly as Mrs Preece was a stickler for punctuality.

On the way back, if they happened to strike the time when the gardeners were leaving for their mid-day dinner break, it seemed like closing time at a factory. The gardeners came pouring out of the south gates in a stream which divided there, some going southwards to their cottages at that end of the village, some turning northward for Headley Common or Warley Hill; folding up their aprons as they emerged, mopping their brows, they greeted the children with pleasure. For they were the most kindly and good-tempered of men, simple in outlook, but knowledgeable, skilful and humorous. Daddy Potter, with his trained mongoose which made short work of the rats in the stables, would be walking down to his cottage on Headley Common, and several of the foremen lived in the larger cottages on the road to Warley Barracks; and then there were the young gardeners who lived in the Bothy, including the foreign gardeners such as Monsieur Renault, who in the annual photograph in which he appears has managed to tilt his boater to a rakish un-British angle. (Preece was very uncomfortable with these foreign gardeners: he could not understand a word they said, and was very doubtful if his efforts to train them got through at all.) With an escort such as this the children passed the Scotch bullocks without even noticing them.

On Sundays the routine was different. Dressed in their best—the boys in sailor (later Norfolk) suits whatever the season, the girls in summer wearing dresses of jap silk or nun's veiling, and leghorn hats with silk ruching under the brims, in winter sailor suits with white vests and box-pleated skirts—they set out for church. The girls carried sunshades and looked most unaccustomedly demure. Sometimes they went to Christ Church on Warley Hill, and sometimes to Heseltine's—but the favourite was Warley Barracks church, because the band played there. On Hospital Sunday they took flowers with them to church. Then back home for Sunday dinner—usually a huge sirloin or a nice joint of pork in the Preece household—and in the afternoon they were sent off to Sunday School, which was held in a building by Brentwood Station. After tea, if the weather was fine, the whole family went for a walk. No one could say that the children lacked for exercise, and no one seemed to worry about the effects of long walks taken on a full stomach. Something else is worth recording. Miss Willmott, it seems, had a serious talk with James Preece in the course of which she suggested that the entire Preece family should become Roman Catholics. With the utmost deference and yet sufficiently firmly to prevent the subject from being re-opened, Preece indicated that this was something he could not contemplate. The sheer effrontery of the suggestion, and the lack of contact with the real world that it evinces, is almost as remarkable as Preece's courage and moral toughness in a situation where a refusal might easily have cost him his job, so mercurial and unreasonable could his employer be.

The Preeces were not the only family who took a walk on Sunday evenings. Families from as far away as Warley Hill set out, parents behind and children in front in a little crocodile, all dressed in Sunday clothes, to walk as far as the north gates of the estate and peer through them, hoping for a glimpse of the gentry within—much to the disgust of the estate workers.

When Miss Willmott was away the children had the run of the estate—but not all the children (those who lived in the Headley garden cottages in any case preferred to play on the common, which was close at hand) and not all the estate. They had to keep well away from the parts of the garden where skilled work was going on, such as the alpine garden, the walled garden and the nursery area, visiting these only under escort. But this still left them with the fields, where there was plenty of scope. And there was one memorable summer when there was scarlet fever and diphtheria at Christ Church School, and the estate children were not only permitted, but positively encouraged by Miss Willmott to keep away from other village children, and for the whole ten weeks to play in the estate fields. Perhaps at the back of her mind persisted the memory of her sister Ada. Everyone on the estate had a thoroughly healthy and happy summer, and no one caught either disease.

As the summer holidays progressed, preparations began in earnest for the most exciting and important event of the summer, the climax of everyone's efforts: the Annual Show and Sports Day, held in the field in front of Warley Place. Cottagers tended their gardens, front for the flowers and back for the vegetables, so that their efforts could be judged both *in situ* by Preece and his foremen, and in the show tent, where fruit and vegetables, bursting with health and lovingly washed and polished, were carefully arranged on the tables in tall pyramids. Flowers, too, went to the show in huge quantities, and great was the dismay if some treasured bloom burst into flower too early or lingered too late. The children gathered wild flowers, many picked weeks, even months beforehand, and carefully pressed between the pages of a book. The date was usually fixed for the end of August or beginning of September, and a surviving programme for the sports part of it, beautifully printed (perhaps on Miss Willmott's Holtzapffel Monotype Printing Press?), states on the cover, beside a photograph of the mansion: 'Great and Little Warley Cottage Garden Show—Village Sports—Captain: R. V. Berkeley.' Obviously, Rose and Robert were expected to do their bit on this occasion as residents, even if only part-timers. A couple of days before the show, two marquees were erected in the south field—a large circular tent, resplendent with a Union Jack flying from the crest, and a smaller rectangular one. James Preece and his men then arranged a magnificent display in the large marquee. The centre pole was surrounded by palms, tall lilies in pots, chrysanthemums, ferns and cacti, while the pole itself was swathed with ivy, and ropes of ivy overhead stretched away to the far corners. On the walls were hung, as in a Greek frieze, in perfect classical beauty and lacking only acanthus leaves, great bunches of purple grapes, their richness and bloom enhanced by the dim light of the tent, and beneath them on trestle tables the plunder of the orchards and hedgerows, apples and pears and quinces, blackberries and sloe and crab apples, in every variety.

When the day at last came, a long procession wound its way through the south gates during the morning, carefully bearing the various entries and exhibits; by lunchtime everything was in place, and at two o'clock everyone from both villages must have been gathered in the field. The proceedings were opened, very grandly, not by one but by two military bands from Warley Barracks, one marching through the north gates and past the mansion, the other approaching along the main road to turn in at the south gates and join forces in the sports field with its counterpart. They met just by the marquees, lending a splendid military flourish to the start of the races. These took place on the level ground at the top of the field, near the walnut tree which was held together with iron hoops made by Coe the blacksmith. The Willmott party could reach this spot by taking the path opposite the house, stepping over the ha-ha, all heedless of the grass snakes sleeping there in the sun, and entering the field by a gate near an enormous mulberry tree. Captain Berkeley was soon ready with his starting pistol, and the races were off. And what races they were! 100 Yards—All Fours; Roll Eating Contest; Frogs in Wheelbarrows; Race, Pipe Smoking; Race Skipping, Girls; and, most remarkable of all, 100 Yards for Women over 60, in which the dignified Warley Place domestic staff and elderly village ladies took part with the greatest good humour, tucking up their skirts to give themselves a better chance of victory. The gardeners played happily to the gallery, causing the children to squeal with excitement and jump up and down in glee as they watched the men pillow-fighting on greasy poles over an improvised bath of water, and the village women trying to catch the greasy pig. There was even a tug-of-war on donkeys, a strange experience for those normally peaceful animals. 'The Prizes will consist of useful articles', says Rule 6 on the back of the programme—but it is nice to think that the useful article was nearly always money.

Meanwhile, Preece and his foremen were out looking over the cottage gardens with a practised and professional eye; while inside the marquee the vegetable foreman attempted to assess the merits of serried ranks and gorgeous pyramids of vegetables; and the housekeeper from Warley Place, Mrs McCullum, was working her way through the pots of honey, the pots of jam (held carefully up to the light to see that the fruit was properly distributed), dripping cakes, gingerbread, and so on; and some other ladies, now forgotten, bent their attention to earnest comparison of cross-stitch with cross-stitch, stocking-stitch with stocking-stitch, and egg cosies, pen wipers, pin cushions and needle books, each with its kind. Some who were children then can still remember the thrill of winning prizes: when she was ten years old Nellie Preece won 2nd Prize for four books of pressed flowers, being beaten to the 1st Prize by Harry Hurcombe, who went one better by printing all the flower names in Latin. Later, in 1910, she won 1st Prize for her collection of 123 varieties of wild flower. Jim Robinson, on the other hand, remembers that he upset his father by refusing to run in the 200 Yards Race. The 1st Prize for everything seems to have been 5s, the other prizes tailing off and ending up at about 2s. As the day rose to a crescendo with the prize-giving, it grew stifling hot in the tent, and mothers at least cannot have been altogether sorry when it was all over. Then at once a hubbub of excited voices broke out, echoing round the tent, so full of the smells of grass and earth, baking and flowers and humanity, and the inhabitants of the Warleys began to pour out, clutching the hands of their pink-cheeked and sticky children, who in their turn, if they had been lucky, clutched precious prize money. Outside there would be a slight feel of autumn in the air, and since on that day all the gardens in the villages were open to everyone, it made a good airing before bedtime to take a walk round to see where the prizes had been bestowed and whether local opinion agreed with Preece and his foremen. For some, there was the clearing up in the marquees to be done, and it seems more than likely that a good few of the partakers in the races had a powerful thirst to drown in the Thatchers' Arms afterwards.

With this grand climax the summer was almost over, school started again, the nights grew chilly and the village began to prepare for winter. Winter coats came out of mothballs, woollen hoods, scarves and gloves muffled up the children. Families made their own entertainment—playing games, organizing musical evenings. Christmas came. Miss Willmott was often away in late autumn, and then went to spend Christmas with the Berkeleys at Spetchley, but wherever she was, there were certain traditions which she always kept. Orders went to Farmer Browne to kill a certain number of sheep, and these were divided up strictly in order of precedence, and under Robinson's supervision, so that the most important families on the estate got the choicest cuts. Sometimes venison was sent down from Spetchley Park, and that too was divided up with scrupulous fairness—though not everyone was as enthusiastic about this once it had been hung. As Christmas drew near, North Lodge was a fine sight. Throughout the year Preece kept two barrels of beer in the scullery, pale at one end and dark at the other, and now these were joined by three turkeys, supplied as a Christmas gift by Woods, the firm patronized by Preece for plant pots and other garden supplies. In contrast to their secular gift, this firm also gave religious medallions to the children. Backhouses of York, architects of the alpine garden, and from whom came the sharp sand used on the estate, contributed a large tin of tea, with a fascinating double lid, a square one on top and a tight round one inside to keep the flavour in. Warley Place kitchen presented a large mince tart on a flat plate to each household on the estate. For the children Miss Willmott organized (or perhaps it would be more accurate to say 'caused to be organized', for the hand of Robinson seems to be detectable again) a memorable Christmas party. In their best dresses and suits they trooped up to the mansion, feeling exceedingly awkward and shy, and were rewarded by a most sumptuous tea and sometimes a magic-lantern show given by Miss Willmott herself. And every child on the estate had a Christmas present: a large and beautifully bound Annual—*Chums, Boys' Holiday Annual,* or *Lister's Holiday Annual.*

In all these festivities, the children retained only a vague sense of the presence of the Lady: the moving spirits of the feast, the bringers of jollity, were the cheerful Mrs McCullum, the jovial figure of James Preece, the benign Robinson—all presiding with the greatest cheerfulness over the events of summer and winter alike. It was not that Ellen Willmott gave any sign of actively disliking children—indeed, she was known to be much attached to her nephew and nieces—but she did prefer children who were not related to her and were of a different social class to be articulate and intelligent, and she may have mistaken shyness for stupidity. So she remained aloof and the estate children curtseyed to her, while her real qualities and sympathies were kept for her sister Rose's children and for the Russells, who still remember the consignments of expensive books and toys which Ellen Willmott used to send them at Christmas time. And yet, the estate children remembered these Christmases all their lives; and going home hand in hand, watching their breath rise in front of them in the cold air, they felt ready to turn cartwheels with excitement—but contented themselves with having a slide on the Headley Pond, if the ice was ready to bear. Prudently, the girls let the boys go first: the pond was *not* ready to bear, feet got wet; sanctimoniously, the girls pushed their brothers ahead of them into the house, and some mild scolding took place. But it was Christmas, it was well past bedtime, and mischief could be overlooked. Within an hour the houses were dark: the gardeners had to be at work at six the next day.

CHAPTER VIII

In the South

The swimming vapour slopes athwart the glen,
Puts forth an arm, and creeps from pine to pine,
And loiters, slowly drawn. On either hand
The lawns and meadow-ledges midway down
Hang rich in flowers. . . .
TENNYSON, Oenone

Where was Ellen Willmott when absent from these festivities?
Almost certainly at Tresserve, or possibly at her new property in
Italy. After so many visits to the Hanburys at La Mortola in the early
1900s, listening to Sir Thomas as he talked of his Chinese treasures in
the cool marble rooms of the Palazzo Orengo, or running down the
steps in the garden to join him in examining the latest and most
gorgeous arrival from the East or distant Mexico, and choosing a
spot where it would show to its best advantage, she had finally fallen
so deeply under the spell of that ancient coastline that she felt coming
over her a familiar and irresistible feeling: she *had* to own land there
herself. In 1905 she at last found the right property, but there is some
uncertainty as to whether the price of 12,950 lire refers only to land
which she bought to landward of the road from Latte to Ventimiglia,
or to the whole of the property, most of which lay to seaward, barely
two miles from La Mortola. Boccanegra is a house which turns its
back to the road with a high blank wall, twenty or thirty yards long;
only the square turret which surmounts it, topped by a miniature
wrought-iron spire and containing a look-out room, can be seen.
Today the solid stone gateposts, topped by terracotta urns and
decorated by strange black wrought-iron bird shapes, flank a for-
midably thick steel gate and ornamental screen. The name of the
house is partly chipped away and partly obscured both by trailing

ivy and by the '*Abbandonata*' sticker of the Istituto Vigilanza of San Remo. Beneath it is carved in the stonework 'PROPRIETA TREMAYNE'.

The land enjoys almost the same aspect as La Mortola, shelving steeply down to the sea, and catching the full sun for most of the day; from the road, the garden presents an appearance much like that of I Giardini Hanbury, but on a smaller scale. A cypress stands on either side of the gate, and beyond them a tall poplar and an acacia, agave and aloe beneath them. But Ellen Willmott's first concern when she came to the house was not with planting, but with watering: in July 1906 she wrote to Professor Sargent that she was making water tanks in different places, so that when the rain descended in torrents as was its habit she could engineer the paths nearby and pile the soil in natural forms against walls, after which the rest could follow at leisure. She added that she was rather laughed at for doing the most uninteresting and costly work first—but perhaps she said this to make clear that her new venture was an expensive one, needing all the resources she could muster. She thus added lustre to her own image as a woman of discrimination with a well-developed sense of priorities in putting her contribution of £200 towards Wilson's Chinese journey, in spite of the other demands on her purse. It is interesting indeed that she had found a garden where she could start from scratch and from which she obviously drew a great deal of satisfaction, for, as she said, she could now work in a garden of her own the whole year round. Once the outline of the garden had been determined, the ordering began—and it was ordering on no mean scale.

Chiefly, Ellen Willmott bought from Hickel Brothers at Beaulieu sur Mer, whose services she also used as landscape gardeners. She seems early in her life at Boccanegra to have taken an intense dislike to the railway which ran through her property, a dislike increased by some expropriations of land made by the Italian Railways in 1908, and to conceal its presence became an obsession with her. She therefore caused the Hickel Brothers to devise various plantings which would make a screen, partly of dactylifera (probably *Phoenix dactylifera,* the date palm), and partly of strong quick-growing eucalyptus, which would in a short time grow to hide the railway line altogether—though they admitted that 'the second discovered part of the line offers many difficulties to be hidden as trees can not be planted in the same way as in the first case because the land where trees would have to go, belongs to the Government. . . .' They had another scheme to offer, with taller trees planted at a greater distance from the line. They also, rather perilously, attempted negotiations with the engineer of the railway, 'who refused the plantation in the land of the company in account of the danger resulting from the stay of strong plants near the rails in the first way and the risk of the plantation in account of the very rapid descent of the land'. It is to be hoped that the trees fulfilled their purpose, for in the two years they were expected to need in order to reach a useful height, much was to happen.

Ellen Willmott spent huge sums of money with the firm of Hickel Brothers: her statement for 1906 ran to three and a half quarto pages; for 1907 it was two and a half pages, and for 1908 two. And her purchases ranged from a single casuarina or dracaena to 100 *Mahonia aquifolia,* 300 cannas, 600 *Tulipa clusiana,* and aloe and agave in consignments often or so at a time, literally by the hundred: Hickels' foreman seems also to have spent a good many days at work at Boccanegra, planning, planting and presumably also arguing with the railway engineer. Yet, by degrees and alas, as usual, Ellen Willmott's relations with this helpful and knowledgeable supplier deteriorated: she would not settle her bills in full and in reasonable time; she would change her mind; she would leave the nursery to house and tend plants which she had ordered and then would say (often quite accurately, but nevertheless very annoyingly) that her garden was not ready to take them; she complained, unjustifiably, and asked the Hickel Brothers to take items back and refund money, also unjustifiably. In the end, but only with difficulty, a settlement was reached, and relations were then broken off altogether. She dealt with other nurserymen too, spreading her orders, paying a little on account here and a little there: she bought from Penco in Ventimiglia, from Billés and Maison Bensa in Menton, and from Augier (speciahst in coconut palms), André and Troncy at Cannes. She ordered everything that flourished in the region—figs, opuntia, bignonia (now *Campsis*), acacia, orange trees, bay trees, pittosporum by the hundred, cedars, eleagnus, yuccas, and so on and so on, until her garden must have been a sight of unbelievable and flamboyant beauty. The bills for this prodigality of bloom over the period from the purchase of the house until 1909 amounted to nearly £2,000 from her local suppliers alone (and she certainly ordered for Boccanegra from other nurserymen too)—an amount which must have produced a garden rivalling La Mortola in magnificence. And that was for the garden alone. The cost of furnishing the house must at least have equalled the cost of stocking the garden. And then there was the gardener/caretaker: Clodoveo (with his family) makes an appearance on the scene in 1909, and remained (at least on paper) Ellen Willmott's '*devotissimo ed umilissimo servo*' until the end of her ownership, behaving in such a way that he managed to keep all possible rivals for his job at bay, since they simply refused to come anywhere near him.

In 1906 the Italian coast was beautiful and uncluttered, and the road which wound past the wall of Boccanegra was still a country road from which the dust rose with every passing cart, accounting perhaps for the lack of windows facing the road. Far down the slope to the sea, the track of the ancient Via Julia Augusta crossed the garden as it did at La Mortola: a narrow road off the main Via Aurelia which ended at Pisa, it formed the main route connecting the Rome of classical times with its distant trading post at Marseilles. The strange, narrow path carries its own atmosphere, of something very, very old: it has an intent feel to it, as though it still holds echoes of the preoccupations of hot and thirsty legionaries, of merchants with their mules stumbling under the ferocity of the *ponente* blowing from the west and their carts rocking crazily, the contents in danger of rolling seawards.

Ellen Willmott's arrival on her visits to Boccanegra was more prosaic: she came by train, the railway by that time having been extended from Marseilles as far as Ventimiglia. To smooth her path and prepare the house in the pre-Clodoveo days, Robinson travelled out a week in advance; it does not seem that he was proficient in Italian but, as in many other situations, he just had to manage. From his room at the top of the square turret he looked out on to the dusty road, and doubtless thought he would rather have been sitting in his properly organized pantry at Warley; but even he, leaning on a wall at the top of the Porta Canarda hill, smoking one of his favourite Toscana cigars, had to admit that on a spring evening in early March—before the worst of the plague of mosquitoes had set in for the year, and the weather being warm, agreeable and still—Italy was in its way as good a place as Essex.

Ellen Willmott had early begun to make a habit of visiting Boccanegra twice a year, the first visit being in early spring, so that, each year, she had two seasons of spring bulbs, one in Italy and then the more extensive and beautiful display at Warley. In a good year bulbs were showing above the ground early in January, and the swallows came at the beginning of March. The garden at Boccanegra, like that at La Mortola, contained many ancient olive trees (one of them, Miss Willmott gleefully reported to Kew 'had Mr Ellis' red mistletoe growing in it') and the crop was usually harvested in April, so in a year when the spring was late in Essex she could stay to see the task completed, returning to witness the even more beautiful sequence of bloom at Warley. And then, in October or November, when the worst of the year's tidying-up had been finished at Warley, and decisions made on the planting for next spring, she returned to Italy to catch the warm autumn days—and, of course, the days of continuous rain. November was not always a good time for going abroad, and in 1909 she was writing to Professor Sargent that she had been quite knocked over by a very bad cold and confined to the house for a week, where she had got on with her writing—presumably for the rose book.

If not at Boccanegra, Ellen Willmott may have been at Tresserve. With three gardens to tend, how could she be sure of catching the best of all? Usually she would try to see her splendid collection of *Iris* in bloom, and at least the beginning of the clematis and rose species. William Gumbleton credited her with having 11,000 rose trees here—and also implied that she more or less kept some members of the nursery trade going, since her last order for Tresserve from a Cork nurseryman comprised four hundredweight of bulbs! 'He would like to find some more like you,' Gumbleton added. The establishment at Tresserve was naturally a much more permanent affair than the house on the Riviera. Across the road from the Château lived the gardener, Claud Meunier, and his sister Gasparine, who looked after the household. Both were devoted servants of Miss Willmott, and (in spite of the fact that she ungratefully grumbled about the incompetence of her garden staff) Claude was an extremely knowledgeable gardener with whom, when away, Ellen Willmott maintained a steady stream of correspondence—as well she might, with the specialist collections under his care, and the seeds and plants which she was trying out in the special conditions of

Tresserve. Notice of the imminent arrival of the Willmott entourage caused a tremendous flurry and *branle-bas:* polishing of furniture, sprucing of rooms, making of beds, and a grand clear-up in the garden. The very young daughter of the schoolmistress (who, living opposite the Château, was the nearest neighbour) was allowed to 'help'; now, as an old lady, she remembers the arrival of the Willmott party complete with Robinson (who, no doubt thankfully, did not have to precede the others on these occasions) and whichever other servants were detailed to accompany their mistress. Gasparine evidently did the cooking, for a letter survives written by Claude in his spidery, decorative hand and dated 1913, remarking that with only a *'fille* de peine' in the kitchen *'evidemment elle ne pourra faire de la fine cuisine mats Mademoiselle a des gouts si simples'*. Perhaps there would be a French servant who had spent a few months at Warley returning home; or perhaps Blanc, the son of the Tresserve butcher who worked at Warley for a time, was allowed a trip to visit his parents and work in the garden under Meunier's supervision. Jim Robinson remembers being taken to Tresserve with his father at the age of about five, and watching the gardeners treading the grapes for the wine made from the Château's harvest. And he can remember Miss Willmott going into Aix and returning with a small wheelbarrow in which he collected conkers from the chestnut trees in the front courtyard.

The arrival would have been a heartwarming moment for Ellen Willmott: in many ways this house must have seemed like home—and then the welcome was so whole-hearted and there was so much to look at in the garden. When visitors arrived, their carriages drew up opposite the Château in the Meuniers' courtyard, much to the enormous interest of the village. Canon Ellacombe has described an arrival at Tresserve:

> Went up after breakfast and found Miss Willmott and the Berkeleys ready for us [i.e. for the Canon and Mr and Mrs Hiatt Baker who came with him]. The place is a delightful one: the house on the top of a low hill and the garden reaching down to the pretty lake Bourget, which, with the fine hills behind, that separate the lake from the Rhone, makes an ideal setting for the garden. The garden is intersected throughout by long shady walks, and there is a marvellous abundance of flowers revelling in

the soil and climate. We had come at the exact time for the irises of which there is a splendid collection: also a great variety of roses, but we were too early for the great collection. But after seeing the Les Barres [Maurice de Vilmorin] and Tresserve collections of roses I have come to the conclusion that, as I have long suspected, I know very little about roses; and I really think there is no one who is a complete master of them!

Professor Sargent stayed at Tresserve at least once, in terrible weather, and there were yet other botanical guests.

Tresserve also made an easy starting point for spectacular excursions. As far back as 1900 Ellen Willmott had set out late in May by an early train to visit Chamonix and Mégève. She joined a party of friends and they stayed overnight at Chamonix: she rose at 4.30 a.m., went to the church and then up to the pine woods on the way to the Brevant, where she watched the sun rise and reflect on Mont Blanc. Later in the day the whole party toiled up through the pine forests: the way had only been open for ten days, and they went by cuttings in the snow. They sat outside the hotel at the top, gazing at the Mer de Glace—a splendid sight, grand and beautiful—but there was no time to cross it, for they had to start back to reach Tresserve by dark.

A holiday at Zermatt in July of the same year was full of colourful incidents. Mules and ponies awaited Ellen Willmott's party, but she let hers follow behind and walked all the way except the last bit (this was not the only occasion on which she lent or abandoned her pony, but even she had to admit that 'keeping up with the mules pressed one'). Ellen at forty-one was still a venturesome woman and obviously enjoyed being roped together with other members of the party, and jumping across crevasses whose depths could not be guessed. It was a highly successful trip: for most of the time the weather was beautiful; they watched with awe spectacular sunrises and sunsets, clambered across glaciers and streams, explored the quaint old town of Brigue with its Ursuline church, and were enchanted by the party of children waiting by the railway line at St Nicholas with plates of cherries, wild raspberries and flowers to sell to the travellers. From the plant-hunting point of view all went well, too: they found *Gentiana bavarica, Veronica saxatilis* (now *fruticans*), *Senecio uniflorus* growing everywhere between the rocks, *Senecio subalpinus*, and on the Rhône Glacier *Campanula pusilla (coch-*

learifolia). Not even the fighting finish could really spoil things—though 'the Calais boat was delayed 60 minutes in coaling—no foreman at hand and the whole affair disgraceful. The boat disgustingly dirty and no attempt to clean up after the last trip. Crossing very rough.'

The doings at the Château were very much part of village life: Ellen Willmott attended the Catholic church in the village, where she had seats marked with her name, and at the feast of Corpus Christi she had her gardeners build a huge altar under the trees in the courtyard. Splendid with candelabra on its many tiers, it was topped with palm, decked with countless vases of roses, and hung with lace; a carpet was laid before it, and plants in tubs grouped around. On this feast day all the village were for once allowed to enter the ancient oak door in the high wall which protected the Château from the road, and wander through the gardens. The children on their way back from First Communion in the village were invited to the Château, and Ellen Willmott gave each of them a book. It seems as though she felt particularly that Tresserve was the place in which to practise her religion, for she had a chapel built on a piece of land near the farm, and there she spent time in prayer and meditation—much more, in fact, than she seems to have spent at Warley. One senses that a great deal depended on how well she got on with the parish priests concerned. In addition, at Tresserve she had a close friend, a nun who was Russian by birth, in the convent at Chambéry, with whom she could discuss problems of all kinds, and this is possibly what brought a spark to her religious life in France; and then perhaps the atmosphere of tranquillity so characteristic of Tresserve fostered this more sacramental frame of mind.

In the autumn of 1907 a sudden and terrible event disrupted the peaceful routine of the village. A servant's candle, taken up to her room, set light to the Château and a spectacular fire devastated the house. Rose and Robert Berkeley were certainly resident at the time, and possibly Ellen Willmott too. The resulting rebuilding—and the house was uninsured, which Ellen Willmott held to be the fault of Dixson, her man of business—took up so much of her time and energy that Professor Sargent was alarmed on her account; and Ellen and Rose, whenever the latter could spare the time, searched all France for beautiful and unusual decoration for the rebuilt house. The carved stone overmantel for the hall of the house is said to have been transported from the Château of Chinon, and the oak linenfold panelling, splendidly carved, must have come from some grand house, while at least one immensely solid wooden door bearing a cross in its centre is thought to have come from an abbey in Switzerland. At this time, too, it seems likely that the bathroom was installed on the first floor of the Château, neatly concealed behind panelling. The whole building, though it looks imposing, is not enormous: to the left of the entrance hall three beautifully proportioned rooms lead out of each other, the last of them being the Grand Salon—now used as the ceremonial room of the *mairie,* where weddings are performed—which leads on to a balcony with huge clusters of campsis spilling over its low parapet and a magnificent view over the lawns and trees and the haze-filled valley, so often completely concealing the lake, to the heights of the Dent du Chat opposite.

In Tresserve as at Warley, Ellen Willmott would rise early to get in a good day's gardening, for there was much to do, and her natural habit fitted well with the early-vanishing daylight of the mountain-locked valley. Much of her hybridizing work was carried out on the rose collection at Tresserve, and there was also work to be done on the Jordan collection of *Sempervivum* which she had bought in 1897 from the botanist Alexis Jordan of Lyons. Some of this had been moved to Warley, but much of it had remained in the Tresserve alpine garden under Meunier's supervision. The work which went on was well understood by the local people, who brought in for Miss Willmott's inspection plants which they thought might interest her—she described to Professor Sargent a plant of *Euonymus* which came to her in this way, brought from the mountain by a peasant, and Sargent told her that it was sold by nurserymen under the name of E. *americanus.*

At Tresserve she seems to have become a different person—and perhaps one who recalled, better than the Ellen Willmott of Warley Place, the beautiful young woman of the 1880s and 1890s. A description of her survives: 'slight, always dressed in black, unpretentious-looking', which contrasts interestingly with her Essex persona: 'slim, rather beady-eyed, with gingerish tendrils of hair escaping from under her hat, always in a hurry', a much more peppery and energetic sort of presence. It was a pity that the woman of Tresserve, the much more gentle and well-loved mistress of the Château who welcomed to her house all the members of local society, French and

English, should have had to merge entirely into the Lady of Warley
Place.

But England and Warley may not have seemed as far away as all
that to Ellen Willmott. An early and successful idea of hers was to
have postcards printed with the addresses of her houses, so that her
gardeners at any one of her gardens could communicate with her at
any other. Thus she kept herself informed of what was going on: she
knew which plants were in bloom at any given time, what the
weather was doing to the garden, which plants had been delivered;
and she could send hasty notes back, chiding, harrying, or simply
telling the gardeners where to set new arrivals. A series of these
postcards sent to Aix by Candler remains to us. Candler chronicles
the moving of paeonies from the fruit garden to the lower garden,
the planting of phlox under the rose pergola and the completion of
the new stone garden. He was, it seems, full of resource and certainly
not above making suggestions as to what should be done in the
garden: 'Am busy re-arranging the Jordan collection in the lower
garden', he commented, 'many of the weedy things are running all
over the place so that we ought to decide which to remove another
year . . . if the labels are satisfactory for the Sempervivum it would
perhaps be as well to get them for the other collection too as most are
now with wooden labels.' Jacob, too, wrote careful postcards detail-
ing developments in the alpine garden:

> The rockry is at present very nice, Daphne cneorum are at its
> best with a mass of flowers, Aubrietias still continue Souvenir
> of W Ingram is one of the best. On a batch of Viola pedata
> in the new rockry were 45 flowers together open, and worth
> mention are Ononis rotundifolia, Claytonia sibirica, Oxalis
> floribunda, O. atropurpurea, Tulipa Mauriana, T. Marjoletti,
> Androsace hirtella, A. villosa, Primula longiflora and japonica,
> Cortusa pubens Cytisus Ravensis Genista pilosa, Waldsteinia
> fragarioides, Sax. Corsica, Dodecatheons, Viola latisepala rosea,
> Potentilla opaca Camassia Fraseri, Genista purgens a very nice
> clump of Iris bosniaca with 18 flowers open today, Arnebia
> echiroides, Allium Noccanium, Cyclamen hederafolium and hed.
> album, Polemonium coeruleum P. campanulatum, Aquilegias in a
> great many varieties, Helianthemums e.t.c.

It was thus that Ellen Willmott came to be credited by her friends with knowing the exact whereabouts of every plant in her garden, for she insisted that she should supervise or advise on every planting, even from so far away.

Unfortunately for everyone, visits to Tresserve and to Boccanegra lasted for no more than a month or so at a time; and the upheaval of the journey got worse, took longer to recover from, and was even becoming quite expensive: £41 os 9d for her household to travel out to Aix in May 1906. And so, late in 1906, Ellen Willmott indulged in one of her memorable extravagances: a large chain-driven Charron car, complete with black chauffeur from Mozambique and his white French wife—Monsieur and Madame Frédéric. It seems likely that this '*équipage*' was acquired at Ventimiglia, where citizens from such colonies would have been more in evidence than in Savoy. Did Robinson have a chance to telegraph to Warley and warn Hurcombe, the coachman, what was afoot? One can only guess that he managed it somehow, before climbing in with Ellen Willmott and as much baggage as could be piled in, gritting his teeth and pulling the dust shield round his head before they set off into the early morning for the long, long drive back to Warley—and the remaining servants thankfully boarded the train instead.

CHAPTER IX

The Distant Storm

Even preceded by a warning, the arrival of the car at Warley, and the descent therefrom of Miss Willmott, travel-worn but triumphant, and of Robinson—merely travel-worn—must have caused astonishment and perhaps even dismay. Where was it to be garaged? The coach-house was already full. Where were Monsieur and Madame Frédéric, new to England and born to the heat of Mozambique, to be housed? Rumour had it that Monsieur Frédéric had once saved Miss Willmott's life, and if this were true, then obviously no pains were to be spared in solving the problem. Hurcombe, a stolid man not easily put off, had also to be considered. He must have realized, looking with interest at this snorting, over-heated metal monster, that the days of carriage and horse were numbered.

Gradually, the various problems disappeared. Those carriages which were only infrequently used were packed a little more closely into the coach-house (one or two may even have been sold at this point), and the new car occupied the forward position. As for M. and Mme Frédéric, they were accommodated in the Bothy, and settled in very comfortably: though an incongruous sight in an Essex village, M. Frédéric was well liked, and Madame his wife taught French to various people in the village, including Hurcombe's daughter May. Frédéric, a methodical worker, has left behind him, carefully written in very large handwriting, an inventory of all the *Accessoires, Outillages* and *Pièces Détachées* of the two cars—the Charron Landaulette and the Limousine—in his care, including a battery belonging to a 'Mr Joncson, Brentwood'.

The car was used a fair deal for longer journeys, including visits to London: a surviving letter from Ellen Willmott to Mr Rehder, the American botanist, suggests that they should motor back to Warley together, as she was coming up by car to the Royal Horticultural

Society meeting. The Charron, however, was not always very reliable, and there was at least one occasion when it broke down when she was being driven home after a visit to Covent Garden: perhaps this was why a second, larger car was later purchased. No wonder Ellen Willmott joined the Automobile Association (then fairly new) which even at that time provided patrolmen specially selected for their ability to undertake minor roadside repairs. With two cars in use, it seems more than likely that M. Frédéric and his successors spent all their time keeping them on the road, so that there is no need to speculate on how the chauffeur filled his day when not actually at the wheel.

For local visiting the carriages were still used, and Ellen Willmott is still remembered by a Swiss visitor, who was much impressed to see her, as late as 1911, on her way to Brent wood Station attended by coachman and footman. Long-distance journeys were usually made by train—Ellen certainly used this means when travelling to Worcester to visit her sister. In later years she used to require her housekeeper to put her on the train at Paddington, but in the years before the First World War Robinson often travelled with her, especially in the summer, when he and Lalla (the Berkeley children's name for Eliza Burge, the lady's maid) were often lent to help Stephens, the Berkeley's butler, with the arrangements for the cricket weeks held at Spetchley. No doubt Robinson gained something by being present at these occasions, but he seems to have been kept too busy with the organizing to pay much heed to the actual play. However, one year, as a reward for his services, he was given a pair of antlers from the Spetchley deer as a present for his son Jim.

Ellen Willmott spent a great deal of time in London. She was a life member of the Royal Institution—she regularly attended lectures there and she certainly got through a good deal of the Institution's writing paper, as a number of her surviving letters are penned, obviously in a great hurry, from the Institution's Albemarle Street premises. No doubt its connection with the great botanist, Sir Joseph Banks of Spring Grove, attracted her too. She was much to be seen in London: at Covent Garden, dining with friends, always at the Royal Academy Private View, and at rehearsals of the Bach Choir, and of various madrigal societies. In 1911, when she was already fifty-two, she had been introduced by the Hon. Spencer Lyttelton to the Bach Choir, and passed Dr Allen's examination, which probably consisted of singing a few scales and arpeggios, with a little sight-reading. Not wishing to let them down, and in spite of her many engagements, she attended assiduously on Tuesday evenings unless she was actually at Boccanegra or Tresserve. Also, those members who did not attend regularly soon received tart and businesslike notes from the Secretary, saying 'in consequence of continued absences from the choir practices you are requested to return your ticket of membership.' The first concert in which she sang took place at the Queen's Hall on 30 January 1912, the programme consisting of only one work: César Franck's *Beatitudes*, conducted by Dr Allen.

Friendship with Sir Walter Parratt, who in 1908 had become Professor of Music at Oxford, must have opened many doors for her, though tantalizingly no details are left to us, only a friend's recollection of her sadness when three of her musical friends—Sir Walter Parratt, Sir Charles Stanford and Sir Frederick Bridge—died within a fortnight of each other in 1924. A close friend of Sir Walter was Sir Arthur Bigge who later, as Lord Stamfordham and Private Secretary to King George V, was to help Ellen Willmott out of a difficult situation and fully to justify the *Dictionary of National Biography*'s assessment of his tact and wisdom, sagacity and resourcefulness. When the Ainslie Hights came to live in Oxford in 1916, they also became involved with the Bach Choir and Ellen Willmott often stayed with them. The Revd H. J. Bidder, Bursar of St John's College, was also a good friend: one June—so often only the month and not the year appears on letters written in Edwardian times—he was collecting her Oxford friends to give them all a luncheon party on the occasion of a Bach Choir concert at Oxford, and 'if you don't receive a more eligible invitation' offering to put her up in a humble way at his home in Museum Road. His is evidently the taste that fashioned the College garden at St John's, for he petitioned her to bring him 'something choice, as the first bloom will be over'; in a slightly earlier letter he mentions that the iris 'Mrs Berkeley' is in gorgeous bloom and that 'Miss Willmott' will be out shortly.

Then there was Miss Venables, so involved in the organizing of the affairs of the Bach Choir, but always writing letters full of news, with the ever-ready offer of a bed whether Ellen Willmott was actually singing in a performance by the Choir or would simply be in the audience. Mary Venables was the sort of woman who made a perfect foil for Ellen Willmott: always sympathetic, always admiring, generous, organized, always ready to overlook forgetfulness, never expecting punctuality . . . if only Ellen Willmott had been surrounded by such people all her life how different things might have been. However, when not staying with Miss Venables, there are strange tales of how she often slept curled up on a bench in St Martin-in-the-Fields, in order to save the cost of a night's lodging *en route* for Oxford; or, even more bizarre, that she once lay down to sleep on the top step of the Judges' Lodgings at Oxford after a concert, because the friends with whom she had hoped to find a bed had proved to be away. (To ask why she did not check this simple fact first would be fruitless: it was just not her way of doing things.) On this occasion a policeman approached her at 2.30 a.m. and offered to let her sleep in the lock-up—she graciously assented. It was fortunate that she did not care a rap about her appearance: at worst she looked like a tramp, and at best was adequately dressed, but never elegant. She told a tale against herself very well: witty and malicious, she savoured these stories, adding to them with an artist's hand so that frequently what began as a matter of genuine amusement became eventually part of the formidable legend of eccentricity which was beginning to crystallize round her. It amused her very much indeed to watch people react to the clothes rather than to the person, and then be forced to change their manner as her presence revealed itself.

Another musical friend of Ellen Willmott was Dame Ethel Smyth: the two women, so alike in many ways—the one mettlesome and the other forceful, both creative and both temperamental—enjoyed each other's company and their shared interests in music and women's rights. Dame Ethel used to visit Warley Place, where she and Ellen Willmott played the organ (and indeed in 1909 Ellen was sufficiently enthusiastic to go to London to take lessons from a Miss Thorne). Probably all unsuspected by the two ladies, these visits were a sore trial to Robinson, for the gas engine on which the organ blowing device operated, a temperamental beast, had to be activated for the occasion. With hard words and help from one of the footmen, the half-horse power Crossley Bros 'Otto' Gas Engine, No. 36857, was eventually coaxed into life. The problem was that a Bunsen burner had to be used for this, and since the house was supplied partly by Company gas and partly by the home-made acetylene variety, both rather unreliable, the lighting-up was a chancy business.

Besides her regular musical pursuits in Oxford and London, Ellen Willmott went farther afield in search of musical interest. The Leeds Festival attracted her, and the Three Choirs Festival could be combined with a stay at Spetchley Park, where much entertaining went on when the Festival took place, every third year, in Worcester. At Spetchley she would have made the acquaintance of Sir Edward Elgar, who had as a child spent a year at the Roman Catholic school run by the Robert Berkeley of the time, and who later returned as the guest of Robert and Rose Berkeley. How Ellen would have sorted with that touchy, rumbustious genius is interesting to speculate.

She was constant in her attendance at Committee meetings and shows at the Royal Horticultural Society's premises: and a great many of her gardening transactions seem to have been carried out in the intervals of official business at 'the Hall'—one hasty note adjured the Director of the University Botanic Garden, Cambridge, to bring a plant of *Nierembergia* to her there if he could spare it, since the rabbits had all hers down to the roots (how regretfully she must have recalled the 6th Foot and their rabbit-shoots in the Warley Garden)!

Ellen Willmott dashed off many letters to Kew in her swift, flowing hand, her thoughts tripping over her pen so that sometimes she wrote a word twice over. She addressed Sir William Thiselton-Dyer, and then his successor, Lt-Col Prain, on a variety of subjects: the continuing saga of her supplement to Pritzel, good wishes on Sir William's retirement, a mild rebuke to Prain for not being available on two days in the same week when she visited Kew, and a faintly reproving expression of sorrow that he was again unavailable, this time to join a tour of Sir Dighton Probyn's garden at Windsor, which she thought was much improved (perhaps as a result of his visits to Warley?). Meanwhile, Ellen Willmott was nothing if not generous in her gifts of plants to Kew—feeling, as she often wrote, that it was an honour to be able to send anything which was acceptable at Kew. Surprisingly, she received very little in return. In 1911 she presented Kew with the Herbarium she had bought from Alexis Jordan, and in 1913 she offered a set of the *Sempervivum* which were to have provided the material for a monograph—the writing of which she had neither the time nor the inclination to take over from him along with the plants. (By 1921 Kew had received not only the Jordan Herbarium but also the *Herbarium Warleyense*—15,000 sheets from many parts of Europe, particularly France, most of it purchased.) She sometimes sent to Kew large numbers of plants: 300 pink Verbena 'Ellen Willmott' ('more if needed'); some *Crocus scharojanii* offered (perhaps not accepted) from Aix; 'a few tulips'; double white hepatica; Iris *warleyensis*. In return, only one gift in reverse is mentioned in correspondence at Kew: but it was a rather fine magnolia, and she was very pleased with it. Kew did, however, repay her by the number of plants which they identified for her, amongst them *Dichondra repens, Rudbeckia laciniata* and various pelargoniums. Sometimes a cross little note appears in the Kew record: 'T. A. S.' is disgusted with the 'miserable scrap' of *Berberis stenophylla* from which she had expected him to make an identification. Occasionally she has a question: where can she find a nursery in England which will supply *Bougainvillea lateritia* (now *B. spectabilis var. lateritia*) and *B. braziliensis?* Her efforts and interest were undoubtedly remarked and appreciated at Kew, and on 15 November 1912, Mr Bean wrote: 'I am glad you are having a busy time, that means good work is being done.'

She kept very closely in touch with the various botanical gardens in England, by letter and in person. Lists of exchanges with the National Botanic Gardens, Glasnevin, Dublin, are still kept: they were heavily weighted in the Ireland-to-Warley direction (seeds, pelargoniums, various primula, *Pasithea coerulea, Anemone obtusiloba var. patula)*; the return traffic consisted mainly of seeds, followed by a selection of shrubs and herbaceous plants in April 1915 and some pelargoniums later in the year. The shipments then came to a complete halt. With the Royal Botanic Garden, Edinburgh, there was also a constant exchange from about 1900 to the early 1930s. Seeds, herbaceous and alpine plants were sent to Warley Place, and back came a very various collection of seeds, producing varying results—of one consignment received in 1927 the larger part did not germinate. However, *Campanula lactiflora* germinated and lasted for eleven years and *Dianthus neglectus* var. *carthusianorum* survived until 1945. Visiting both Oxford and Cambridge often, she could personally keep an eye on developments in both of these botanic gardens. Writing to Professor Sargent, she records with satisfaction a triumph at Oxford: 'The Curator was quite pleased with me because I happened to be able to tell him the name of a plant when he asked me which he had for years shown to visitors and enquired the name—Watson, Irving and several others among them.'

And there were more exotic contacts. In 1913 she received an invitation to attend a reception to mark the bicentenary of the Imperial Botanic Garden at St Petersburg, founded by Peter the Great in 1713. Did she go? One supposes not, since no echoes of such a journey are to be discerned—but how much she must have been tempted (though in its way it seems to have been a rather strangely constituted occasion, beginning with a solemn Te *Deum,* and apparently offering guests only a single refreshment—tea at the end of the first day). Her contact with the Palace gardener at Sofia, Alaricus Delmard, is interesting, for she clearly corresponded with him in his own right, in spite of the fact that Henri Correvon was allegedly the agent of King Ferdinand of Bulgaria, and that it was the King's Secretary whom she later put in touch with Kew at the suggestion of the invaluable Mr Bean, who was sure that the Director would be very happy to enter into a relationship with Bulgaria, 'where so many fine things are to be got'. Delmard describes the decorations which he has arranged for the hall in which Queen Eleanore was holding a bazaar in aid of crippled soldiers. There were baskets of cane and brown rushes filled with flowers from the mountains, the prettiest being the purple orchis and lily-of-the-valley, also baskets of yellow straw full of red cherries with knots of ribbon grass and beautiful *Paeonia tenuifolia.* There were irises of every shade on some of the stalls, pink and white carnations, and tall white columns surmounted by jardinières full of guelder roses and blue hydrangeas. Interesting too is her correspondence with the Californian nurseryman Carl Purdy. Here she achieved an excellent system whereby she supplied him with various collections which he either had not seen or could not easily obtain, and in 1912 was making arrangements to ship a collection of old florists' tulips, of *Iris Germanica* and *I. pumila,* and of crocus, together with *Tritonia crocata* 'Prince of Orange' (for which she was to receive an Award of Merit from the RHS in 1916), and some prostrate veronicas. Through Sargent she had attempted to sell Purdy some of her surplus daffodil bulbs, but there is no indication that this potentially lucrative idea succeeded as it had with other nurserymen in England. Purdy offered to try and sell some copies of *The Genus Rosa* but it is doubtful whether he succeeded. A charming letter from Lord Kilbracken reveals plans for a visit by Ellen Willmott and several friends to Holland in 1913, but he felt himself forced to withdraw at the last moment from the enterprise.

The question of correspondence is worth a small digression. The amount of letter-writing in which Ellen Willmott engaged must have made very considerable demands on her time and energies, in spite of the speed and fluency with which she wrote. She herself estimated that on average she wrote twenty-one letters a day. (It is to be hoped that few recipients replied as ungraciously as W. E. Gumbleton: '. . . but what an *un* interesting letter you send me full of a long *rigmarole* about Coleridge and the Liverpool Merchant instead of interesting tidings of . . . any new plants you may have bloomed lately.') And while she could and did leave the packing and dispatch of plants to her gardeners (though her complaints of incompetence were manifold, and it does seem that they lost or mixed up rather a lot of plant labels, especially considering the fact that they were labels beautifully and specially made for Warley Place), no one could write her letters for her. Professor Sargent, using every tone from light teasing to moderate rebuke, suggested in vain that she might acquire a secretary to lighten the load and (one would guess) to remind her about things like acknowledging shipments of plants, paying contributions to expedition funds and settling freight charges promptly; but though at that time she was extravagant about most other things, she still continued to burden herself with much writing and carelessly to forget about money she owed. Mrs Slater, the agency typist whom she had so castigated over inverted commas, but who was of a forgiving nature, continued to type indexes and lists for her, and offered in times of difficulty to 'make me a willow cabin at your gate'—but she was not encouraged in this. In general Miss Willmott spurned modern aids, worked from choice without any help, and refused to have a telephone installed—any member of the household wishing to make a telephone call had to walk down to the post office and use the public call box there. Would a telephone have reduced her huge expenditure on telegrams? I doubt it. On one occasion, writing to Sargent, she remarked in off-hand fashion that she had 'written and telegraphed to several places' to try and get him a book on General de Boygne, which she knew he wanted, before he left Europe. Since she was at Tresserve at the time, these places probably included London and Paris. She also had rather grand ideas about telegraphic addresses, considering that 'Willmott, Ventimiglia' was sufficient identification for the Italians to work on.

A typewriter she must have owned, as it appears in the sale

catalogue of the contents of Warley Place, presumably used by Mrs Slater on days when she was needed to work at Warley. But Ellen Willmott cerainly left it strictly alone, and longhand remained her preferred method until the day she died. There was also, mysteriously, an adding machine in the house: perhaps it was useful to Robinson in such tasks as working out the amounts of Christmas mutton to go to the various estate families.

From fairly early days Ellen Willmott used the morning-room as her work-room. It faced south over the lawns, thus allowing her to keep an eagle eye on at least some of her gardeners at work, and it adjoined the music-room. It was also fairly small and easy to heat. In later years this room, and the conservatory which led out of it, were the only rooms in the house which were kept heated in the winter. The conservatory had a semi-circular vent in the floor round the edges of the room for the heating; in this room, Miss Willmott, and her nieces or anyone else who could face staying at Warley Place in the winter months, took their meals. French windows led to the terrace on the south side of the room, so that Miss Willmott could easily get to the garden; coming indoors again she would kick off like a child the sabots she always wore for gardening, to be picked up and cleaned by Robinson.

The gardening world had not finished its recognition of her work. At Christmas 1907 came two dedications. One was in the last issue of *The Garden:* the dedication, accompanied by a reproduction of the portrait in pastel attributed to Signora Gutti, was prosy and unexciting. It praised her as a conscientious and painstaking botanist, for giving the greater part of her life and strength to the production of serious scientific work and for 'her great knowledge so freely given and her enthusiasm in promoting a love of flowers and their ways in this and other countries'. It contains no memorable phrases. *The Botanical Magazine* did better: opposite a full-page reproduction of a portrait in oils it declared in an altogether more lively fashion:

To Miss E A Willmott FLS VMH
of Warley Place, Essex
whose skill in gardening is only surpassed
by the generosity with which she dispenses the treasures
of her gardens and accords to others the benefits of her
experience, this volume is gratefully dedicated

Miss Willmott had only just returned from Italy to spend Christmas with the Berkeleys at Spetchley Park. The aftermath of the fire at Tresserve had made it a taxing year, and this unexpected pleasure at the end of it lifted her spirits, so that she wrote excitedly to Colonel Prain, saying that she was 'overpowered' at the honour (a curious slip for 'overwhelmed'). Nor had this series of honours come to an end. In 1910 her gardening connections in Holland brought her membership of the Jury of the great Exhibition at Haarlem, arranged by the General Bulbgrowers' Society. And then in 1912, following publication of the early parts of *The Genus Rosa,* the Société d'Acclimatation de France accorded Ellen Willmott the honour of the Grande Médaille Geoffroy Saint-Hilaire: the nurseryman Maurice de Vilmorin was, apparently, the leading spirit in this. The Société is now defunct so that it is impossible to trace the citation, but since the name of Saint-Hilaire is associated with early nineteenth-century ideas on the formation of new species, it seems very probable that her rose book earned her this distinction.

Then there is the story, with no date and no details attached to it, but yet bearing the ring of truth, that Ellen Willmott was asked by the Emperor of Japan to go and lay out a garden for him—a matter of enormous interest, and extremely lucrative—but that she turned it down because she had too much to do in Europe. And indeed she very probably did have too many commitments simply to disappear to the ends of the earth for a long period, even though a sight of the flora of Japan must have made the offer tempting and exciting almost beyond bearing. It was, however, one thing to be out of reach of telegrams because she herself chose to vanish somewhere in Europe, but quite another thing to be *really* out of reach and unable to intervene in things which concerned her. The refusal, however, shows how little she cared for money as such, for at whatever date the offer was made she could certainly have done with a replenishment of her resources.

There has never been just acknowledgement of the work which Ellen Willmott undertook for others, both in and out of the garden: the commissions she carried out in London for her sister; and the number of times Eliza Burge was dispatched to shepherd a Berkeley child round London and once, in the depths of winter, to bring Eleanor back from Rome; the training jobs which she found for young boys in her own and others' gardens—Phillibert, a Swiss boy, and Philip, a German, come to mind; the efforts that she made to raise money among members of the RHS to save the Secretary, the Revd Wilks, from having part of his garden sold by auction; the endless sacks of plants and sets of photographs sent to friends in whose gardens she had walked and to whom she had dispensed wise advice. At the height of her fame she was even asked if she could find some garden owner in Essex who could find material for a wood-louse paper to be presented to the Selborne Society by Mr Wilfrid Webb; for apparently a rare species of woodlouse was once to be found in Great Warley. And then there were the numerous visitors to her garden—most were welcome guests but some were not, and she refers rather bitterly to the fact that she had stood guarantor to Wood, landlord of the Thatchers' Arms at Great Warley, because she thought he would not be the kind of man who would have 'tribes of trippers down all summer'. (In fact, the guarantee was called in and she had to pay up.) Presumably she had experience of missing plants and trampled borders. All these and many more tasks she gladly took on, and it should stand to her credit that the letters of her friends are full of admiration for her talents, achievements and kindnesses, and delight in the pleasure which her lively presence in their households obviously gave to them. Henri Correvon summed it all up by saying how much the Correvon family looked forward to seeing her 'pas a *la course mats* "staying"'.

The happy progress up to the award of the Geoffroy Saint-Hilaire Medal was soon to be spoiled by an unpleasant quarrel which developed with frightening speed from small beginnings. It was a pity that Ellen Willmott's propensity for taking sides, and thereafter for supporting her chosen side with ill-judged and blind enthusiasm, drove her to take part. 'The Crispian Row' has been fully and vividly described in Mea Allan's *E. A. Bowles and his Garden at Myddelton House*. Briefly, its course was that Sir Frank Crisp, who had been among those who had supported Ellen Willmott's candidature as a Fellow of the Linnaean Society, had created in his garden at Friar Park a faithful miniature copy of the Matterhorn on which he had set a superb collection of alpine plants and which he had decorated with tin representations of chamois. This was too much for Reginald Farrer, who with very ill judgment chose the preface which he had been asked to write for his friend E. A. Bowles's book *My Garden in Spring* as a platform for a piece of mockery which was furiously resented by Crisp. Without waiting for his rage to subside, the latter rushed into print, producing a little booklet entitled *Mr E. A. Bowles and his garden, a New Parable of the Pharisee and the Publican.* In this Bowles, most unjustly, was blamed for the content of the preface written by Farrer, and the little publication was distributed at the gates of the Chelsea Show by Ellen Willmott, who was carrying a supply in a bookmaker's leather bag. Why did she do this? She must have been aware that Bowles was quite blameless in the affair. The only explanation seems to be that she felt slighted by either Bowles or Farrer or both, and that she was taking her revenge. She did in fact admire Crisp's garden, as did her sister Rose, with whom Bowles was *persona non grata* since she felt that in his writings he did not sufficiently acknowledge his debt to Ellen.

Ellen Willmott had earlier attempted to persuade (one could almost say 'lure') Bowles to Warley for a week-end to be devoted to daffodils, and had herself visited Myddelton House, writing a letter of thanks for the visit which demonstrated her tendency to behave in an extraordinarily gauche fashion at times when her interest was aroused. Accustomed to dealing with men on equal terms, she found it rather hard to take a softer line and let it sound natural. She had, she said, had the pleasure of seeing a friend in his house, surrounded by the things which make his life; and she ended, 'reserving all else till we meet'. This sort of thing did not do for Bowles, who was not at his ease with women, however much he had in common with Ellen Willmott, and he did not take kindly either to Farrer's suggestion that he should 'marry the cankered Ellen at once, and save further trouble'. So (always assuming that she understood the psychology of what was going on) Ellen Willmott had some reason for feeling slighted, even if she had brought it upon herself. Reginald Farrer she simply did not like, for whatever reason. But the fact that she had so miscalculated the likely reaction to her behaviour is disquieting: she seemed to show the same complete inability to size up a situation and set herself a realistic goal that had marked her attempt to convert the Preece family to Roman Catholicism. In the event, however, Bowles published a mild disclaimer in *Gardening Illustrated,* and shortly afterwards went to Switzerland plant-hunting, after which the whole distasteful business gently fizzled out, though not without some lasting damage to Ellen Willmott's reputation. And Crisp later wrote to her: 'I confess I had the malicious intention to make it imply

7. *The south front of Warley Place in high summer, when agapanthus replaced agave in the tubs. To the left is the conservatory, then comes the french window leading from the morning room, and on the right are the drawing room windows. Below the mansion is the Pleasaunce, Cardinal's Walk, the bowling green and, just out of sight, the alpine garden beyond.*

8. *Jacob Maurer has recruited some help from his eldest son Max to clean out the South Pond below the alpine garden.*

9. *The entrance to the Château at Tresserve: the ornamental fanlight and well-estab-lished climbers show that this photograph was taken before the fire of 1907.*

that it was Bowles though not saying so, but it is better to put it straight.' By March 1914 the matter seemed to have completely blown over, and Bowles, quite back in his light-hearted vein, was writing cheerfully to Ellen Willmott about *Galanthus* species, inviting her to come 'and have a raid and carry off some loot to make things a little more fair a little more *take* on your side— and *some* give on mine': so long as the 'loot' was not to be E. A. Bowles himself, all was well. He also reports, with some glee: 'You will be glad to hear my father has allowed me to move the rails of the meadow by the rock garden—at last. Chiefly because his farm horses broke some of them down and ate up half the kitchen garden and rolled on the rest—Bravo GeeGees! says I.'

The Essex Field Club was a flourishing local organization, and it is strange that Ellen Willmott waited until 1907 before she joined it, together with Guglielma Lister—my cologist and botanical artist and a cousin of the Hanburys—who had also become a Fellow of the Linnaean Society in 1905. This presumably was a membership valuable to Ellen Willmott, giving her access to many gardens she might not otherwise have seen, and also to the club, whose members were thereafter able to make an annual tour of the Warley Garden conducted by its indefatigable owner. This was written up in the Essex *Naturalist* with every sign of appreciation. In 1912 these short notes were supplemented by a much longer and more detailed article by J. C. Shenstone, FLS, which describes the garden and the plants it contained in detail, and is the most reliable written source of information on Warley Garden in its heyday: and Ellen Willmott circulated offprints to her friends, while occasionally remarking that she was not entirely satisfied with the article. The garden was open to the public once each year, usually in June, the profits being given to a local (probably Roman Catholic) charity. A rather reluctant recruit to the post of footman at Warley Place, Robinson's son Jim, then aged about seventeen, remembers standing at the gate with a tin collecting the entrance money.

It would seem, however, that the contents of the collecting tin might have been better applied to the owner of Warley Place herself, for it was in 1907 that the first signs began to appear that all was not well with Ellen Willmott's finances. On 22 March in that year she borrowed the sum of £15,000 at 4 per cent interest, secured upon Warley Place, Warley Lea, Warley Place Farm, the Headley garden and several of the cottages. The money was borrowed from J. J. Stokes, senior partner of Frederick Willmott's old firm, and J. G. Tasker, thought to be a cousin of the Countess Tasker. Obviously the cost of the new establishment at Boccanegra had rather exceeded estimates, and for the rest it seems to have been a matter of a gradual build-up of regular expenditure until it went far beyond income. It must have been at about this time, too, that the number of gardeners at Warley Place rose to the maximum of 104, and this again must have placed an impossible strain on finances. It is instructive to look at the amount which Ellen Willmott spent on subscriptions and donations in 1906—taken singly none of these was very large, but in total they were quite frightening. She subscribed to the Glamorgan Daffodil and Spring Flower Society, the Folk Song Society, the United Kingdom Beneficent Association, the Lincolnshire Daffodil Society, the United Kingdom Railway Officers' and Servants' Association, the Musical Association, the Devon Daffodil and Spring Flower Society, the National Auricula and Primula Society, the North Lonsdale Rose Society, the Midland Carnation and Picotee Society—the list is endless. Nearer home there was the Essex County Automobile Club (cars could break down near to Warley as well as in more distant parts), the Brentwood Chrysanthemum Society (where the hand of Preece must have been at work), the Warley District Nurses' Fund, the Soldiers' Home, Warley and, in unexpectedly ecumenical fashion, she contributed to Christ Church, Warley. Some of these subscriptions were clearly the inheritance of her father's obligations, some the result of mild pressure brought to bear when she went to judge at shows of all kinds round the country, and some simply because her sympathies were engaged. Some were for very humble amounts—10s for the Cornwall Daffodil and Spring Flower Society, and 5s for the Southampton Royal Horticultural Society—and some, like the Midland Daffodil Society, demanded an extortionate £5 a year; but most asked a guinea. There were overseas subscriptions to be reckoned with, too: the Association Horticole Lyonnaise (12 francs), the Bulletin de l'Herbier Boissier (a rather stiff 100 francs for two years), the Automobile Club du Rhône (*membre étranger*) 30 francs, and the Deutsche Kakteen-Gesellschaft. Her subscription to the London Library of £3 a year was obviously of very great value to her. Then there were donations: to the Dean Medal Fund, London Dahlia Union, the Primrose League, the Brentwood

Division of Police, the Brentwood District Cottage Hospital, and (somewhat surprisingly) the Brentwood St Thomas' Football Club. The reckless and indiscriminate way in which these small but rapidly mounting sums were dispensed is indicative of the way in which Ellen Willmott lived. For they formed only a very small part of her total expenses.

Looking at other bills—why, for example, did she need to buy shrimps and prawns from Groves in New Bond Street, when there were perfectly adequate fish shops in Brentwood? Or to have her shoes repaired in Queen Victoria Street? Thoughtlessness and her own immediate convenience governed her expenditure. As early as the 1890s she had taken to running up very large annual accounts with Parkers, the jewellers in Vigo Street: these mainly listed repairs, silver mountings for the numerous beakers of various sorts and ages which she bought, the setting of stones and making of necklaces. Large items were billed individually, and there were many of them: antique diamond necklace, £383; fine lozenge-shaped diamond ring, £325; antique candlesticks, £113 10s; silver dinner plates, £337 10s. Her hair was looked after by Sutterlin's in Maddox Street, whose bills included charges for combs, slides, setting lotion, clasps, and papier poudré, as well as attendance charges. Some of her clothes were bought in the rue Royale in Paris, and here, at Raudnitz, she had alterations carried out and dresses and blouses made. In Paris she also bought the large hats with tussore draperies which she favoured. Wherever she went, she seems to have acquired silver buckles— every pair of shoes and every belt she owned must have sported one. Quarterly statements from Quaritch the bookseller in the early 1900s show that she normally had a balance owing to them of anything from £200 to £900. She bought from them many costly botanical works—a *Herbarius* at £151, a copy of Flore *Portugaise* at £40—and many rare madrigals: an entry in 1905 shows 'Gibbon, Madrigals etc—£530'. Thus was her library built up: and in short, whenever she wanted something, she bought it. Payment was another matter. Extremely casual and careless, she usually only paid sums on account, rarely settling a bill in its entirety, and practically never doing so immediately. Many are the surviving letters which request in varying tones the settlement of *'petits comptes'* of a few francs. English tradesmen seem to have waited longer before pressing for payment: perhaps they felt they had Ellen Willmott sufficiently under their eye to allow them to wait. Her extravagance was evidently proverbial among her friends and others with whom she came in contact, and their views were well expressed by William Robinson, who in August 1910 wrote to her: 'I have always been greatly impressed by your expenditure and thought that only a millionaire could afford it', adding, unhelpfully, 'the way to get into trouble is to have several homes.'

The final extravagance came with the lavish redecoration of Warley Place in the spring of 1906, by Amédée Joubert & Son's Chelsea branch. Cowtans, who had been good enough for her parents, would not do for Ellen Willmott: it had to be a French firm. They made a thorough job of the main ground-floor rooms, painting the drawing-room, staircase and hall, fitting an antique white statuary marble chimney-piece with steel grate in the drawing-room, and providing wall hangings and silk curtains, and a carved gilt mirror. They made new cabinets and provided new door furniture. But the bulk of the work consisted of extensive structural alterations in the music-room, including the 'removal of the present ceiling and its replacement with a new one ornamented with fibrous plaster enrichments' and the making of an ornamental dome. A new organ front was constructed and the organ pipes gilded. The whole specification for the work sounds rather like something carried out at Xanadu for Kubla Khan. The total cost was £1, 131. It may well have been the last straw.

And this fateful March, though never recognized as such, was the turning point of Ellen Willmott's life. She had inherited none of her father's financial acumen, but simply felt that her commitments had outrun her. In turning for help to James John Stokes, whom she had known from childhood, she was simply turning to the nearest substitute she could find for her father's advice. Even if Stokes tried to persuade Ellen to curb her expenditure, his efforts were unsuccessful. There was nothing she could give up, or at any rate was prepared to give up. So Stokes gave her the next best advice that he could: she should use her assets to provide her with capital, which advice was probably intended to extinguish her debts and to provide her with a little extra to get her affairs straight—after which the capital could slowly be paid back. But borrowing money is a heady feeling, especially when its results can be measured in terms of a beautiful house and garden—which were really the only things that Ellen

Willmott cared about. Seen from her point of view, the issue was simple. How *could* she reduce expenditure at Warley, in view of its immense horticultural value? How could she be expected to give up a Mediterranean garden only just started, on which a great deal of money, time and care had been lavished? Surely Mr Stokes must understand this (however stupid he might be, her face and manner may have implied). Stokes would not have been the first man to end up, after such an interview, genuinely believing that everything that had gone wrong was his own fault. So, far from repaying anything, Ellen Willmott merely borrowed more: £3,000 in December of 1907, also from Stokes and Tasker, who, resigned but cautious, took Shenfield Lodge as further security, and spread the risk by passing a share in the loan to Henry Dixson, their clerk, and to Colvin Brandreth, a partner in Messrs Peirs Ellis & Co.

It seems unlikely that this charge upon the estate was broadcast in any way by Ellen Willmott, but one person did know, for his signature appears on the principal indenture: this was James Robinson. Robinson, who now had another son, Frank, and a daughter, Mary, must have been heavily burdened by this knowledge, and perhaps he shared it with his wife, who in her long years in service with the aristocracy had learned to be discreet. Although he knew that the Red House was not directly involved in the mortgage deed, Robinson was under no illusion about his employer's ways with money, and could hardly have expected the mortgage to be redeemed; that it should remain at its current level must have been the most that his devout prayers would have been aimed at. Meanwhile, there was nothing that he could do except hang on—an increasing number of years at Warley Place (he was then forty-seven) could only be helpful in finding another place for himself, if ultimately the household disintegrated. But in truth he did not want to leave Warley: well established, he enjoyed village life, and his attitude to his employer was one of tolerance for her feelings, respect for her abilities, and genuine liking.

The Robinson family were not the only ones affected: by 1911 the decline in Miss Willmott's fortunes resulted in a disaster which could not entirely be concealed from the outside world—Preece had to be asked to find another post. This decision must have been extraordinarily hard to reach, and still harder to explain: for there were a hundred minor economies which Ellen Willmott could have made which would have been less detrimental to the running of the estate than the loss of Preece. Besides, the fact that he would no longer be competing at shows up and down the country in his capacity as Head of the Gardens at Warley Place would surely make it known in the horticultural world as swiftly and certainly as could be that Ellen Willmott, that most liberal and extravagant of gardeners, was at last beginning to feel the pinch. Preece was known by name at Kew, too: there are little notes on letters saying 'ask Preece to . . .' (send something, pack something, tell them something). But, nevertheless, by March 1911 the unbelievable had happened, and the Preece family were out of North Lodge and temporarily housed at Ivy Cottage near Headley Common. By then the elder Preece children were nearly grown up: Charlie had left the Warley Garden, accompanied by testimonials from Jacob Maurer, Thos H. Candler, and his father, to work for James Veitch & Sons Ltd, that most famous nursery, in Chelsea; Nellie, aged sixteen, had just about finished her dressmaking apprenticeship in Brentwood—a hard worker, and good at her job, she was unlikely to cause any problems. Of the younger ones, Maurice and Sid were already at work at Warley Place, while Fred (he who had been handy with a knife in the leaf-mould pit) worked for a butcher in Brentwood until he died at the age of nineteen of peritonitis. In 1911 Preece wrote to his son Charlie to tell of an interview with Miss Willmott, who had said she was doing her utmost to find him another place. The letter does not make it clear whether Preece was still working at Warley Place or whether he was 'resting'. In the end Miss Willmott did not find him another place, but instead allowed him (presumably on a fixed rent) to take over the Headley garden as a going concern and run it commercially under his own name. Letterheads still survive showing the firm's name— James Preece & Sons, Fruit and Chrysanthemum Growers, Headley Garden, Brentwood, Essex. It was indeed a brilliant idea, for at one and the same time it relieved Miss Willmott of the necessity of doing anything further for Preece, brought in some much-needed income from rent, ensured that this piece of her garden was properly looked after, and reduced the number of gardeners (including Preece's sons) she needed to employ. But for some reason it was not a success, and in due course Preece found a post in Barnet and moved his family there. He did not long survive the move, but died in the influenza epidemic of 1918, aged only fifty-two.

Preece's work was taken over by Fielder, a spry little man awarded the VM H in 1910 who had worked for many years at North Mimms in Hertfordshire, and who came to Ellen Willmott's employment in 1911 to live on the other side of the road from South Lodge. Fielder was a competent gardener who quickly accustomed himself to his employer's ways, and in particular early grasped the importance of keeping her informed by postcard. More important, his arrival at Warley Place was quickly followed by several significant awards from the RHS, all of them for plants introduced from China by E. H. Wilson: *Corylopsis warleyensis* was given an Award of Merit by unanimous consent in March 1912, and *Primula warleyensis* in April (19 votes in favour). Also in April, *Deutzia longifolia* was unanimously accorded an Award of Merit, and a note appears in the RHS Proceedings that it forces well and the flowers remain in good condition for a considerable period. There were four other important awards for Ellen Willmott in 1912, making it a very good year for her and for Wilson's plants—though *Tropaeolum albiflorum*, which gained an Award of Merit, is described as 'a rare greenhouse climber from Chile or Peru', and therefore presumably cannot be credited to Wilson. Next, however, came the beautiful hardy *Lilium warleyense*—' a strong and good grower' with flowers three inches across, reddish orange with brown spots—it was awarded a First Class Certificate in July 1912. A small diversion is in order here. Ellen Willmott, as early as 1910, was supplying bulbs of *Lilium myriophyllum* and *Lilium leucanthum* to the trade, but it now seems probable that these lilies were in fact wrongly named at the time and should have been called *Lilium regale* and *Lilium sargentiae*. 'As indeed anyone looking at the bulb could see for himself, said the amateur lily grower Arthur Grove, writing to Ellen Willmott in 1912. He thought (privately) that Wilson was not altogether as careful as he might be over his lilies—and this surmise was proved to be right, for Wilson in his monograph *The Lilies of Eastern Asia*, published in 1925, admitted that the two lilies had earlier been distributed under the erroneous names. Since Messrs Veitch were responsible for raising the first bulbs it seems probable that this firm, rather than Wilson himself, was at fault.

A Botanical Certificate was awarded to Ellen Willmott for *Deinanthe caerulea*, and finally an Award of Merit for *Patrinia palmata*. Fielder's services were transferred to the Royal Horticultural Society almost full-time in the summer of 1912 and for the next year the RHS awards for Warley Place were fewer. In mid-1913, however, they picked up again with Awards of Merit for *Aethionema armenum* 'Warley Hybrid', unanimously acclaimed and described as 'a charming sub-shrubby alpine growing about six inches high, and bearing crowded terminal racemes of rose-pink flowers in great profusion'; *Styrax wilsonii and Lysionotus warleyensis*. Awards of Merit were received in 1914 for *Rhododendron moupinense*, another of Wilson's introductions; *Clematis sieboldii*, a very pretty hardy climber introduced from Japan by von Siebold; *Iris chrysographus; Michauxia tchihatcheffii*, a very interesting hardy plant from Asia Minor; and the beautiful *Verbascum* 'Warley Rose', growing to a height of four or five feet, and bearing its flowers of a lovely old rose colour in branched panicles. From which the reader will note that Ellen Willmott did not in any way go in for the 'Tush and Pooh plants' of no kind of value or interest, so often and so much despised by her forthright correspondent William Gumbleton. Fielder went on to do useful work for the Royal Horticultural Society: he even gave lectures. '*Trees and Shrubs for Autumn and Winter Effects*', published in the RHS Proceedings, was very adequate but not very inspired.

About this time Candler, too, left Warley Place for a job at Medmenham: he was annoyed that after so many years at Warley Ellen Willmott refused to give him an open testimonial, and a cross and desultory correspondence faltered on between them. Without Preece, her next most trusted aide was Jacob Maurer. Jacob's preferred life was to get on with his work steadily and quietly amongst the familiar plants in the alpine garden, tending, propagating, cleaning the stream and pools, and stopping now and again to watch the butterflies which hovered ceaselessly over this favoured spot. Most of the time he preferred to work on his own, but occasionally he found a young gardener whose work he approved and whose company he enjoyed. The best of these was a young German called Carl, who after a year or two left for Australia and was never heard of again—but who left in Jacob's mind a persistent, mocking dream of this distant land. Jacob was immensely proud of his family but away from them he was shy and rather unsociable; his English, fluent when writing, deserted him while speaking, and to the end of his life he could never manage his 'th' sounds, to the great embarrassment of his children on those occasions when he drew the task of thanking

Mrs Heseltine, one of the grand ladies of Great Warley, at the Christmas tea which she gave to the villagers each year. 'Your father speaks funny,' the others teased. But it was lucky for the young Maurers that an occasional party of this sort came their way, for at home the fare was very plain indeed. Feeding his four sons, born before the First World War, on a wage of 18s 6d a week, which only rose to 35s towards the end of Jacob's service, was not easy. Not for the Maurers the daily basket of fruit which had been delivered to the Preeces' back door. Times had changed since then, and the back garden at South Lodge—which lay beyond a small yard in which washing flapped continually on the line, and a little hedge—was crammed with leeks, onions and greens, and tended by Jacob in the evenings. In a shed in the Maurer garden, Mr Say wood of the Bothy, an old man with a long white beard, cleaned out flowerpots, pausing to refresh himself from time to time with some brown liquid. 'What's that?' asked the Maurer children, curious as always. 'Cold tea,' replied old Say wood briefly. But they were sure it was beer. The space available was certainly not large enough for all that Jacob needed to grow; and so to supplement it he quietly appropriated a piece of land alongside the path which led near the smithy to the Well Mead garden. Here he grew potatoes and nothing else, wheeling a barrow down to collect a load of them, and pushing it back uphill, steadied by one or more of the boys. And on this very sparse diet, supplementing what groceries the family could afford, they had to manage. As soon as the boys were old enough—about ten—they were encouraged to take on little jobs in rich houses in Great Warley.

So, as the old Europe gradually approached its fate, Ellen Willmott's fortunes also began to show the deep inroads which had been made by twelve years of spending on a grand and profligate scale; and even she must have realized, however much she pushed the unwelcome thought away, that retrenchments and economies had come to stay. Life must have moved in the most extraordinary way along parallel channels: in the one, expenditure must be cut back, the number of gardeners reduced, only one car used, few visits made; but in the other, Ellen Willmott was still a distinguished horticulturist, and this was something which lack of money could not touch. In 1913, as the world was slipping towards the brink of war, Ellen Willmott was again writing to Kew on the subject of the King of Bulgaria: the King was, she said, most anxious to get in touch with

Kew and his Intendent had invoked her good offices to help him to do so. A letter written by Dr Berger, Curator of the La Mortola Garden, confirms that King Ferdinand was at this time planning to create a botanical garden on his Aegean coast. From Oporto the Baron de Soutellinho was writing to Ellen Willmott asking her if she would like the seeds of a beautiful white broom called *Retama monosperma* (now *Genista monosperma*) (he has sent her some seeds anyhow) to grow in her Italian garden. E. H. Wilson wrote from the Arnold Arboretum to express his satisfaction that she would allow her name to be given to the Chinese lily (*Lilium Willmottiae*). This was the level at which Ellen Willmott naturally moved by the time she was fifty-five, and after twenty years' steady, practical experience of gardening she felt it her due to move with royalty and with the distinguished minds of her day: with this neither war, nor financial problems, were to be allowed to interfere.

But the warning voices continued to beset her: Sir Frank Crisp of Ashurst, Morris, Crisp & Co., who took an interest in her affairs as friend and adviser rather than as solicitor, and whom she had originally consulted at the suggestion of William Robinson, pleaded with her in the plainest terms to try and understand the realities of her situation and to come to grips with it. She just did not have the income to equal her wealth of commitments, and borrowing more money simply meant further interest to be paid, which in turn reduced the funds available for the upkeep of the properties and the possibility of the repayment of debts. The problems arising from the fire at Tresserve in 1907 immeasurably complicated and worsened matters: the insurance company involved had, it was said, 'been good to her' in spite of the insurance bungled by Dixson—and Rose Berkeley's insurers also paid up to some extent—but what this may have meant in terms of hard cash is not clear. Sir Frank spelled the situation out for her; the long-suffering bank manager, Mr Morgan of the Pall Mall Branch of the London Joint City and Midland Bank Limited (in which had been incorporated the London Joint Stock Bank Limited), spelled it out again; and so did Mr Arthur Forster of Messrs Frere Cholmeley, a firm of solicitors whom she was just starting to consult on the recommendation of her gardening friends the Lilfords—a matter which made Sir Frank Crisp's unofficial status rather difficult both for him and for Frere Cholmeley. In some ways it seems completely unbelievable that a woman so intelligent and in such a dire financial situation could fail to grasp its simple arithmetic; but she did so fail, and the reason was partly the belief remaining from her childhood that money was something which would always be there and which other people would handle. Could they not understand, she inwardly argued, that she had on her mind exacting and worthwhile tasks from which she must not be deflected—certainly not by anything so tedious and bothersome as bills and bank accounts? Intermittently, when forced to dwell on the subject, her fertile mind devised ways of raising funds or of solving problems, which took no account of ordinary financial processes, and she was then at once out of patience when her suggestions were considered impracticable or, worse, went unheeded. From this time onward, she was never again to live out of the shadow of money worries: her ability to confront her problem squarely on the facts was greatly impaired by her highly emotional reactions, the residue of her childhood feelings, her well-developed sense of what was due to her, her pride in the position she had attained in the eyes of the world, and a certain innate recklessness. All these combined to make her deaf to the voice of common sense and moderation and blind to the message of figures on a page of paper. She would not, and could not, comprehend, and retrenchment was for her the deepest of disgraces.

Nevertheless, her solicitors did their best, but by 1913 it was no longer possible even for Ellen Willmott to set aside the unwelcome problem of money, in spite of writing in her diary, 'Prosit Neujahr' (perhaps to keep her spirits up). With hindsight it seems incredible that she could not bring herself to dispose of one at least of her properties: she thought no doubt of the houses and gardens which she had laboured for so long to make beautiful, and perhaps she considered Gasparine and Claude at Tresserve, looking eagerly for her return, or wondered whether Clodoveo at Boccanegra could really be selling off her possessions to pay his wages; and at Warley itself she had no desire to lose face to a greater extent than had already happened with the dismissal of Preece—so she did not contemplate selling any of her houses. Her thoughts went round in circles: she had really no idea at all of what to do, and though there were plenty of people whom she could approach for advice, there was nobody to suffer and rehearse the problem with her, over and over again, until the solution emerged. To everyone else, the answer was obvious: sell the overseas properties and reduce outgoings so that a comfortable life could be maintained at Warley and the debt on the estate be gradually extinguished. But Ellen Willmott did not see things in this way: she thought that by hanging on to the houses, and renting them, she could win an income for herself and still retain the houses and gardens, while ultimately paying off her debt. She had failed to take into account three things: the outgoings on the houses, and the maintenance of the gardens to her own standard; the extent to which her friends would trade on her good nature and lack of business sense in the matter of rent; and (worst of all) the annoyances, petty arguments and time-consuming details in which her life as landlord would involve her, distracting her attention from matters she found so much more worth while. She sat desolate and debated with herself. The nuns in convents where she was well known prayed for her, and lit lamps before the statue of St Anthony, but few others knew the extent of her worry—not even her sister Rose, with whom she had shared so much else.

In 1913 she sold one of her Amati violins, together with a Stradivarius which she had acquired at some time since her Amati purchases of 1889/90. (But she still had her Amati viola in 1917, for a letter survives from the young and later well-known viola player Lionel Tertis, thanking her for allowing him to use it.) And by March 1913 she had brought herself to the point of trying to let Warley Lea, The Croft and The Glen all together for £500 a year. The attempt cost her a lot of painful effort, and was unsuccessful.

It was good to be able to escape into the garden, and here at least the sights and sounds around her were soothing and reassuring. Her manner towards her friends remained outwardly calm and cheerful. Her engagement diary for the year reads much as usual: her nieces' and nephew's birthdays recorded; numerous RHS and other shows noted—Gladiolus, Sweet Pea, Tulip, Rhododendron; the Bach Choir, 'Zia's Madrigals'; the Magpies; to Sir Dighton Probyn's garden; to Friar Park; lunch with 'Lady Scarborough', Kitten's wedding. What could she have been doing at Canvey Island on 16 August? Or at the Brewers' Hall on 22 February? As the year progresses the entries get fewer and more sober: it was a sign of the times—and of the change that was taking place, so unwelcome and so dreaded, in her life.

CHAPTER X

No Armour against Fate

The year 1914 started with an icy January, but the weather very soon moved into a pattern which always swung back into heat-wave conditions. In May, temperatures were abnormally high by day, plummeting at night to register ten degrees of frost. In June the heat was fierce, with the highest temperatures on record. And in June, events in her life took a dramatic turn which must have profoundly shaken Ellen Willmott's confidence: this had nothing to do with the approaching conflict, but concerned an institution which had been firm ground under her feet since she was a child—her father's firm. She still thought of it as that, although since her father's day it had undergone several changes of name: after Frederick Willmott's retirement in 1879 it became first Hawks, Stokes & McKewan and then, after the death of Hawks in 1880 and the entry of Stokes's two sons into the partnership, Hawks, Stokes & Sons. On 24 June 1914 the blow fell: Stokes was adjudicated bankrupt, but the papers relating to the bankruptcy proceedings have since been destroyed, so it will never be possible to know exactly what happened. But even seventy-five years after the Solicitors' Act of 1843 had started a fairly disreputable profession on the path of probity and the Larcency Act of 1901 had made it much more difficult for solicitors to embezzle their clients' money, it was still possible, and seems the most likely cause of Stokes's downfall. Ellen Willmott's solicitors pounced. By the greatest good luck Arthur Forster of Frere Cholmeley's had, in April, managed to arrange for Lord Lilford, a gardening friend of Ellen Willmott, to take over her £18,000 mortgage, on the understanding that it would be repaid when Tresserve was sold. So evidently Ellen Willmott had been brought to the point of agreeing to this—but how, or when, is not known. It is also clear from the tone of Forster's letter that there had already been trouble of some sort with

Hawks & Co., and that he would be glad to get her loan out of their hands. Smitten with painful neuralgia, the result of an abscess, Ellen Willmott could hardly take in what was happening, let alone respond to it. She went before a Commissioner of Oaths and swore a proof that money was owing to her from Stokes & Co. as instructed.

Rose, who was on a visit to Aix with Robert, wrote to say how dreadfully distressed they were at the news of her illness, and recommending 'asperin tabloids'. She reported that it was raining in torrents, that she was sending Ellen a red linen dress to wear in the garden when there were visitors, and that she and Claude had dug up several bits of the prettiest of the irises and taken them down to Amédine to send off to Warley. She told Ellen how beautiful the garden was looking and how effective the deutzias appeared, planted in front of the house in corbeilles: the plants, a little larger than usual and a little ragged, made a beautiful soft effect in the hazy light of the Tresserve evening. During the Berkeleys' stay at Aix a tea party had been held at Tresserve—Lord and Lady Enfield, Mr and Mrs Paul Foley and a friend. 'Claude and Gasparine were enchanted with the party and would like one every afternoon', she said, adding, 'unfortunately there is no one worthy'. She could hardly have realized how deeply such news, and such a picture of the beauty of her garden, would strike home to Ellen, for she had no idea how desperate her sister's situation had grown. It must all have sounded like another world to Ellen, whose troubles were multiplying with astonishing speed. Mr Morgan, of the London Joint City and Midland Bank wrote reminding her of an earlier promise, which no doubt she had forgotten, to repay her debt to the Bank (probably about £8,000) when her warehouse property at Great Guildford Street was finally bought by the Corporation of London for the purposes of the approach to the proposed St Paul's Bridge. Somehow, Ellen Willmott parried this request, and it was not till the following year that shares were sold to pay off the debt—Argentine Railways shares, which her father had bought for her in 1886. But to Ellen Willmott in 1914, the loss of the firm which she had known for so long, even though she no longer used their legal services, was a very sad affair. The declaration of Stokes's bankruptcy seemed the signal for worse to come, and from all sides.

It was scarcely surprising that M. Durand-Dronchat at Chambéry did not receive answers to his urgent letters written in early June concerning a pending lawsuit arising from building work undertaken after the fire at Tresserve. Ellen Willmott, infuriatingly, would not decide which of various remaining items she wanted done, and then used the resulting delay as a reason for failing to pay M. Louis Goddard for the work already completed. And this was only the beginning of the trouble that was to come at Tresserve, for her debts there were all the time building up until in 1917 they amounted to 15,000 francs, and M. Durand-Dronchat was suggesting that he should be given authority to supervise Claude Meunier's stewardship and receive a fee of 500 francs a year for doing so.

Then everything else was swept aside, for suddenly, in July, Rose Berkeley had to go into a nursing home for an operation. The Berkeley children all went to stay at Warley for a time. Rose had cancer. It was an appalling shock for everyone. Thereafter she carried on as normally as possible, but radium treatment went on for the remaining years of her life, depleting her vitality and draining her of energy. Hardly was this personal shock over than, succeeding the assassination of the Archduke Franz Ferdinand of Austria at Sarajevo, there came the swift acceleration of events through the hot, breathless summer to the beginning of August and the outbreak of war. The only bright spot in this disastrous period was a visit from Professor Sargent, whom Ellen Willmott had not seen for some considerable time.

The current belief that much of Ellen Willmott's inherited money was invested in Germany and was for this reason lost during the war seems to have no known foundation. These 'investments', in fact, probably provided a face-saving story which could be put about to cover the situation at Warley Place, and to that extent the war was a saving measure for her: it could be made an excuse for the reduction in her style of living at Warley, which instead was the result of a dramatic curtailment in income, the outward signs of which were slow and inexorable rather than dramatic. Many years afterwards she wrote to Colonel Prain about the herbarium which she had given to Kew in 1911: 'I never made a list, which was one of the things the war stopped, among the many troubles it brought me.' The war did indeed bring her troubles, quite apart from the sadness and the slaughter, and in May 1915 her financial problems came to a head: there was just no money coming in with which to run Warley Place. Sir Frank Crisp, who had evidently been lending Ellen Willmott money against the security of her Italian property, proposed getting together a small group of friends who would contribute towards the running costs of Warley Place (and thus, tacitly, towards the living expenses of Ellen herself). He had approached William Robinson, and received from him at first an equivocal answer, and later, an offer to join in with a contribution if others would do the same. The matter of Robinson's contribution, if there was one, is a puzzle. Much earlier he had written to Ellen Willmott: 'Five pounds a week is a big lot when a man is poor, but I will see how my balance comes out soon and if I may help.' Yet in 1916 she stated that Robinson had offered a mortgage of £1,000 and then withdrew the offer. The balance of probabilities seems to be that his contribution, if made at all, was only a small one. On 3 May Ellen Willmott wrote to Frank Crisp: 'It is these next few weeks. I am in a pretty bad hole for the moment.' Crisp urged her to write to other friends, and he himself, ceding his prior claim on her Italian property, approached Lord and Lady Mount Stephen for a short-term loan, saying that, even though Miss Willmott had reduced her outgoings to the point where she was suffering considerable privation, she still needed £25 a week in order to keep Warley going. Presumably the money was forthcoming. And one other relief was at hand: the offer of Lord Lilford to take over the mortgage on her property was still open, and after an interim period when the loan passed into other legal hands, reflecting the bankruptcy of Stokes and the death of Brandreth, Lord Lilford's offer was taken up. It included a merciful clause allowing interest on the loan to be capitalized, and thus lifted the burden of interest, at least, from Ellen Willmott's shoulders.

But there were still the running expenses of Warley Place to be found. Some of these must have come from the group of supporting friends, and some may have come from an unexpected source of support—the Army, which now took over Warley Lea and Shenfield Lodge, and later other properties, and embarked thereafter on a running battle with Ellen Willmott about repairs and furnishings. She, on her side, was receiving the same sort of treatment from Mrs Thomas, the tenant of the tearooms, who complained bitterly that the cooking arrangements in her kitchen were so much in need of replacement and the fuel costs were therefore so high that she could make no profit from the food that she served her customers. She was also unlucky in leasing one of her houses to an 'unspeakable tenant',

Lady Angela Forbes by name, who, she alleged, destroyed her collection of rose species. Presumably she was referring to the collection in the Well Mead garden, but it seems extraordinary that such a thing could have been done barely half a mile from Warley Place, even though Lady Angela apparently employed an ignorant gardener who connived at this. Casting round all the time for new ideas, Ellen Willmott had begun to toy with the thought of starting a School of Gardening, and wrote to Cécile Gradwell, a girlhood friend, asking for advice. Cécile thought that such a school, if run under Ellen Willmott's name, would certainly succeed, so long as it was aimed at those who did not have to earn their living, for she foresaw a need after the war for unmarried upper-class daughters to take a largé part in the running of family estates. She sent a prospectus of Lady Wolseley's Glynde School of Gardening: perhaps that put Ellen off, for there was silence on the idea—for a time (Ellen Willmott later became a patroness of the School).

Then there came an even more desperate period, in which Ellen Willmott was hard put to it to show a serene face to the world. It appeared that not only at the London Joint City and Midland Bank, but also at Barclays Bank, she had a loan outstanding. This latter declared its intention to put an execution in at Warley Place and take her effects. Sir Frank Crisp commented that in more than fifty years in the City he had never known such harsh treatment of a defaulting customer, especially as the security of the Italian property had been offered. Forster, urgently consulted, was against her offering as security to the Bank her shares of the leasehold properties at Newcomen Street and 59 Borough High Street which she owned jointly with her sister, because of the moral understanding with Lord Lilford that his security extended to all her property, unspecified as well as specified. Surely, said Forster, she must have had a back history of a writ and various approaches from the Bank pressing her to pay? Her reply to this does not survive—and indeed it is perfectly possible that she had received such approaches and had set them aside. She had a gift for forgetting what she did not want to remember, and further, she had much on her mind with the running of her estate, quite apart from her personal worries. But one thing is certain: she *believed* the Bank's letter to have come out of the blue, for she wrote thus to Miss Gilpin, châtelaine of William Robinson's household at Gravetye, the estate in Sussex where he so successfully realized his unique and imaginative vision of a beautiful garden: 'When that awful letter came I went out weeding, as the only way to bring me a little relief. Being RC the two ways that are often chosen, making away with oneself, or drowning misery in drink, are not allowed to us and indeed neither way appeals to me. . . . I have not said a word to a soul nor shall I do so just wait until the awful thing comes and then go through with all the horrors and not let anyone know that I mind. . . .' She certainly expected bailiffs in the house. Forster suggested, gently, that an approach to Rose might be the easiest way out of the problem. Meanwhile, the last of the Argentine Bonds were sold to clear, finally, Ellen Willmott's debt to the London Joint City and Midland Bank.

Problems of every kind beset her: Austin, the most reliable gardener left at Warley, was wanted for military service, and she had personally to attend the Tribunal so that the best possible case for retaining his services might be put forward: worried and overworked, Austin increased her troubles by himself turning obdurate. One of her tenants, Rainbird, was complaining about the boiler which needed repairs; and, ironically enough in her penurious situation, the tax inspector sent her a super-tax form to complete. This she felt, reasonably enough, to be too much, but Forster assured her that it had to be completed if she wanted to be left alone by the tax inspectors. Within the short space of a month, in June 1916, matters crystallized. Arthur Forster wrote to her at length, sensibly, soberly, compassionately. Unless the two plans she had put forward for keeping Warley Place going succeeded—the School of Gardening, in which she had now apparently interested a lady called Mrs Scott, and the finding of a paying guest (of a superior kind, for she would be asked to contribute to the upkeep of the estate to the tune of £1,000 a year)—he could not see how she could possibly go on living at Warley Place, and indeed without Sir Frank Crisp's contributions the whole estate would have collapsed long ago.

He went on to point out that there were two possible courses which she could follow: she could sell Warley Place by auction (which at that time would probably not even repay Lord Lilford), or she could sell the best part of the contents to pay the mortgage partially or to provide income. Lord Lilford would give her two to three weeks to arrange the lease of gardens and farm, find a paying guest or shut the house, and thereafter seek a purchaser. If Mrs

Scott's proposal was to come to anything then guarantors, or at least unimpeachable references, must be obtained. Forster was obviously not at all happy with the idea, seeing it as a potential money-waster, and realizing all too well that in this sort of undertaking a business acumen a good deal more acute than Ellen Willmott's was required. He took therefore a step which should have been taken long before: he told Rose what had happened. Although he warned Ellen Willmott of what he was about to do, this must have been a most bitter pill for her to swallow. She had for so long faced her consuming worries courageously on her own, working out what she considered to be sensible schemes for solving her problems and determined not to burden Rose, who had troubles of her own with her illness and over the running of Spetchley with few servants and gardeners, Stephens the butler having gone to work in a munitions factory; and with the constant worry for the safety of Rob, who had gone to the war. And Rose, moreover, had been wearing herself out with organizing an entertainment for the troops, which had been an enormous success and had been reported at length in *The Times*—but which had taken a toll of her scanty physical reserves. Nevertheless, Rose had stamina. Arthur Forster must have made a good job of explaining the situation to her, which he did without attempting to conceal its gravity, and yet without generating undue drama. Rose went away and in the course of a sleepless night worked out what she felt would be the best line for Ellen to take. She suggesting renting everything except the mansion, Lodges and the Red House. She, Rose, would contribute a small sum towards expenses, and thought that produce from the garden could be sold to add to income. Also she felt that Ellen could 'part with a thing here and a thing there', which she herself would sell in order not to make the decline of Warley Place too obvious. But the cornerstone of her advice was that Ellen should trust Mr Forster and Lord Lilford entirely, leaving it to them to work everything out for the best. It is certainly the same Rose who had written to her mother from Aix in the 1880s complaining that to her always fell the job of reminding Ellie to take her cough mixture every four hours, who now wrote to her sister: 'I am sure you won't like my advice but surely it is worth making a *supreme* effort now to straighten matters, and you can well put it down to the War.' In this last suggestion, at least, Ellen took her sister's advice. Perhaps Rose's offer of a small income saved her, and certainly there is talk later of 'Mrs Berkeley's mortgage' which may have followed on. However this may have been, Warley Place was not sold up and nor were its contents, and Barclays Bank did nothing so dramatic as to turn Ellen Willmott out of her home.

She did, however, lack the unquestioning support given by the presence of 'Lalla' whose death in 1916 symbolized the end of an era. Eliza Burge had been Ellen Willmott's lady's maid for very many years—perhaps even back into the 1890s—and she had become part of the Willmott family life. She underwent an operation for cancer at the Middlesex Hospital, and briefly returned to Warley: Ellen Willmott was away from home, but Robinson was sufficiently alarmed by Eliza's appearance to write and report how ill she looked. She went to live out her last days with her sister at Chippenham, where she died in the late spring of 1916. She was not replaced. No one, in fact, could have taken the place of such an old and loyal servant.

Although she still had a roof over her head, Ellen Willmott built up a picture of herself as a poor lone woman, spending an icy Christmas at Warley in 1916, with only an oil stove to heat the house—' trying to prevent murder between man and maid, putting up with the bad cooking and getting on with mending'. A fearsome picture indeed—but with Robinson about, could it really have been as bad as all that?

But a breathing space had arrived, and as spring came Ellen Willmott could once more thankfully go out into the sunshine and see how the garden was getting on. It was amazing how quickly problems could be forgotten in the absorption of watching some obstinate seed finally coaxed out of the ground, or some rarity from China or South America persuaded to flower. A letter received from her old and valued friend Dr Norman Moore at about this time expresses most happily this state of mind: 'A day like this', he writes, 'with a bright sun and pleasant turf and a beautiful distant view reminds me of Warley more than twenty years ago and your mother in her chair and you full of happiness and activity and the cottagers coming up in the evening.'

There came to her, too, some wholly unexpected family support: her cousin Charlie, son of Uncle Charles Willmott, came over from New Zealand—though it is not clear whether he saw any active service in the New Zealand Expeditionary Force, he was evidently entitled to use their postcards, and sent one to Ellen thanking her for the happy time she had given him on one of his leaves. He returned to New Zealand late in the war, and promised to send Ellie seeds on his return: perhaps he did so, and he certainly did not lack the opportunity, for he long outlived his English cousins.

There were, however, some problems out of doors. The gardening staff was gradually dwindling: some volunteered for war service with Ellen Willmott's blessing, but the rest found their services were no longer needed. A minor scandal was caused by the case of Mrs Gooch, which was taken up by *John Bull* in a short article entitled 'An Englishwoman's Home—Essex Lady's Piecrust Promise to Soldier'. It appeared that Ellen Willmott, hearing that Gooch was off to join the RAMC, had written from Spetchley to wish him God speed and to say that the best way she could help his wife would be to let her stay on in the cottage near Headley garden rent free. Three weeks later she changed her mind, giving Mrs Gooch three weeks' notice to quit; typically, she declined *John Bull's* offer of an opportunity to explain herself. It seems more than likely that she was too deeply enmeshed in her financial troubles to have been conscious of the passage of time in matters like this, and she may have been driven to give Mrs Gooch notice for financial reasons too, which she would naturally not wish to explain in public. It was months before she realized that it would have been to her advantage to give such an explanation earlier. Even so, there were in 1914 still quite enough gardeners to keep the grounds, though perhaps not quite so weedless as before, at least in reasonably good trim.

In 1914 gardeners still had their own area of work in the Warley Garden. Apart from excursions in a punt to cut branches overhanging the pond, a young gardener who spent a year at Warley in 1914, Hugh Balls, spent some of his time working in the old orchard, where there were still trees believed to be the Essex D'Arcy spice apple, covered with clematis and mistletoe and iron pergolas carrying pears and apples trained over them. The herbaceous beds in this garden were still at their peak and the phlox, small collections of which were sent across the Atlantic to Sargent at the Arnold Arboretum and to Carl Purdy the nurseryman, made a special impression on the young gardener. These sets presumably included the phlox 'Ellen Willmott', with its pale ageratum-blue flowers, which had received an Award of Merit from the Royal Horticultural Society in 1910. Hugh Balls also worked in the nursery area, amongst the frames where tomatoes and cucumbers were grown, and remembers that there were bee-hives in that part of the garden.

But there was no Preece now to pull the whole thing together, and Fielder, after only a year at Warley, moved on to the RHS staff as an adviser for five days out of seven each week, and so hardly spent any time in the Warley Garden. So, to a large extent, Preece's mantle fell on Ellen Willmott's own shoulders, and she certainly set an example of industry, for when her gardeners arrived at 8 a.m. for work (somehow working hours seem to have slipped since Preece's day) they often found her already busy with her trowel and trug, doing some weeding or transplanting plants along the side of the drive. At this time she is described as being 'plump and [of] fresh complexion'—strange that a young gardener should see her in this way, when other scanty descriptions sketch in a slight, brisk, hurrying figure. Certainly she got through an immense amount of work. At about this time she decided to invest in a donkey for fetching and carrying: Isabel Russell teased her that a husband might do the same job better—but eventually it was a donkey who joined the household.

In the alpine garden Jacob Maurer plodded steadily on. He had his problems. In the period just before and during the war his five daughters were born—all of them christened with flower names—Rose, Violet, Lily, Margrit and Iris. The last birth was too much for young Rosina Maurer, who developed tuberculosis: for eighteen months she hovered between life and death, in and out of hospital, stoutly refusing to go into a sanatorium. Ellen Willmott, beset with her own troubles, did what she could to help, but she could not persuade the county authorities to provide an outside shelter for Mrs Maurer; and although the doctor pointed out that the shady situation of South Lodge under trees was not likely to aid the patient's recovery, Ellen Willmott obviously did not feel moved to provide other accommodation for the family. Rosina died in 1918, aged only thirty-three. The care of nine children was quite beyond Jacob, and so a cousin, Freddi, came from Switzerland to help him look after them. The boys did not do anything much to help their father in the garden. At home, their main interest and occupation was to play or simply to stand watching by the railings of the back drive: a splendid vantage point, both for the comings and goings of Warley Place, and also for whatever was afoot in the village. Max, however, had one weekly task which was a duty rather than a job, since it was unpaid, untipped, and entirely taken for granted. This was to go up to the mansion, neatly dressed, in the early evening on a Sunday, and stand waiting outside the French windows on the south side of the house, cap in hand, until Miss Willmott chose to emerge with the letters for post. These he took from her and then walked all the way to Brentwood to put them into the evening post—a task he deeply resented.

Meanwhile, Jacob continued his skilled and patient work in the alpine garden at Warley Place. The visitors from Kew, botanists from universities in Britain and abroad, members of learned societies, and royalty, all came to talk to Jacob and admire the slopes and gullies of the alpine garden, so filled with beauties and rarities: the Chinese garden, the Japanese garden and the fern cave. Talking to them, absorbed in his subject, Jacob forgot that he was speaking an alien tongue and became fluent and excited. The visitors went away impressed by his knowledge and skill, which in this area of practical work clearly equalled Ellen Willmott's; but yet, when house guests came to leave, it was always Robinson who was standing by on the front doorstep with coats and baggage, and into whose hand the grand tip was pressed—Jacob, working quietly away in his corner, was forgotten, and the only extra which came his way was an occasional batch of partridge eggs which he used to find on the edges of the South Pond. Jacob was not a vindictive man, but the difference rankled . . . just a little. It was much less easily forgivable than the remarks made to him in all good faith by Mrs Berkeley (to his way of thinking an altogether gentler and more ladylike person than her sister Ellen): 'My poor sister, she is living on her capital'—for it would be wrong, and in any case impossible, to expect a lady to understand how nice it would be to have any capital at all to live on. Such 'let them eat cake' comments were only to be expected from the gentry. With these thoughts in his mind Jacob laboured on in the alpine garden, outwardly submissive, inwardly dreaming of Australia as he cleaned out the pond.

There is little doubt that his attitude brought out the very worst in his employer: it was an invitation to trample, and trample she did, though probably no more so than others of her generation with their servants. She would never actually cross the threshold of South Lodge, for it would have seemed to her a very undignified thing to do. Instead, she approached as nearly as she felt she could do without loss of face and, standing just inside the yard but not inside the bounds of the little hedge which separated off the vegetable garden, she would call 'Jacob! Jacob!' in a high-pitched, authoritative staccato. At whatever time of the day or night and whether or no he was in the middle of a meal, Jacob hastened to the call: he was bred to obey, and she expected it of him.

Ellen Willmott could never resist interfering in other people's garden arrangements. Apart from her first, and most advantageous move—the tempting of Jacob Maurer away from M. Correvon's garden—there were a good number of similar incidents. It cannot have made for friendly relations to remove a young gardener from a nearby house. On one occasion she tried to suggest to the 22-year-old Percy Picton, now running the Old Court Nurseries at Colwall but at that time working for William Robinson at Gravetye, that he might like to work at Warley—' But I refused,' he says. Things however did sometimes work the other way round. Even if she was unsuccessful in finding a place for James Preece, Ellen Willmott did find a gardener for Bodnant, and in rather a strange way. She was godmother to the present Lord Aberconway who, having difficulty with a birthday thank-you letter, filled up space by saying that the head gardener had died and his father was looking for a new one. Ellen Willmott wrote at once to the boy's father to inquire whether this was true and, if so, to recommend a Mr F. C. Puddle for the job. So in due course Mr Puddle became the first of three generations of the Puddle family at Bodnant. Again, Ellen Willmott was to be found writing hopefully to Professor Sargent that owing to Mr Barbey's giving up his Chambéry garden because his son did not care for plants, 'that nice gardener is looking out for a place'.

Kew, needless to say, kept going steadily during the war, and in October 1914 Ellen Willmott was writing to Colonel Prain asking him to spare Mr Bean from Kew to visit Spetchley Park, which she is sure he will find an interesting garden. She mentions that John Evelyn the diarist, who had owned Warley Place, was a great friend of a former Robert Berkeley. She adds an interesting comment about the plumbago (*Ceratostigma willmottianum*) which is now so often to be found in English gardens: it was raised from seed obtained from E. H. Wilson's first trip to China on behalf of the Arnold Arboretum—only two seeds germinated, one being grown on at

Warley and one at Spetchley. How many plants are descended from these two ancestors, one wonders? Seed lists were still produced at Warley, and consignments sent away, despite shortage of labour. One plant at least was accepted graciously and with great pleasure: Princess Victoria wrote a card in curly, hard-to-decipher handwriting, to thank for an illegible tree which 'just brightens up my garden on the windowsill'.

Most of the societies of which Ellen Willmott was a member kept going, but in a diminished sort of way and with patriotic overtones. The Bach Choir continued to meet regularly, many of its concerts being based on patriotic themes or containing works like *Songs of the Fleet*. In 1917 there was a special concert entitled 'A choral commemoration of heroic deeds of the first seven divisions, Mons to Ypres', and during the programme there were special readings on the history of the first seven divisions.

During the war years an old and much-loved friend and visitor had died. Ellen Willmott records that on 1 October 1915 the Bristol Madrigal Society, which she apparently accompanied (though she could not have been a member, as they did not admit women), made a pilgrimage to Bitton and Willsbridge, to sing there some of Pearsail's madrigals. Canon Ellacombe, as bright and well as ever, welcomed the party to the vicarage, but this was the last of these gatherings, for in February 1916 a sad letter came from his neighbours at Bitton Grange to tell her, gently, of the Canon's death and to offer her hospitality over the time of his funeral. Ellen Willmott, who sincerely mourned this old and valued friend, attended the funeral on 13 February, and contributed extensively to the memorial volume Henry *Nicholson Ellacombe: A Memoir,* edited by A. W. Hill and published in 1919. Ellen Willmott's correspondence with Arthur Hill is interesting. She evidently liked Hill, and as a result shows a curious clumsiness in her dealings with him. She had become so accustomed to being brilliantly in the lead in every conversation, so used to battling with problems on her own, that she had to think herself into a feminine role—and thought is no substitute for reaction. *She* invites *him,* having missed him elsewhere, 'Could we meet somewhere for a little supper afterwards'. Later, accepting an invitation, she uses one of her standard, and perhaps gauche, comments: 'All else when we meet.' Perhaps A. W. Hill was a sturdy character and able to take this sort of manoeuvring with amusement, while not losing sight of Ellen Willmott's qualities. The meetings must have concerned her contribution to the Ellacombe memorial volume. 'I fear it reads like twaddle and piffle', she remarks modestly, but somehow hitting the same false note. And yet her contribution does not read thus, but instead achieves, apparently unawares, simple feeling straight from the heart, rare for her: 'The master has gone and Bitton can never be the same again, nor in our time is it ever likely that such another garden can arise, for it needed the man, the soil, the climate and fifty years' love and work to make it.'

Such writing is entirely free of the purely mischievous and divisive note of so many of her other comments. Just a year previously, she had written to Hill: 'Mr Vicary Gibbs has written Mr Graham Smith a very nasty letter, he writes too of the many plants and cuttings he sent to Britton which are only in his imagination, not a word about the many rare plants he had from them. I was reminded of a remark by a mutual friend "his character is as ugly as his garden".' Poor Mr Vicary Gibbs. (Of Mr Graham Smith nothing is known; Mr Britton is believed to have been an American botanist.) This letter, however, is Ellen Willmott writing in a style in which she felt much more comfortable: downright, partisan, battlesome and uncaring for the feelings of others. So much energy and genuine feeling deserved a better fate than to display themselves in so distorted a fashion. A letter to Lt-Col Prain in March 1919 also shows this mischievous and inflammatory tone. She grumbled that even mutual friends had begged pieces of her new plants which she intended to exhibit when in character and name verified, grown it on themselves, exhibited as theirs, and got an Award of Merit. She felt the plants should have Kew's imprimatur or a provisional name before receiving an Award of Merit. Bitterly (and, theoretically at least, in confidence), she commented that all this was not surprising when one knew the members of the committees personally. Erudition or fitness was one of the last qualifications necessary, one only needed to be a friend of . . . or . . . etc. to be eligible. The committees as at present constituted were not competent to deal with the subjects put before them. . . . But one might as well talk to the table as to the RHS. She may well have been right. . . . But did it do any good to fuel the fire of warring factions in this way? Looking briefly back to her early years the contrast in her attitudes, built up by slow changes over the years, suddenly leaps to the eye. The girl who wrote with such joyful enthusiasm of her first visit to Paris, and the disenchanted elderly lady, are painfully different.

The end of the war left Ellen Willmott weary. Again writing to A. W. Hill, early in 1918, she says: 'I have been talking to my only man left . . . everything is so difficult in war time and I am at my wits' end sometimes how to manage.' The Only man' was presumably Jacob, and since it is known that Jacob was never entirely without help, this must again have been an exaggeration. Nevertheless, it must often have seemed that she was in the same situation in which she felt herself to be when trying to persuade Wilson to go to China—namely, pushing a large stone up a hill and keeping it there.

The uncertainties and sadnesses of war had their effect on the family. Ellen Willmott's nephew Rob went safely through the war, as did Robinson's son Jim. Rose Berkeley found it increasingly difficult to run Spetchley Park. Exhausted by the radium treatment, worn out by a succession of heavy colds, and with only very inadequate help in house and garden, she struggled on. Rose, when she so wished, could turn an even more devastating, if less extravagant, phrase than her sister. Here she is on maids: 'As soon as the Archbishop's visit is over I am going to get rid of Margaret and Marion. The latter is too awfully destructive and the former tiresome.' Robert Berkeley was none too well either: he suffered from persistent giddiness which could be very alarming.

Ellen Willmott's very existence at Warley was still threatened. Towards the end of the war she did manage to find paying guests sufficiently respectable to meet all criteria: Sir Francis and Lady Younghusband. And for a while, perhaps from 1918 to 1919, between her war-time job as a VAD and a peace-time training for work at St Dunstan's, Eleanor Berkeley came to live at Warley. Neither arrangement lasted for very long, the Younghusbands presumably leaving when the war was over, and Eleanor finding the life at Warley, which was predominantly geared to survival and the garden, boring for a young woman with lively social inclinations.

Some considerable efforts were still being made to reduce expenditure. Ellen Willmott tried (a vain attempt) to sell the victoria to the Army and Navy Stores, but they agreed to have the dog cart (subject to its size) in their show-room, and sell it on 10 per cent commission. It was not very helpful. She still had Army tenants at The Glen and The Croft, though they could raise problems too—Colonel and Mrs

Turner, moving into The Glen, very reasonably asked for certain repairs to be carried out.

A sad blow came in 1919: her old and trusted friend Sir Frank Crisp died in April. *Country Life's* editor asked her to write a short article on Friar Park but the article when it appeared bore the initials 'H.C' not 'E.A.W.' Did she repay the money she had borrowed from him? It is too late now to tell.

During the early part of 1920 Hamptons tried to let Warley Place, but were unsuccessful. Also during 1920 there is some rather tenuous evidence, impossible to check, that Ellen Willmott may have been discussing a handing-over of the Warley Garden to Kew—but nothing came of it. At the same time she was pursuing her aim of finding a suitable paying guest on a long-term basis through the Williams Agency, and was agreeing with them that the advertisement which they had been using might better attract the right kind of applicant if the word 'American' were added—for then, as now, Americans were considered to be in a better position than the English to contribute £1,000 a year towards expenses. Evidently the change can have had no effect, since no one suitable came forward. Miss Willmott wrote intermittently to friends and acquaintances asking for their help—with money or advice—and it is sobering to see the kind of response she got. Vicary Gibbs could not stand guarantor for anyone, the articles of his partnership in the family firm of merchant bankers forbade it; Sir Isaac Bayley Balfour at the Edinburgh Botanic Garden did not understand English law, and so could not advise her; super-tax and his responsibilities for his relatives prevented Lord Ducie from offering help; Mrs Ainslie Hight, without much thought, wished her 'better luck soon' adding, infuriatingly, that there were always compensations. She wrote to her friend Alice de Rothschild, asking if she would like to buy Boccanegra; Alice replied; 'Why not sell a picture?'—one of the very few practical suggestions she received, and one which she perhaps followed. In a roundabout way, associating her request with potential income from *The Genus Rosa,* she tried to borrow money from John Murray, but he wrote saying that he had recently bought up a smaller publishing firm and was himself a borrower. Many made the war their excuse. Perhaps she asked the wrong people, and perhaps the Mary Venables of this world might have been more constant in upholding a friend. But she must have found it supremely difficult to approach anyone, and the fact that she did so at all reveals at least determination and courage.

In May 1920, Apple Tree Cottage was advertised in the Morning Post as being available for renting. And at the same time the decision must, finally, have been taken on Warley Place, for particulars were printed of a sale by auction to take place on Wednesday, 9 June; but this, apparently, never happened. The reason for this may not be far to seek. Ellen Willmott had been making serious attempts to sell her property at Tresserve, as well as Boccanegra. It is not certain when she last visited either (the last mention of her presence comes late in 1913 apparently in response to an urgent request from Sir Frank Crisp for the deeds of Boccanegra, without which he could not arrange a loan on it), and the thought of both her cherished gardens in a decayed and neglected state must have saddened her immeasurably. During the war she had been receiving regular postcards and lists of accounts from Clodoveo, to whom she seems according to her habit to have sent small sums of money from time to time—enough to keep him hoping but never enough to pay his salary and all the bills up to date. He received a certain income from selling flowers to Monsieur Tissot at the Orphélinat nursery at Chambéry, but this cannot have gone far.

For some years, beginning about 1913, she had let Boccanegra periodically to Lady Menzies and her daughter, who had written to her at length during their tenancies, praising the house and garden but also somehow managing to inject a large element of complaint into the letters. Why did the water supply work in the apartment by the front door, but not in the main cistern? Could Ellie please supply a proper wash basin? 'Dear Boccanegra' was so cold in the winter that the resulting feverish cold had driven Lady Menzies to seek refuge in a hotel for some weeks. And yet, in January 1920, Lady Menzies was asking for a fifteen-year lease, and at the same time wanting to know the present purchase price of the property. The letter from her agents, Benecke & Hey wood of San Remo, makes sad reading. The garden during the previous five years has been utterly neglected and is in dreadful disorder, a great number of plants are dying or dead, and the olive trees untended: Lady Menzies would take all in hand, asking only that for the first two years, while rehabilitation was going on, she should pay a nominal rent of 1,000 lire, and thereafter 5,000 lire a year. It was a very small sum, but it was at least something tangible, and carried the hope of something better. Lady Menzies did not get her fifteen-year lease, nor did she buy the property: after a prolonged struggle, involving much unpleasantness and difficulty with Clodoveo, whose protracted responsibilities, lack of wages and general state of hope deferred had turned him from a '*devotissimo ed umilissimo servo*' into a worried and obstructive old man, the estate finally changed hands and became the 'Proprieta Tremayne', remaining so ever since. To Ellen Willmott, after eighteen years of ownership, it must have been sad that relief should have been the dominating emotion.

But Tresserve? During the early part of 1920 Ellen Willmott received an offer of 40,000 francs for the Château from an unnamed Frenchman. Very probably it was this that prevented the sale of Warley Place from going through: but salvation was at hand from a more reliable source. Lord Berkeley who, having no son of his own, had decided to make Rob Berkeley his heir, had heard of Ellen Willmott's troubles and of the impending sale of the Château; and he now came forward with an offer to exceed the amount offered by the Frenchman, and the possibility of helping her further with her mortgages. Even in the poor bargaining position in which she found herself, Ellen Willmott was still astute enough (as she could be, in business matters, by fits and starts) to make the point that the Frenchman's offer was less than market price. Lord Berkeley replied that he did not know how to assess a market price, but that he was willing to pay slightly more than the Frenchman offered, and to safeguard Ellen Willmott's interest by offering her half of the profits on any resale which he might make in the following few years. And so the problem was solved—but at great human cost, and particularly to Claude and Gasparine who were heartbroken at the turn of events. By 1921 Ellen Willmott was writing to her friend Alice de Rothschild that she intended never to go abroad again.

Early in 1921 Ellen Willmott's mortgage was transferred from Lord Lilford to Lord Berkeley: its amount was much reduced, reflecting the sales of Tresserve and Boccanegra. It seems possible that some of the profit from the sales was used to pay off the Barclays Bank loan, and that some may have been invested to provide a small income.

Here *The Genus Rosa* made its way once again to the forefront of Ellen Willmott's life. She had, she thought, got a promising offer from Wesley, the bookseller, for sales in America, and wanted to take over the unsold parts of the work from Murrays' keeping. After the earlier flurry of activity, the grand names bandied to and fro, the sense of frenetic promotion and sales, it comes as a great surprise to find that anything from 200 to 500 copies of each part remained unsold. John Murray had in every respect done more than his duty to a very difficult author and felt that a commission of 5 per cent on the remaining stock was a fair one, as they had held it for so long: he wrote with great dignity and firmness to Miss Willmott on the subject. It is sad to record that after their long association they parted so stiffly. But Ellen Willmott needed money, and thought she saw a way of recouping some of her outlay on *The Genus Rosa*. It is doubtful whether she managed to do so.

And so Warley Place settled down again, though at a level sadly lowered from that of earlier times. The lamps before the statue of St Anthony had done their work. Ellen Willmott must have felt, briefly, that life had started afresh, and made a new effort to run her affairs in a more organized and less stormy fashion. In 1914, besides Robinson, Warley Place staff had consisted of a non-resident foot-man, chauffeur and night-watchman; resident were a cook, lady's maid, parlourmaid and housemaid. By 1918, it seems likely that the footman had departed, never to return, and that the parlourmaid's services had been dispensed with also; but there was certainly a long unbroken line of cooks from the time the Willmotts first came to Warley Place, and 'Lilian Turner, housemaid to Miss Willmott' witnessed the new will she made on her sixtieth birthday in August 1918, so we know that at least the mansion was kept dusted. When young Jim Robinson came back from the war in 1920 he did not return to his position with the Percy family in Devon, but instead was given some casual jobs around the estate—soldering up all the watering cans, every one with a hole in it, was one such job. From this he progressed to the post of chauffeur to Colonel Turner, of The Glen. Jacob Maurer was also most probably provided with a little extra labour after the war, as the surviving gardeners returned to Great Warley, but the garden had to be maintained with the absolute minimum of labour. During the war there had been some female gardeners, but the end of hostilities seemed to have seen the end of them too. The essential jobs were also the most time-consuming: the pruning of all the roses and shrubs on the estate once a year took

Jacob and another gardener three weeks; and mowing the lawns and paths with a motor mower, including trimming the edges, took three days. Thus the immediate appearance of the gardens was saved, and of course, whatever else happened, Jacob would never let the alpine garden suffer. The approaches to it were still mowed by hand, and the orange trees still stood in their tubs on the lawn above. The rest had to take its chance, getting done whenever there was labour to do it, and otherwise getting left.

Ellen Willmott herself, of course, got through an enormous amount of garden work—but her over-riding interest was her experimental work. And she still kept up her judging. She is remembered at the Rose Show by the Revd James Jacobs as a gracious, benevolent presence; and in 1924 the National Rose Society honoured her with the Dean Hole Medal, the Society's highest award, and she is to this day the only lady to be honoured in this way. She is also remembered by one of the Gascoigne children, recently married, on an occasion in about 1924 when she was expected to judge at the York Show, as she had done every year since at least 1914. Having at first said she would arrive by the 1 p.m. train, she countermanded this by telegram; expected then to arrive at 6 p. m., she finally appeared by lunch-time on the following day, perfectly serene and oblivious of the chaos caused, and very faintly reproving towards her hosts, whom she obviously considered to be making a great deal of fuss about nothing. The 3rd of June followed so closely on 2 June in the calendar, she explained, that she found it impossible to keep up.

Early in 1920 Ellen Willmott was asked to take on the job of advising on plantings for the garden of Anne Hathaway's cottage at Stratford-on-Avon. She was offered plants from many private gardens, including Knole in Kent, home of the Sackville-West family, but it was a job which required a lot of co-ordinating and there were pitfalls and problems. However, by April, Colonel Prain was congratulating her on a job well done, adding that he was certain she should not work so hard.

Ellen Willmott's relations with the Berkeley family were growing more distant as their interests diverged. Her nephew Rob was grown up, still in the Army, and did not often come to Warley; Eleanor, now nearly thirty, was still a disorganized girl who was fond of horses; and Betty, now twenty, was the most like her aunt of all of

10. *The garden at Boccanegra, carefully planted but wild and beautiful: the paths were made by Ellen Willmott to follow the channels carved out by heavy rainstorms down to the little beach and the sea.*

11. *Kaufmanniana tulips: one of the many flower studies among Ellen Willmott's photographs. Criticisms of her work made by 'the best photographer in Cork' were faithfully relayed to her by W. E. Gumbleton, but this study does not seem to bear any of the blemishes he mentions.*

12. *The best of the Warleys' produce arranged with care for the annual show.*

them, with a will of her own. Rob was the only one who had inherited the gardening skills of his mother and aunt. The days were gone when the Russell children were invited over and the two families played croquet on the south lawns, or tennis on a court without a net, but the young Russells still kept up their visits to Warley Place.

Rose Berkeley was sixty in September 1921; for some considerable time she had been unable to do anything in the garden: she was so tired, and suffered so much pain. On the day after her thirty-first wedding anniversary—21 August 1922—she died. Her death was a great grief to her husband and children, but to Ellen Willmott, who could never remember life without her sister, it was a blow scarcely to be borne. In all the important happenings of her life, Rose's full attention and sympathy had been hers, and as the elder sister she had never looked to have to live without her, though strangely Rose, even before she developed cancer, was sure that she would die first. As so often happened when Ellen Willmott's feelings were deeply involved, she expressed herself very badly on paper, and the obituary which she wrote for the Essex *Naturalist* is stilted and formal in tone:

A fit memento to one whose life was spent for others and whose greatest pleasure was her garden, are the beautiful lines of Jamman Shud now on the alcove overlooking the Fountain garden scene:

> *The Moon of Heaven is rising once again*
> *How oft hereafter rising shall she look*
> *Through this same garden after me—in vain.*

Simpler, and much more convincing, is her comment to the Russell family—'Now there is no one to send the first snowdrops to'—and with Rose's death there was a change in Ellen Willmott, a loss of some remaining gentleness, which nothing was to reverse, for two years her writing paper carried black borders.

CHAPTER XI

The Straitened Days

If Ellen Willmott felt like walking back from Brentwood Station at close on midnight, she walked, the whole mile and a half, rather than call out the chauffeur and the remaining ancient Charron (in a burst of economy the other one, long since beyond repair, had been dismantled and the chassis sold). It did not matter if it were raining or blowing a gale, it was all one to her; nor did the wearing of evening clothes make any difference. She still went frequently to London, for Bach Choir rehearsals and on other occasions. The walk from Brentwood Station leads first up the fairly steep slope of Warley Hill, past the Roman Catholic church on the right and Christ Church opposite it and then, as the houses thin out, follows a road with wide curves, the ground keeping its gentle upward slope with each dip and rise, past Headley Common, finally reaching Great Warley and the main gates of Warley Place. In Ellen Willmott's day there were two large gas-lit lamps on the gateposts, and these were kept burning through the night (though the families in the Lodges had to manage with oil lamps). It was a long, lonely, eerie walk past shuttered cottages; and on one fine clear night, as she was walking back *en grande tenue* after attending a reception in aid of the National Art-Collections Fund she thought she heard someone following her: footsteps seemed to be echoing faintly along the road behind her. Up till then she had been carrying her tiara in a brown paper bag stuffed carelessly into her large coat pocket but, fearing she might be set upon and robbed, she hastily pushed the package into the hedgerow for retrieval the following morning by Robinson, and reached the house without mishap.

Robinson must have been thankful that it did not fall to him to wait up for 'the Lady' after these expeditions. By the front door there was a loose brick in the house wall, behind which the house key was hidden; the door was usually bolted on the inside by the time Miss Willmott reached the house, however, and so she pulled a special bell which rang in a room, once, in grander days, the footman's bedroom, and now allotted to one of the youngest gardeners—often only fourteen or fifteen years old. He, roused from his slumbers, stumbled out to admit the mistress and rebolt the door after her. Miss Willmott thanked him, retired immediately and went straight to bed. Muddy hems and scuffed shoes were no concern of hers: although the days of Eliza Burge were over, she still continued to behave as though she had a lady's maid. And so, in a way, she had—in Robinson, who had taken on that task too as part of his multi-faceted role in the house. He did, however, get some help from anyone among the changing population of housemaids, cook-housekeepers and others who showed any aptitude in that direction.

Of the outdoor staff, the coachman, groom and stable-boy had gone, and in the garden only Jacob and a few others remained; while the chauffeurs had been replaced by a mechanic/driver who slouched around in the stable in dirty overalls with a cigarette always dangling from his mouth. Robinson, to whom he was anathema, nicknamed him 'Greasy'.

One evening early in 1924, Miss Willmott dined in London at the house of Mr Ernest Law, whose learned work on Hampton Court graced the shelves of her library and who had been working with her in the planning of Anne Hathaway's garden. The following day at breakfast she told Robinson, as he waited on her, that she had found a new housekeeper the previous evening who would be coming the next week, with her mother. Robinson received this news with a straight face and mixed feelings. Long ago he had faced and come to terms with the fact that his mistress was a born director, but not—except when it suited her—a born oiler of wheels. Robinson recognized that it was his task in life to act as *continuo* in the household at Warley Place, and indeed this was nothing new to him—only now the task was much harder, and the support much less. He sighed inwardly and waited for the worst.

Miss Annie Cotterell had been working as cook to Mr Law, but she was suffering from the effects of blood poisoning and the doctor had warned that she must get away from London. Hearing this, Miss Willmott had on impulse offered her the job of housekeeper at Warley Place. 'It's a healthy place,' she said. Seeing the girl hang back, and learning that she had an elderly mother whose home in London had just been condemned, she suggested that they both come, remarking that there was plenty of room. And indeed there was, since most of the bedrooms had been locked for months. The previous housekeeper had been unsatisfactory to the point at which Robinson had suspected her of stealing, and she had been dismissed. He was not at all sure how he would feel about two women coming to disturb the precarious balance of the household.

Annie Cotterell and her mother arrived at Brentwood Station on a cold dull day in February: it was just as well that their trunk had been sent on by carrier, for there was no one to meet them. Finally they found a taxi, and as they drove out into the cold, dank countryside and up the long drive to the side door of Warley Place they heartily wished themselves back in warm, familiar London. Nor was their welcome very reassuring. 'You're the two I've been expecting, I suppose,' said Robinson as he opened the door. He led them downstairs to the large, cold kitchen with barred windows, in the centre of which stood an ancient disused kitchen range, with barred front and rusty doors. Their spirits sank. Next came the climb up three flights of stairs to the bedrooms, where they were invited to choose a room for themselves. They found one looking over the roofs which seemed less neglected than the others. It was hardly an auspicious beginning.

In the morning things looked rather better, though their first job was a baffling one. Miss Willmott appeared, bearing a large box full of a jumble of keys which she set down on the kitchen table, announcing that all the rooms were locked and that the keys needed sorting. This task took the Cotterells nearly a fortnight. When it was done, they were astounded at the sight which met their eyes. The bedrooms were all named: the Rose Room, the Blue Room, the Buff Room, Ilex Room, and so on. Each was beautifully furnished with antique furniture including a four-poster bed, and with blankets and linen to match the colour of the room, but moth, dust and damp were everywhere. The Cotterells had to wait until the weather became warmer before they could open the windows to air the rooms and hang the blankets outside in the fresh air. The whole house seemed icy. There being no longer housemaids to labour up from the basement with copper hot-water cans for the bedrooms, the marooned bathroom was more than ever a nuisance. Miss Willmott, in fact, did not take baths: she preferred to wash all over instead, frequently saying that she did not feel the cold. But Annie Cotterell was a Londoner accustomed to speaking her mind. She wanted a bath, and she wanted hot water for cleaning: at once. Eventually Miss Willmott capitulated, the range was put in order and its chimney cleared of jackdaws' nests, and soon there was hot water and also some warmth in the kitchen. Gradually Robinson realized that the new regime was a good deal better than the old one and, instead of sleeping in the house, as he had done since the last housekeeper departed, he began to return to his own house in the evenings. The Cotterells, meanwhile, hovered between horror at the dirt in the house, and astonishment at the grandeur of the furnishings. Mrs Cotterell's brother was an antique dealer in Seymour Place in London; he came once to visit his sister and left visibly shaken. Curious, the Cotterells asked him the value of the contents of the house: he refused point blank even to try and put a figure to it.

Ellen Willmott still rose at dawn to work in the garden, though she did concede a short nap after lunch. She often went along to harass Jacob Maurer, but he, after more than thirty years at Warley Place, was just beginning to acquire some grasp of tactics. He would suggest some slight innovation in the garden, whereupon Miss Willmott would automatically and vigorously respond, 'I'm not having *that*, Jacob'. There followed a short exchange, also along well-practised lines, after which Miss Willmott would go away and Jacob would quietly do what he had intended to do in the first place. No further comment was made on the change by either party. In 1927 Jacob remarried, and perhaps this had bolstered his confidence; his new wife was Maggie Saywood, daughter of old Saywood, the 'cold tea' man. She made an enormous difference to the pleasure and comfort of Jacob's life and cared for his family devotedly.

When gardening, Miss Willmott wore an old brown serge skirt, sabots and a serge jacket; the long hours in the open air had their effect on her complexion, which was becoming coarse and weather-beaten. As she worked in the garden, a young boy followed her around and helped her with jobs she gave him: this was David Rolt, then about twelve, the son of Canon Rolt who lived at The Glen. Ellen Willmott talked to the boy as if her were an adult. Much of what she said went over his head, but the quality of it was clear even to a child, and the blazing brown eyes were hypnotic. Part of her fascination for the young was that she herself retained so many childlike qualities, good as well as bad: but these, in the end, were her undoing. Another young person who was very close to her, her niece Betty Berkeley, took a step at this time which caused Ellen Willmott much distress. At the time of Rose Willmott's marriage the Berkeley tradition of one son or daughter in each generation entering the Church had seemed very distant and impossible, and in any case both a son and a daughter in Rose's generation had been so called, and therefore could surely bear witness for the next generation as well. That Betty, who was half a Willmott, should decide to enter the Order of Notre Dame de Sion, seemed to Ellen unthinkable. But it happened. She did not write to Betty during the latter's novitiate.

One of the young Berkeley ladies privately asked Annie Cotterell to keep an eye on Miss Willmott's appearance, so that she was properly dressed when she went out. The housekeeper thus gradually found herself taking over some of the work of a lady's maid, making sure that when Miss Willmott left the house to go visiting she had a scarf, gloves and a handkerchief. Earlier, there had been an incident when Ellen had gone to London to see Queen Mary and, finding that she had forgotten her gloves, borrowed a pair from a friend whom she met on the station platform. These gloves turned out to be rather full of holes, and it was felt on all sides that a repetition of this incident would do the family's reputation no good.

Ever since her mother died, Ellen Willmott had made full use of the extraordinary amount of freedom which she enjoyed. When difficulties arose in her life, as far as possible she ignored them; when someone annoyed her, she said so: she saw no need for diplomacy, and did not employ it. But now, in 1928, trouble came: she dealt with it in her own way, caring little for its effect on her personality and reputation. Rather did she concentrate on extracting the last ounce of triumph and amusement from it.

Ellen Willmott could be fervent in her devotion to causes. The case of Violet Douglas-Pennant, who had been appointed Commandant of the Women's Royal Air Force in 1918 and dismissed a few months later on grounds never clearly defined, was something which attracted Ellen Willmott's passionate indignation. Here, she felt, was a piece of sheer injustice, coupled with an injury to a woman because she was a woman, inflicted by male colleagues out of malice—and this spoke to Ellen Willmott's latent feminism. The period from

1918 to 1928, during which this case and its ramifications dragged on, was the time at which women were moving from the limited suffrage granted in 1918 to full suffrage, and it was a time when such events easily sparked off public indignation. Miss Willmott went often to London to attend the meetings of a committee dedicated to restoring Violet Douglas-Pennant's good name. (Violet Douglas-Pennant did not forget the support she received: she and Ellen became friends, and she was one of the chief mourners at Ellen's funeral.)

On one of these visits, arriving a little early for the meeting, Miss Willmott hastened off to do some shopping at the Galeries Lafayette in Regent Street. She ordered some scarves to be charged to her account, and on the way out her eye was caught by another scarf which she bought and paid for, either dropping or not bothering to pick up the till receipt. Outside the building a store detective stopped her, claiming that she had not paid for her purchase and, since she was unable to produce the receipt, she was asked to accompany him to the manager's office. The latter, on being asked what he intended to do, replied that he would charge her with shoplifting. It happened that on this occasion Miss Willmott was not dressed in such a way as to appear a person of consequence, and so it was not until she had asked to use the telephone and was heard speaking to Queen Mary that the manager realized that he had provoked an incident which was about to take on a life of its own. The King's Private Secretary, Lord Stamfordham, arrived post-haste on the scene, and the manager begged Miss Willmott to accept his apologies and went on to offer her immediate compensation if she would allow him to drop the matter. 'No,' said Ellen Willmott at once, following this up with comments to the effect that he had started this, and must now accept the consequences. The accounts of what happened next are difficult to disentangle, but the most likely version is that Miss Willmott, insisting on being publicly cleared of the charge of shoplifting, spent the night at Marlborough Street Police Station and was brought up before the magistrates on the following morning.

At Warley Place, Robinson and Annie Cotterell had been in the kitchen while this drama was taking place in Regent Street, Robinson cleaning the silver and Annie Cotterell starting on the preparations for dinner. There was a knock on the side door, and the local police constable came in and told them what had happened—he thought they might well not see 'the Lady' again that night, and he was right. Annie Cotterell, aghast, could only keep on repeating that she had put a scarf in Miss Willmott's bag for her, and why should she want another; Robinson needed longer to take in what had happened, and his real anger broke when, early next morning, reporters appeared on the front doorstep. 'Clear off, I'm not talking to you,' he shouted, enraged, his normal decorum deserting him.

Meanwhile, in court, Ellen Willmott was defended by Sir Henry Curtis-Bennett, K C, and eminent people—Lord Stamfordham, the Lord Lieutenant and the Chief Constable of Essex—gave evidence of unimpeachable character. She was acquitted. She then delivered an impassioned speech on women's rights, in which she pointed out how fortunate it was that, for once, such a thing had happened to someone well able to defend herself. An inarticulate woman in poor circumstances, she said, would certainly have been convicted. It was a telling point, and indeed she had stoutly defended a cause which needed all the help it could get.

Ellen Willmott went home well satisfied with her efforts, but unaware that this, like so many others, was a Pyrrhic victory. Others benefited, but at her expense. The line between the defender of justice and the woman who needed to be able to boast of another battle won, is very finely drawn: and battle for its own sake ultimately came to play almost too great a part in Ellen Willmott's life. But in the meantime, immensely enjoying herself, gleeful at the discomfiture of the Galeries Lafayette and delighted with the opportunity for publicity on women's rights, Ellen Willmott went hotfoot on her return to give the story to the Rolt family.

A year later, the debt, as Ellen Willmott saw it, was honourably settled. *The Times* of 15 January 1929 reported under the heading 'MISTAKEN CHARGE OF SHOPLIFTING' the story of the civil action:

> Civil action settled
>
> A settlement was announced before MR JUSTICE AVORY yesterday of an action in which Miss Ellen Willmott of Warley Place, Great Warley, Essex, claimed from Galeries Lafayette Ltd of 190 Regent Street, W damages for alleged false imprisonment and malicious prosecution.
>
> Lord ERLEIGH, for Miss Willmott, said that she entered the

defendants' premises in February of last year, and on leaving she was followed by a detective and arrested on a charge of theft. She was subsequently brought up at Marlborough Street Police Station and acquitted. After she had issued the writ in the present proceedings the defendant had explained to her the difficult position in which a West End store was placed with regard to the problem of pilfering.

Miss Willmott was satisfied that a genuine mistake had been made, and in the circumstances the defendants had agreed to pay her out of pocket expenses and to offer an apology in open court. On her part she desired to withdraw the allegation that the defendants were actuated by malice.

Mr Walter Frampton, for Galeries Lafayette Ltd, agreed that a mistake had been made, and apologised on behalf of his clients.

This was very probably not her only appearance in court, for it is said that she was regularly summoned for non-payment of rates—a deliberate act to avoid jury service.

While the shoplifting affair was in train, Ellen Willmott's finances were taking another sinister turn. She was becoming almost paranoid about money; gone were the days when the Robinsons, father and son, went to draw the wages from the bank at Brentwood—there was no longer an account there. Money appeared only after her visits to London, and her housekeeper noticed that she often took a small parcel with her, and that afterwards some small item of gold or jewellery had disappeared. A delicately phrased and merciful letter from one of Queen Mary's Ladies in Waiting survives: 'The Queen well understands that one is obliged to sometimes sell one's family treasures, and as the Queen collects things of Royal interest, it might well be that this case would do for Her Majesty's Collection.' Ellen Willmott certainly sold books which in earlier days she had been reluctant to part with, even to the Arnold Arboretum, and one of the dealers to whom she quietly sold books from her library can remember how, as a very young member of the firm, he delivered the proceeds in cash to her at a rehearsal of the Bach Choir, and thought her a very rude and unpleasant old woman. Robinson often had to remind his mistress that he needed money in order to pay the gardeners, and Annie Cotterell's wages were sometimes in arrears. Miss Willmott had accounts at several London shops besides the ill-fated Galeries Lafayette, and there was a kitchen account at the village shop which had to be presented to her each time it reached a certain sum, so that she could check it before paying. In the house she became suspicious, complaining that money was disappearing: she even hid it from Robinson. She constantly made confidences to Annie Cotterell, adding conspiratorially, 'But don't tell Robinson.' Annie, squirming under the burden of some piece of information which she knew very well she would blurt out to Robinson in the end, hastened out of her way as soon as possible. Uncomfortable as the situation was for Annie, it must have been far worse for Robinson, who had to witness this deterioration and to suffer being played off against the housekeeper. In spite of all this Ellen Willmott still spent, if not prodigally, at least more than she could reasonably afford, on any rare plant which she coveted. She was also greatly tempted to buy another violin, which would have been the fourth to pass through her ownership. Tantalizingly, no details of this violin are known: could it be that she had heard of the Willemotte Guarneri, a famous instrument, the property of a Belgian industrialist and later of the violinist Ysaÿe who used it for most of his professional life? But the owner of this mysterious instrument would not part with it unless Miss Willmott were to give up her remaining Amati, which she refused to do. So, fortunately for Ellen Willmott's finances, the negotiations lapsed.

It was not only in money matters that Miss Willmott was becoming suspicious. As far back as the turn of the century she made the Head of the Gardens fix up around the daffodils in the fields trip-wires which would set off air guns and frighten the life out of anyone hoping to pick a bunch surreptitiously. And although other staff had been drastically reduced she still kept a night watchman with a dog. On one occasion, up very early in the morning, she found the unfortunate man asleep, and he woke to the sound of himself being sacked. In the late 1920s attention was turned to the security of the mansion itself, but it was typical of Ellen Willmott's state of mind at the time that, instead of taking moderate and reasonable precautions, she rushed to the other extreme and adopted some bizarre methods of protection. The Cotterells were fascinated by the alarm bells fitted to all the window shutters, and Ellen Willmott herself kept a hand-bell in her bedroom, presumably to disconcert intruders. An equally primitive, and equally effective alarm operated in the strong room which had been built where the old kitchen had been. In her early days at Warley Place, Annie Cotterell, blundering around in the dark, unlocked a door in the passage, setting off such a shrill pealing of bells as to scare her out of her wits and bring Robinson at a run. Later, when they had all recovered from the shock, he took her into the strong room and showed her its contents. There were gold and silver cups which Ellen Willmott had won at shows, medals, canteens of silver, a huge silver bowl with a design of chrysanthemums chased on the outside, and the massive, ornate silver dinner service with its twelve place-settings which took him a full day to clean, and which gave him his most satisfying task. Robinson regarded the protection of this strong room as a solemn trust, and he would certainly have guarded it with his life. In fact he kept a gun, not only for the protection of the valuables but also to shoot rabbits, pheasant and partridge for the table. Nor was he the only member of the household to be armed, for one morning after Ellen Willmott had returned to the house unusually late at night, Annie Cotterell, remembering promises she had made to the Berkeley ladies, suggested that Miss Willmott might at least take off her jewellery before she started her walk from Brentwood Station, and stow it away safely—or at least more safely, since it would attract less attention—in the large handbag which she carried. Her employer when going to London always wore a diamond brooch in the shape of a bow pinned conspicuously in the front of her hat, and several valuable rings—surprisingly, in view of the long hours of gardening and the appalling chilblains from which she had suffered for years, she still had good hands (kept so by the use of heavy leather gardening gloves). Miss Willmott's response sent a shiver down the spine: 'Whoever comes near me will get the worst of it,' she remarked grimly, displaying a loaded revolver lying loose at the bottom of her handbag. (It must have jostled her lunch on days when she went to Kew, for she told Sir David Prain that she always took her lunch with her 'and ate it walking about'.) She alleged that she knew how to use this weapon, and neither Robinson nor Annie Cotterell could convince her that it would be better left at home. They knew that she sometimes imagined that people were creeping along behind the hedge shadowing her, and did not know quite how to cope with this.

Warley Place, thus protected and managed, could still when necessary present a relatively prosperous face to the world. Ellen Willmott kept up her friendships with the Royal Family: but the housekeeper can only remember one occasion on which Princess Victoria came to Warley Place and another when Queen Mary's expected arrival to lunch in November 1925 was cancelled by a telegram announcing Queen Alexandra's death. This news saddened Miss Willmott greatly, as she had felt real affection for the charming and dignified Queen Mother, whom she had so often accompanied to Rose Shows. A few days afterwards a small packet arrived in the post. It contained an ivory paper-knife, inlaid with jewels and showing signs of daily use, which had belonged to Queen Alexandra. A letter from one of the Ladies in Waiting came with it telling Ellen Willmott, who was deeply touched, that the Queen had wanted her to have it as a token of her regard. Once, when King George and Queen Mary were to visit her at Warley and she was late in meeting them at Brentwood Station, a well-meaning policeman who was controlling the small crowd which had gathered said to her, 'You can't go there, Ma'am.' 'Oh, but I must,' she replied, enjoying the situation, 'they are coming to have tea with me.'

Guests other than royalty were also received and feasted in considerable style when this was felt to be fitting. Robinson spent days polishing the silver, removing any scratches with jeweller's rouge or with specially made hard rubber blocks. The parquet floors shone with care and attention, and the cascade curtains of cream satin gimp at the front windows of the house still kept their opulent appearance, no matter how much dust had to be brushed off them. The last of the hothouses to be maintained was the orchid house, so there was always a magnificent silver bowl of spray orchids on the table, which sparkled and gleamed with its silver and glass. (Help from the village was needed on these occasions, and easy to recruit—everyone liked to know what was going on at Warley Place.) But with Tresserve gone there was no longer wine made on a Willmott estate and bottled by Robinson at Warley. Though there were lunch guests, there were not the dinner parties of earlier days, and hardly anybody came to stay. An exception was Lady Binning, who said that Annie Cotterell could not possibly manage a visitor on her own, and so brought her kitchen-maid with her, who got under the housekeeper's feet to such an extent that the latter, boiling with righteous indignation, told Miss Willmott that she would give in her notice if it happened again (previous housekeepers would have shaken their heads, wondering what things were coming to, and how she dared). Apart from these sporadic entertainments, the house seems to have been kept largely under dustsheets. When she was alone, it was difficult to persuade Miss Willmott to eat anything very much. The one thing she did like inordinately was grouse (apparently Mrs McCullum's farmer brothers kept up an earlier tradition of sending them to her), which she preferred very high indeed: Annie Cotterell hated plucking the birds, as every time she pulled a feather out a couple of maggots came with it. Ellen Willmott also enjoyed a glass of mulled wine in the evenings. But dinner did not always consist of grouse: Peter Coats, garden writer and designer, relates that he was taken as a very small boy with his mother to call on Miss Willmott, and they were invited to share her evening meal—a jug of Bovril.

The centre of Ellen Willmott's horticultural work was now the walled garden at Warley Place. Here she engaged in her hybridization work with roses, making some attempt to compensate for the damage done to her collections of rose species both at Tresserve and at Warley during the war. The deaths of some old friends must greatly have saddened her, for Sir Norman Moore died in 1922, Sir Dighton Probyn in 1924 (depriving him of the privilege of serving Queen Alexandra until her death) and Professor Sargent in 1927: the loss of these appreciative and responsive friends must have taken some of the joy out of the task. As she worked, she must have felt very much the absence of the old purposeful bustle round the potting and packing sheds, the rattle of the boilers being stoked, and the cheerful shouting of gardeners to each other.

Annie Cotterell and her mother would get up at dawn to pick the spring flowers with the dew still on them to bunch and sell at the back door for sixpence each. Although there is no previous record of the sale of Warley Place flowers in the village, they were certainly being sold to Pipers the florists at least ten years earlier, accompanied by arguments and acrimony about the prices offered.

In 1929 the daily running of the household at Warley Place sustained a shock from which it never properly recovered. Annie Cotterell and her mother decided to leave Miss Willmott's service. For quite a long time now the housekeeper had been finding her mistress's ways more and more difficult to deal with: the suspiciousness, eccentricity and rudeness; the constant 'divide and rule' tactics used on herself and Robinson; the capricious behaviour and constant demands were very trying. Perhaps the atmosphere in the house was too much one of old age: for Annie Cotterell did not have a lifetime of service at Warley Place behind her, as did Robinson, nor did she feel his loyalty to the Willmott family. She was still a young woman with plenty of life ahead of her, so it was not surprising that she found it all too heavy a load—and she had taken the eye of Dick Carter, who in young middle age made a good living doing handy-man work around the village. So the Cotterells departed, and after Annie's marriage lived on in Great Warley for a time. And so only Robinson was left at Warley Place.

Then, in the following year, there fell a grievous and unlooked-for blow. Miss Willmott's elder niece, Eleanor, married an Irishman, John Brennan, in February 1930, and died four months later. With this, Ellen Willmott knew finally that there would be no one of her own kin to live at Warley Place and to carry on the traditions of the garden. Only her nephew Rob of her sister's children had inherited the Willmott horticultural gifts, and to him, as heir both of his father's estate and of his distant kinsman, Lord Berkeley, would come in due course both Spetchley Park and Berkeley Castle—task enough for any man, without the care of Warley Place to add to it. But he could have advised Eleanor, until perhaps a child of her own had been born with the gift which she lacked. And now this would never happen, and no one would reap the rewards of the care and effort bestowed on the Warley Garden. Some of the bitterness which had overwhelmed Ellen Willmott when her young niece, Betty, had entered the Order of Notre Dame de Sion, returned to her now.

But she rarely kept this frame of mind for long, and though 'embittered' is a word very often used of Ellen Willmott in her later years, it is much too rigid and blunted a term to describe a character so subtle and complex. Energy, mental and physical, characterized her whole approach to life, even in her sixties and seventies. Sharp and intolerant she could certainly be, but, much more important, she was a fighter—not always too sensitive a fighter, as has been seen from her part in the Farrer/Crisp affair—and her exultation in this was a dominant feature of her old age.

CHAPTER XII

The Spite of Fortune

In 1927 Ellen's nephew, Rob Berkeley, had married the Hon. Myrtle Dormer, daughter of a Catholic peer, Lord Dormer. Their first child, Rosalind, had been born in 1928, on 14 September—one of Ellen Willmott's 'special days' as she had told John Murray when it was put forward as a publication date for the first part of *The Genus Rosa*, and therefore surely a good omen. Now, a few days after Eleanor's death, the Berkeleys' second daughter, Juliet, was born. This did not provide a direct solution to the problem of the inheritance of Warley Place, but it seemed an earnest of hope for the future. For the time being this happier occasion drew the family together again, but nothing could blot out the events of the past weeks, nor soften their consequences for Ellen Willmott. Gradually, a rift between Warley and Spetchley developed. It was thought locally that the Berkeley family neglected their aunt in her last years, leaving her very much to lead her untidy, eccentric life on her own. If this were indeed the case they certainly had reason in plenty for doing so, with their young family and their growing involvement in county affairs. Rob's attention, too, was claimed in preparing for the role he was to take over at Berkeley Castle.

So Ellen Willmott sat for the most part alone in her once-beautiful house; no longer having the means to entertain as in earlier days, she naturally and inevitably ceased to receive visits from those who had once belonged to her active social life. She complained bitterly to a young gardening pupil of the neglect and cold-shouldering she had received from former friends in high places. Without the constant coming and going which she so much valued, with her family distant and preoccupied, and seeing her house fail to receive the attention it needed and her garden visibly deteriorate, she must have felt herself confronting the inevitable end of her active life.

Now entirely without a housekeeper, she relied absolutely on Robinson, who recruited help from the village as required. Who did the cooking? One of the village helpers prepared the breakfast, and perhaps also the lunch, but Miss Willmott, never a great eater, probably scarcely noticed the absence of large meals in her own house (except from a prestige point of view) and at about this time someone coming to call found her at lunch—bread and cheese in the kitchen with Robinson. On her butler now fell all the awkwardnesses of the house—and Ellen Willmott more than likely forgot that he was only three years younger than she was, and expected him to be here, there and everywhere. He was even required to turn his hand to emergency mending: there is a story of how, when Queen Mary came visiting and lost a button from her coat, the only person in the house able to sew it on was Robinson.

Jacob Maurer, with his few gardeners, who were always expected to be in two or three places at once (one of them even died while at work) laboured to keep things going, and Ellen Willmott still laboured with them. By now the orchid house too, had to be abandoned; and another task which was coming gradually to an end during the late 1920s was the packing up and posting of numerous plants all over the world, though contacts with Kew were still going on in a more limited way. Even in 1926 Ellen Willmott was complaining to Sir David Prain: 'I am not only short-handed here but no one will lift a hand to a single job he was not engaged to do. I have no packing cases either.' She was never one to spare her gardeners complaints of laziness, incompetence and knavery. Seed lists, however, were still sent out, and the thirtieth anniversary of the first dispatch, falling in February 1932, was celebrated in Sir William Lawrence's RHS Report in *Gardening Illustrated,* which commented on the fact that the list contained close on 600 names, and was a remarkable achievement. On this occasion Miss Willmott's buttonhole, usually an out-of-the-way flower chosen to puzzle, was a pink Java rhododendron. Not only Jacob Maurer, but also his family, were mobilized to help with sending out the seeds from Warley Place once the requests had arrived. Their job was to fold the seed envelopes in such a way that they could be used again. It was a considerable relief to everyone concerned when the distribution was over for the year.

Although it had lost its former splendour, the Warley Garden still had a magnificence which drew visitors. The alpine garden was unchanged, and the lawns as beautifully kept as ever. The Essex Field Club continued to visit the gardens each year, and accounts appear in the journal of the pleasant afternoons the members spent there, and of the trouble taken by their hostess in talking to them about her plants. Mention is made of several rarities in the garden, including the headache tree (*Umbellularia califomica*), which induced headaches in the unwary, and caused mild hilarity among the visitors. The last recorded visit of the Club members took place only three months before Miss Willmott's death.

It is an interesting reflection on Ellen Willmott's character that, while showing the utmost kindness to her Field Club visitors, who were by no means all expert gardeners, she was at the same time teasing a friend of hers from Oxford Bach Choir days—Miss Beatrix Havergal, founder and Principal of the Waterperry Horticultural Training School—about training young lady gardeners who, she said, would be 'utterly hopeless and unsafe in the borders'. This seems at first to indicate an inconsistency hard to believe, but Ellen Willmott herself had been undertaking the training of some young women, and possibly she spoke from experience, or perhaps she scented competition. One of her gardening pupils, Yella Bullion, who appears to have profited from her stay—for she wrote in affectionate, even adulatory terms afterwards—later laid out a garden for Hitler at Berchtesgaden, but Ellen Willmott did not survive to know of this. Another pupil, Jaqueline Tyrwhitt, who now raises plants in Greece, felt that she had failed to give the kind of response to Ellen Willmott's talk of plant life and habits which would have brought her a rich return in hearing the unique accumulated knowledge of a lifetime.

And indeed Ellen Willmott excelled in this: there was scarcely a plant which was not closely familiar to her—she knew its place in the botanical scheme of things, its history, likes and dislikes, through actually handling it and observing it herself, and then through following up botanical descriptions and figures in her botanical library. There is a story that, when she had a particularly fastidious plant to set in Warley Garden, she would take with her the old aunt of one of her gardeners to help her with the task; but it is surely hard to see what anyone else could add to her own skill and sympathy with plants. And she knew so much: Champion Russell once brought a

South African plant over from Stubbers for her to identify—she could not do so off the cuff, but she knew exactly where to set the ladder in her library so that she could reach down the book in which it was figured.

Mr Alfred Baker tells of a visit made by his mother and Mrs Arthur Booth, both keen amateur gardeners, around this time. Ellen Willmott escorted her guests round the garden 'with great courtesy but also with an eagle eye in case they removed a slip or a head'. Saying good-bye at the end of the tour she offered her gardener to escort them to the rubbish heap where they might find a plant to take away. There was, she said, 'a lot of water buttercup they might like'. This was the sort of treatment which prevented Jacob from getting on with his jobs and caused the visitors themselves to reel under the impact, not quite sure whether to feel grossly insulted, rarely privileged, or just part of some cosmic joke of which Ellen Willmott was the agent. It is, of course, very likely that the slightly overgrown garden may have had a peculiar, crazy charm which was missing in the days of its perfection: perhaps the unguarded comment which Rose Berkeley had once made to Jacob: 'a field of dandelions is much better than all this botanical stuff', hints at the unstudied glory which could arise when a garden of planned deliberate magnificence relaxes and proliferates towards its natural state of beauty and confusion. But to Ellen Willmott it must have seemed a bitter travesty of its former days. Did she, at last, face up to her own part in the deterioration which surrounded her? Perhaps glimpses of her own follies—her extravagance, pride of possession, her wastefulness, her selfishness, disregard for others, the blame she meted out but never took to herself, the enmity she aroused and so much enjoyed—may at times have presented themselves, and their inexorably growing effect, to her mind. But this represented the sort of reality of which human kind cannot bear very much, and it seems that she retreated for reassurance to the normalities of daily life. She may well have felt injured that her relations did not spend more time with her, but perhaps it dawned distantly on her that this too was largely her own fault: who would want much of the company of an eccentric, disagreeable, overbearing aunt? There must come a break-even point at which these qualities were no longer outweighed by the brilliance, sympathy and laughter which for so long had made her, in spite of her faults, a fascinating companion for the young. The Russell family retained towards her the kind of affectionate respect and genuine liking which over-rode their sense of what was unattractive in the face which she presented to the world. They record, with sympathy and amusement, how they took her to the theatre with them: she slept through the performance, afterwards telling them unblushingly how greatly she had enjoyed the evening.

Still suspicious, still ready to believe that people were after her, she shuffled out to dine with neighbours. As a concession she laid aside her day-time wear and donned instead a shapeless black blouse with long skirt and sat at table bedecked and ablaze with splendid jewellery, her old head with its *toupet* slightly cocked to one side, bird-like, sharp, half unaware of what was going on around her and then pouncing with some swift, witty comment—and shaking with deep, satisfying chuckles because she had caught her audience napping. Sparkling and malicious, she exaggerated wildly for the sake of the picture she felt herself building up, adding touches here and there as it pleased her artistic sense. Sometimes it seemed that she answered questions at random: asked once whether she played the organ, as her hands were so like those of an organist known to the inquirer, she replied—in total disregard of the organ-playing sessions with which she so often restored herself after a day's labour—' No, but I can use a spade.'

Her financial affairs had drifted into a state of truce, and she lived somehow on her income. Distressingly, however, she was pursued by the Romford Council for payment of rates, and it is said that only the intervention of Lord Lambourne, Lord Lieutenant of Essex and lately President of the Royal Horticultural Society, extricated her from this trouble. She wrote to the long-suffering bank manager, Mr Morgan, and received a reply written from his home address in which he said, with evident relief, that the time of his usefulness to her was over. He suggested that she should take her brother-in-law into her confidence, and also took the opportunity of advising her to dispose of her property herself, rather than have it done by other hands. The letter sounds as though he had been wanting to write it for many years: perhaps it was the work of a man who, just retired, was feeling reckless.

Another woman might have sought refuge in religion, but Ellen Willmott did not spend any longer about her prayers than she had done in earlier years and, though she continued her weekly attendances at mass, she clearly did not pin her hopes for the future there. 'If ever I get to heaven', she would say, 'it will be no thanks to the nincompoop along here' (pointing to the Roman Catholic church) 'nor' (indicating Christ Church on the other side of the road) 'to the lunatic down there.'

In 1932 she allowed her lathe and a number of her tools to pass to the Lewis Evans Collection at the Museum of the History of Science at Oxford. This came about because Mr R. H. Gunther, the first Curator of this Collection, was taken over to see her by the Russells. To let this prized possession go is as much a tacit admission of diminished energy as anyone was ever likely to extract from Ellen Willmott. Gleefully and to spite Mr Gunther, however, she did ensure that, if she were not to use the lathe herself, then no one else would do so either: for she kept back an essential part, and after her death Mr Gunther wrote to Pamela Russell to see if it could be found. 'No,' said Robinson when asked about it, 'she didn't mean for him to have it.'

She continued to complain about the kind of treatment she received from servants and inferiors of many kinds: one day, passing the village carpenter's shop, she made some comment about the mending of shutters. The carpenter, a taciturn, bearded man, eyed her malevolently and a few seconds passed in silence. 'You bloody fool,' he then offered in terse and level tones. Ellen Willmott turned away. 'You see what I have to put up with,' she said to her companion as they moved slowly off, but her remark did not entirely carry conviction. Some hint of respect and amusement hovered there.

In the evenings she sat quietly, sometimes with Robinson in the house and sometimes quite alone. She wrote letters, read, scanned the newspapers—the *Graphic* and the *Weekly Times* were presumably still the reading at Warley Place—played the organ (the one which did not require Robinson's services to get going) or perhaps she just sat thinking. It would hardly seem possible that she should fail to review the events of her life, and stare into the future bereft of human companionship, which she must have known was of her own making and for which she could blame no one else. Then, as she approached the moment of acknowledging this, back would come daily life flooding in—the distant sound of the cowbells on Lescher's herd, the satisfying memory of a stinging retort to a stupid remark offered to her the evening before at a rehearsal of the Bach Choir, the sudden thought that she must find a buttonhole flower to give her fellow Committee members pause for thought at the show next day—and the bad moment had gone.

She continued to be active over RHS matters, though she no longer competed for awards. In 1930 she was elected to the Floral Committee (Group B), and in 1933 to the Lily Committee—a remarkable testimony to her liveliness of mind at seventy-five, as well as to the breadth of her knowledge. She attended the Lily Conference in July of that year. She continued to attend as many events at 'the Hall' as possible: in 1932, for example, her buttonhole flowers at various events were described by Sir William Lawrence: 'Miss Willmott wore *Columnea Oerstedii* . . . the delicious *Lilium Thomsonianum,* a tall spike with some 16 pale lavender flowers enhanced by pink anthers . . . three magnificent blooms of *Lapageria rosea,* very large, open at the mouth, the throat mottled with white: it grows out of doors at Warley on a North wall . . . a curious pendant form of *Elsholtzia Stauntoni.*' Back from the bustle of a show, and the unmistakable scent of narcissi, or trodden turf and lilies at Chelsea, or the sharp drift of chrysanthemums in autumn—back to the empty, cold house and the solitary, darkened evenings. But then again, on some days she set forth just as she used to do ten years earlier, for a busy day in London, and is remembered standing on the platform at Brent wood Station waiting for the first excursion-ticket train of the day, looking rather haphazardly dressed, but discoursing animatedly to a friend or neighbour. Perhaps she would be visiting Queen Mary or having lunch with friends, followed by an afternoon rest at the Royal Institution (perhaps, at this stage in her life, slumbering peacefully through a learned lecture). Then a meeting at the Royal Horticultural Society Hall, or of the Alpine Garden Society, which she joined in 1932, and on to dinner—perhaps the Linnaean Society dinner at Stewarts, or a dinner of the Horticultural Club or the Garden Club. As she grew older she developed an intense interest in archaeology—the Societies of Essex, Kent, Exeter, Wales and Cambridgeshire all drew her attention—and she was also a keen member of the Selborne Society; but, gradually, the number of excursions in which she could summon energy to take part grew smaller.

It may have been after one of these energetic days in London or farther afield, and perhaps walking home on a chilly evening, that in August 1932 she went down with an attack of bronchial pneumonia.

She refused to retire to bed: a neighbour, coming in to help as best she might, succeeded only in persuading Ellen Willmott to remove the hat which she habitually wore in the house, and to agree that she felt more comfortable without it. This must have been a severe illness, and while it was in progress, one of Ellen Willmott's tenants well remembers a smart chauffeur-driven car drawing up outside his house, and two well-dressed old gentlemen descending from it. Leaning over the gate, the older of the two delivered himself of an inquiry, thus: 'Has that old devil kicked the bucket yet?'

She had not; far from it. Ellen Willmott put in an appearance at the first of the RHS Autumn Shows, and was welcomed back by Sir William Lawrence in his Notes in *Gardening Illustrated:* 'We were all glad to see Miss Willmott back again: she was wearing *Pentapterigonum rugosum,* with striated flowers like Roman glass.'

The year 1932 saw the death of Mr Vicary Gibbs, whose ability as a cultivator was often mentioned by Professor Sargent in the same breath as his comments on Ellen Willmott's own skill—not always, one feels, to her pleasure or satisfaction. And, in December, another death occurred which affected her much more closely: that of Gertrude Jekyll in her ninetieth year. A few months earlier Miss Jekyll had written sadly to her that she could no longer do satisfactorily all the odds and ends about a garden that wanted doing directly you noticed them. In September Miss Jekyll's last surviving and closest brother, Sir Herbert Jekyll, had died suddenly, and with that her hold on life began to slip from her. Writing to Mr Cowley, then editor of *The Garden and Gardening Illustrated,* Ellen Willmott recounted how she 'had a feeling' that it was absolutely necessary to go down to Munstead to see her friend, and wrote of her in eloquent terms—and yet it is interesting to see that even into this genuinely sorrowful letter she still managed to inject a powerful feeling of self-importance: 'She was such a sensitive and great personality. I so thoroughly realised it, perhaps more than others.' There seems no reason for this claim, and yet it was made in absolutely good faith. Both she and William Robinson, neither in very good health, attended the funeral.

After mid-October there are scarcely any entries in her engagement diary, but the year ended with a happy compliment: Sir William Lawrence, writing his piece 'Resolutions and Wishes' in *Gardening Illustrated* on 31 December, begins: 'to Miss Willmott, Lady

Beatrix Stanley . . . and to all the ladies who demonstrate that you can be at once a good gardener and a charming woman, a happy New Year.' It would not have been lost on Ellen Willmott that she came at the head of the list, and would have afforded her much satisfaction. But the constant moving about of her earlier years was slowing down, and her handwriting began to show that she was sometimes tired. The last two letters from her which are preserved at Kew, dated May 1933, show signs of this weariness and another, rather touching quality also creeps in. She had a plant of *Sorbus* which Kew had never seen in flower. 'It is pre-Wilson,' she wrote, 'and if not matched in the Herbarium may it bear my name or Warleys?' She added that she was not going to the Linnaean Society dinner—she did not really feel that the Trocadero or Criterion, which people liked so much, were right for learned Societies, and there were so many crossings to make in order to get there. The *Sorbus* was named by Kew *Sorbus sargentiana* var. *warleyensis*, and was held to be identical with Wilson's No. 3492 (Veitch). She still rarely missed a Bach Choir rehearsal, though it seems likely to have been her musicianship rather than her voice that kept her in the choir in her seventies. These concerts were demanding, and no matter how many times she had sung in the St Matthew Passion, the last occasion, on 18 March 1934, would have needed as much attention to detail as the first. Did she, as the great final chorus 'In tears of grief dear Lord we leave Thee' came to an end, realize that this was the last time for her?

From then on, her path ran steadily downhill though, as must be remembered, it had started at a very high point of activity. She was in her mid-seventies, and had no one really close who could minister to her: for though she had plenty of friends, and a large circle of acquaintances, she seems to have had no intimates except in so far as her servants, who knew well her worst qualities, could qualify. And in the end the picture which she had earlier painted of herself as a lone woman was given its finishing touches and became true: not as a depressed and gloomy figure, but rather as an old lady plotting mischief—a scarecrow, but one still owning the snapping, alert brown eyes of her early portrait, and threatening with a chuckle to haunt Warley Place after her death.

In the end Fate treated her kindly and let her sidestep the confrontation with herself, the uneasy malaise and the mortal fear of a slowly approaching death. Robinson slept in the house as usual on the night of 26 September 1934, and in the morning got up to let in the woman who came up from the village to prepare his mistress's breakfast while he went home for his own. Before long he realized that there was no sound of movement upstairs. Ellen Willmott had died apparently in the early morning, suddenly, dropping dead and lying where she fell. She was seventy-six. The news spread swiftly through the village; the doctor came; a post-mortem examination established the cause of death as an embolus in the coronary artery. Robinson must have telegraphed to Rob Berkeley and presumably that call for help and instruction was answered. Ellen Willmott's body was taken on Sunday evening to the Church of Holy Cross and All Saints on Warley Hill, and then on Monday, 1 October, requiem mass was sung and the coffin, covered with flowers from the Warley Garden, was taken to the burial ground at Brentwood Cathedral and buried in her father's grave, which was lined with evergreens and laurels gathered from the grounds—the last service which the faithful Jacob Maurer performed for his mistress and tormentor. The grave is set in an unostentatious square plot hard up against the wall of the Cathedral, with a kerb, and a cross laid against a central plinth. After her death the words: 'Pray for the repose of the soul of Ellen Ann Willmott of Warley Place, died 27th September 1934'were added to the like words in which Frederick Willmott's death was recorded on the side of the grave. Masses are said in perpetuity around the date of her death each year, but it is sad that on the grave of someone who loved flowers not a flower now grows.

The funeral was attended by Ellen Willmott's widowed brother-in-law, Robert, and by her nephew Rob and his wife; there was also a large number of local people present and friends from outside Essex. On 2 October, in Farm Street Roman Catholic church, a memorial service was held, and in this congregation her gardening friends predominated. All arguments about money now past, her old bank manager, Mr Morgan, also attended. Rob wrote to Sir Arthur Hill, Director of Kew at that time, thanking him for his sympathy, and saying that his aunt had right up to the end been absorbed in the activity she loved best, and that she had felt no pain. Then, over the next weeks, came the obituaries: accurate and inaccurate over facts, some prosaic, some very discerning; but all implicitly recognizing the good and the bad, and celebrating a notable opponent. The notice which would undoubtedly have pleased Ellen Willmott most has already been mentioned: it was written by the geneticist C. C. Hurst for *Nature*. It neglected to deal with such trivia as the circumstances of her life, but plunged straight to the heart of the matter in appraising the great contribution made by *The Genus Rosa* to the literature of the rose. Two other pieces would also have pleased her. One of them was the kindly and straightforward comment which appeared in the *Essex Naturalist* and which referred gratefully to the Club's last visit to Warley Place two months before her death. It says: 'Our Club has to mourn the loss of a respected member of its Council, a member of twenty-seven years' standing and a gracious personality, ever ready to share with others of like tastes those peculiar joys which a love of flowers affords and which she herself enjoyed in such abundant measure.' The other, which appeared in the *Gardeners Chronicle*, contained that touch of asperity which would also have appealed to her: 'Faithful with an equal and emphatic fidelity to her likes and dislikes of people, Miss Willmott did nothing by halves. She would by her incisive judgment suggest to the mind a new version of the divine injunction "Love your enemies", for she undoubtedly got a lot of enjoyment out of them.' This, many would feel, hit the nail on the head. Many organizations and societies must have missed her, the Guild of Blind Gardeners among them. On 24 November an article headed *'Plantae Willmottianae'* appeared in the *Gardeners Chronicle,* and after that public interest died down. The final verdict, however, must be Robinson's: 'There was nothing my Lady could not do.'

Meanwhile, Great Warley was slowly getting used to the fact that the autocratic Lady of Warley Place was no more, and that the small energetic figure, slowed down of late to a shuffling gait, would never again be seen. The Berkeleys, father and son, visited Warley Place far more often than they had done in the previous years, although Rob, rather than his father, seems to have settled all the business. Robinson went up to the house every day, and an immense amount of sorting out took place. Probate of Ellen Willmott's will, which yielded the smallish sum of £12,787 9s od, was granted to Rob on 4 December.

An unsettled and forlorn air hung about the house as the winter progressed, though Robinson tried to keep up appearances as well as possible in spite of the inevitable disorganization of the sorting of the accumulated possessions of the Willmott family. But both to him and to Jacob the house and garden must have seemed uncannily quiet. Jacob suffered greatly from the dismembering of much of the garden which he had tended so faithfully: the Berkeleys walked round the garden deciding which plants should be moved to Spetchley—an eminently sensible thing to do, in view of the impending fate of Warley Place, but the break-up caused Jacob much pain as he sorrowfully packed up his beloved plants. And he had too at the back of his mind the worry of what he was to do when the estate was finally sold, as he had no doubt it would be: he saw the promise of a little house, and the £1 a week pension, which had first persuaded him to leave Geneva, fading before his eyes. He was sixty-nine, had raised nine children, and had worked hard all his life. Now, as Ellen Willmott had done, he saw his life's work crumble. The anxieties pressed too hard: suspicions which had first arisen in his mind during the First World War, when he caught the query and whisper in people's minds—was he a spy?—and the memory of the ignorant questioning of the police, came suddenly crowding in. He began to show fears of being followed and persecuted, the sadder because people in Great Warley liked him and no one would have harmed him or wished him ill.

At last, winter over, the time for the sale arrived and must have come almost as a relief. First, at the end of March, Sotheby's sold a silver and enamel fourteenth-century Gothic crucifix, said to have been part of the treasure of Basle Cathedral, a Swiss Burg Mote horn dated 1495, and an interesting oblong casket, all of which had been on loan to the Victoria and Albert Museum since 1922. At £30, £85 and £62 they seemed rather poorly priced. Then followed on 1,2 and 3 April the sale of the greater part of her books; and on 5 April the more valuable of her musical instruments (those that were left) came under the hammer. The scope of her library, assembled with such care and greed over the years, and in the end never left to the British Museum as had been her oft-repeated intention, was astonishing. It included the exceedingly rare Tenore *Flora Napolitana* (one of her favourite books), the Herbarius of 1485 in both the Paris and the Passau editions, Buchoz's rare eighteenth-century *Herbier colorié de l'Amérique*, the *Flora Rossica* of P. S. Pallas, published in Leningrad in 1784–8, and numerous others. Also for sale were two drawings ascribed to P. J. Redouté, drawings said to be the originals of those for *The Genus* Rosa, and a portfolio of about 180 of Ellen Willmott's own colour drawings, mostly of tulip, iris (presumably for the book she was to have written with Sir Michael Foster), and crocus.

Music was also included in this part of the sale, and so many rare seventeenth-century editions of the work of Thomas Morley, John Ward, John Wilbye and others, as to make improbable the suggestion (even if extensive inquiries had not failed to trace such a bequest) that Ellen Willmott had left a collection of rare madrigals to one of the madrigal societies in existence at that time. She had also owned the only known manuscript of Purcell's only violin sonata, which she had acquired from the private sale of the possessions of Mr Taphouse of Oxford; autograph musical manuscripts of Bach, Mendelssohn, Schubert, Liszt and others; and numerous autograph letters of various composers—and, again, of various botanists. (Earlier, Mr Westley Manning had attempted to buy manuscript letters of Schubert from her: did he succeed?) And there were manuscripts of Laujon's Recueil, bound for Madame du Barry, and of *Airs for the Guitar*, bound for Vicomtesse (Adolphe) du Barry. Last but not least, the library included the famous works on turnery of Plumier and Böckler.

The last day, 5 April, saw the final dispersal of the music-room. Many items were withdrawn after the catalogue was printed. But that still left twenty-one instruments, among them a fine Italian violoncello of c. 1800, a viol d'amore, probably German, of the late eighteenth century, bearing a printed Stradivarius label of 1720 (sold for £7), a hurdy-gurdy of guitar shape, a large viola, Flemish virginals in a highly decorated case, and a fine spinet. These last two each fetched £34, the viola £22, and the other items only single figures. It is sad to think of an eighteenth century musical clock, and 'an 18th century miniature musical spinning wheel, in mahogany with ivory enrichments, containing a small organ which plays when the spinning wheel is revolved' so despitefully used, when they must have been so prized by visiting Berkeley and Russell children. Saddest of all was the sale of Princess Amelia's harpsichord, which more than sixty years earlier had been Frederick Willmott's gift to his young and beautiful daughter and had seemed to herald the opening of a happy and prosperous life for her. 'In fair playing condition' it went for £90. Now, happily, it is at Spetchley Park.

But this sale, though in its way an important breaking-up of a valuable collection, was an impersonal affair, and did not hit home in the same way as the sale of the contents of Warley Place. For six days at the beginning of May 1935 the sale of every item still in the mansion gradually and inexorably went through: it took place in the larger of the ground-floor rooms, overflowing into marquees on the lawn. The catalogue, which must have owed much to Robinson, and which was produced by Kemsleys the auctioneers, was in itself a little masterpiece. Where did all these possessions come from? So many tea and dinner services—in Angoulême porcelain, Crown Derby, Nant-Garw, Royal Worcester, Sèvres, and so on, indefinitely; so many dozens of glasses, custard cups, honey dishes, finger bowls? Thirty-seven decanters, and enough glasses for a sizable party? And the strange items—an adding machine, shoemakers' tools, pruning scissors and thimbles all mixed up together, a set of Chinese chopsticks, a carved ivory model of a human skull with reptile mounts? Villagers and townspeople flocked to the sale to acquire something from among the costly and beautiful collections, or simply to have something which used to belong to 'the Lady'. Robinson could not bear to attend the sale, and either went out walking, or sat at home, while the slow painful dismemberment went on, day after day, and people came pouring out of the gates almost as the gardeners had done in the good days—but carrying not the tools of their trade but items they had bought, their faces lit with pleasure or greed, many of them making a day's outing of it. Again a gap of a few weeks, and then on 28 May Kemsleys were to auction the property itself in seven lots. In the interval, presumably, any of the unsold contents had to be removed to sale rooms and the house, denuded of furniture and its full shabbiness revealed now that the pictures had been removed from the walls, had to be swept and put straight.

Rob Berkeley was using this period to write to Sir Arthur Hill at Kew, urging that he should go and plunder Warley, taking whatever he might want for Kew, 'as time is getting a bit short and Warley may be sold on May 28th'. Mr Coutts, the Curator, was supposed to be making the journey to Warley between 23 and 27 May, but whether this actually came about is not recorded. The truth probably was that the staff at Kew were very well aware of the contents of the Warley Garden and, since they had been generously supplied by Ellen Willmott in the past, were not desperate to dig up any particular item. The sale took place, and all in an afternoon Warley Place was sold to a Mrs Gray, licensee of a local public house (how Ellen Willmott would have hated that, for years previously Mrs Gray had threatened to sue her because the Warley Place Charron had caused a horse to shy, lash out and hurt itself). Others are known to have wanted to buy the estate; but with hindsight, it is so obvious that an infinitely better plan would have been to lease the property to some person, or organization, with the means to restore the garden to its former beauty. But even had the decision gone in this direction, the times were wrong—no one had the money to buy.

Only one comment remains on Mrs Gray's ownership: E. A. Bunyard, in his book *Old Garden* Roses remarked that, through the kindness of the present owner of Warley, Mrs E. A. Gray, he had secured some interesting varieties of Albas from the late Miss Willmott's collection, and hoped in a year or two to add considerably to the present collection.

And so began the plunder and decay of the famous garden. Mrs Gray did not live in the mansion, so there was no protection for the grounds and the merciless dragging up of the bulbs went on. Only the crocus were safe, for yearly they bury themselves deeper in the soil where it is a matter of considerable effort to dig them up. So were the vandals deterred.

Robinson retired at last, his reward the gift of the Red House from the Berkeley family. But so accustomed was he to the round of hard work and responsibility, so closely had his life marched with the life of the Willmott family, that he did not long survive his unaccustomed leisure, or Ellen Willmott, and died peacefully at home, his last thought being with the grandchild he did not survive to see. So ended a lifetime of devoted and faithful service. His son Jim still lives at the Red House.

But Jacob Maurer, as seemed his fate through life, was less fortunate. South Lodge was sold, and the Maurers—by this time only Jacob and his wife—had to leave. What happened about the pension is not known, but the cottage was obviously forgotten; restive and suspicious, in fact behaving much as his employer had behaved in her last years, he could not settle: he went for a time to live with his married son John at Billericay, but in the end his trouble worked on him there too, and he felt the need to return to his native Switzerland. There he lived with his wife Maggie for two unhappy years of increasing mental anguish, until in the summer of 1937 he committed suicide—the bitter end of a lifetime's labour, and a hard reward for a kindly and lovable man.

It seemed barely possible that it was not yet sixty years since Frederick Willmott had stood looking over the land which at last was his and the house in which he had hoped his grandchildren and their children would live for generations. His brilliant daughter had had a different vision of immortality: and she would have appreciated, chuckling happily, the final irony that hers has been the more successful. With her life's work apparently in ruins, her contribution to horticulture is yet certain and supreme: her plants, her standards, her special and characteristic *élan*, have left their mark. She had character, and ability, and she became a legend; she wrote a book which is a classic; she taught others her skills, and left an influence on garden planning and on horticultural methods which is still potent: none could have offered more to the world.

Postlude

And what happened then? Mr A. J. T. Carter, a property developer who had earlier expressed an interest in Warley Place, was asked by the agents for Mrs Gray if he was still prepared to purchase. Inquiries were made of the Brentwood Urban Council as to whether planning permission would be granted for a limited number of well-designed houses to be built to an agreed standard, each with a large plot of ground: the mansion was to be demolished to provide a site for Mr Carter to build a detached house for himself, and he was to retain the pleasaunce, the walled garden and the alpine garden. The Council raised no objection to this, nor did they mention that as early as 1935 they had discussed proposals for including Warley Place in the metropolitan green belt. So in July 1938 Mr Carter acquired the estate for a sum believed to be in excess of £14,000. Detailed plans were submitted to the District Council, who now refused to approve them. Justifiably indignant, Mr Carter appealed to the Minister of Health. The District Council, now realizing that the Minister was likely to allow the appeal, considered buying the property. This was strongly opposed by members of the Council and eventually a compromise was offered by Mr Carter, which provided that if he were to receive permission to develop thirty-three acres of Warley Place he would agree to the Brentwood Council purchasing the twelve and a half acres of land to the south-east of the main road at a price to be fixed by the District Valuer. The Council felt that this area was the most important part of the property to be retained for the green belt. In the event, however, even this suggestion fell by the wayside.

And now the shadow of the Second World War fell across the scene: with its approach no one was any longer interested in buying land or houses, and early in 1939 Warley Place mansion was demolished, just in time to prevent its being requisitioned by one of the Services. And so the estate remained undeveloped and the garden lapsed into wilderness. A stick of bombs fell across the grounds, setting fire to the old coach-house and leaving craters. At the end of the war the Warley Place estate stood derelict and desolate, and worse—from Mr Carter's point of view—the green-belt legislation, which had by now been approved, prevented him from being able, ever, to build on the land. A final application to develop was made to the Brentwood Council and when this was rejected an appeal was made to the Ministry. But this time the appeal was refused. Mr Carter died in 1971 and his son inherited the estate.

Although there was a small amount of income from the rents of the cottages and grazing of the fields it was by now becoming impossible to maintain the property and in 1977 it was decided to lease the area which had at one time formed the gardens of Warley Place to the Essex Naturalist Trust. Now, for the first time in forty years, the sound of axe and saw rang through the grounds. With enthusiastic parties working at week-ends, clearings were made in an attempt to improve the natural habitat and to coax back some of the wild and cultivated flora. Old ponds were dug out, nest-boxes were set up and a bird-hide built. The work was not easy but gradually a nature trail was formed and the Warley Place Reserve was formally opened in April 1978. The walled garden has now largely been cleared of encroaching sycamore, and in spring the ground is brilliantly starred with anemone and chionodoxa. In other parts of the garden the cold frames are emerging, disinterred from the growth of ivy and brush. The birds, foxes and badgers no longer lord it over the forgotten gardens. In the cold, deep spring snow of early 1979, the sky bright blue and the air bitingly cold, Warley Place was taking on a new identity, slowly emerging from the past.

❦ APPENDIX ❦

Plants Named for Miss Willmott and Warley

In this list (which does not claim to be complete) there are two groups of plants: those named for Ellen Willmott by her gardening friends, botanists and nurserymen, and those named by Miss Willmott herself. The latter were usually exhibited by her at Shows of the Royal Horticultural Society in London and in the list below an exhibitor is not quoted for such plants. Short descriptions of the plants have been included where possible.

Aethionema
    'Warley Hybrid', RHS Award of Merit, April 1913.
    Sub-shrubby alpine about 6 inches high, with crowded terminal racemes of rose-pink flowers.
    'Warley', RHS Award of Merit, May 1928, when shown as 'Warley Rose'.
    Of rather dwarf habit, with freely produced flowers of deep purplish-pink.
Anemone pulsatilla (now *Pulsatilla vulgaris*) 'Warley Variety', shown at the RHS in April 1914, but passed over by the Committee.
Auricula 'Warley' (*Primula auricula*), RHS Award of Merit 1910, when shown by Mr J. Douglas, nurseryman of Great Bookham, Surrey.
    A show variety of a delicate mauve colour.
Campanula
    x *haylodgensis* 'Warley White' (listed by Professor W. T. Stearn in his article in The Garden, June 1979).
    pusilla (now *cochlearifolia*) 'Miss Willmott', RHS Award of Merit, June 1915, when shown by Mr Clarence Elliott, writer and

nurseryman, of Stevenage. His letter asking Miss Willmott's permission for its naming survives.

A charming silvery-blue flowered form of *C. pusilla.*

'Warley', RHS Award of Merit, July 1899.

Miss Willmott said that this was a chance seedling found where
C. rotundifolia and *C. fragilis* were growing. The writer of 'Notes
for the Week' *(The Garden,* 29 July 1899) says that, though they
make a pretty group, the plants individually do not seem to be
endowed with much vigour or freedom of flowering.

Of dwarf habit, this very distinct and pretty campanula is an
abundant blossomer with small semi-double deep violet-blue
flowers borne on slender stems.

'Warley Alba', RHS Award of Merit, August 1925, when shown
by Messrs Prichard, nurserymen, of Christchurch, Hants.

A dwarf alpine variety, small-leaved and small-leaved with relatively large
flattish white flowers freely borne.

Ceratostigma willmottianum, RHS Award of Merit, September 1917;
Award of Garden Merit, 1928.

Miss Willmott raised two plants of this species (one of which was
grown at Warley and one at Spetchley) from seed sent from the
Arnold Arboretum. It had been collected by E. H. Wilson in the
dry country of the Min River valley in western Szechuan, China.
From these two plants all the plants in cultivation have been
propagated.

A hardy, shrubby species, 2–4 feet in height, with deep marine-
blue flowers borne in clusters at the end of branches, closely
packed but opening in succession: flowering is continuous for
about six months, from May until the first frosts.

Cheiranthus (wallflower) 'Ellen Willmott', Highly Commended
after trial at Wisley in May 1924. It was sent for trial by Messrs
Watkins and Simpson of Crawley.

A bright ruby-red single variety.

'Warley Bronze', listed in the Warley Place seed list for 1912.

Cistus 'Warley Rose'. Said by Sir Oscar Warburg to be one of the
erroneous names under which *C.* x *pulverulentus* was distributed.

Corylopsis warleyensis (now *willmottiae*), RHS Award of Merit,
March 1912.

This shrub was discovered by E. H. Wilson in 1908 south-west
of Tachien-lu in western Szechuan at 6,000 to 7,000 feet. Two

years later he collected seeds in the same area, from which most plants in existence at the time were raised.

A hardy, bushy, deciduous shrub, 6–12 feet high, with habit resembling that of the hazel. The flowers, soft yellow and very fragrant, appear before the leaves and are borne in numerous pendulous racemes (about 20 flowers on each).

Crocus chrysanthus 'Warley', RHS Award of Merit, February 1905. A handsome variety with medium-sized flowers, white with a yellow base in the centre of the flower, tinged with deep blue on the exterior, and bright red pistils.

Dahlia

The same name has been given to two different cultivars.

'Miss Willmott', Highly Commended after trial at Wisley in 1908. Sent by Messrs Bakers, nurserymen, of Codsall. A cactus dahlia, with yellow flowers, shading to salmon-buff, freely produced. 'Miss Willmott', grown at Wisley in 1922, but no award. Sent by Messrs Cheal, nurserymen, Crawley, Sussex. A single dahlia, of crimson-scarlet with narrow buff tips.

Delphinium 'Miss Willmott', listed in the Warley Place seed list for 1912.

Dianthus 'Miss Willmott', RHS Award of Merit, July 1905, when shown by Mr J. Douglas, nurseryman of Great Bookham.

A border carnation, with exceptionally bright cherry-red flowers.

Epimedium x warleyense

When Dr Steam was working on his monograph of the genus he received this hybrid from Miss Willmott in 1932 as E. perralderianum. It had flourished for over 20 years at Warley Place. Miss Willmott was said to have been thinking before World War I of preparing a work on *Epimedium*, and this plant was one of those she had acquired in preparation for it. Professor Steam suggests that it is a hybrid between *E. alpinum* and *E. pinnatum colchicum*. Sepals are green or purple-tinged, inner sepals orange-pink in effect, and petals (much shorter than the inner sepals) yellow with blunt, occasionally red-streaked spurs.

Iris

'Miss Willmott', in the Wisley trial of 1925–7, but passed over for award. Tall bearded iris, blue-white, May-flowering, 22 inches high.

warleyensis, ensis, RHS First Class Certificate, March 1902.

A Juno iris collected in Bokhara in 1901 by van Tubergens' collector, Kronenburg. Miss Willmott was the first to flower it in England and the plant was shown at the RHS Show in March 1902. The flowers, faintly violet-scented, are pale blue with a conspicuous golden-yellow blotch in the centre of the rich purple falls.

x warlsind (*I. warleyensis x I. sindjarensis*). A hybrid catalogued by van Tubergen in 1936.

willmottiana, RHS Award of Merit, April 1901.

A Juno iris from east Turkestan collected for van Tubergen in 1899. The flowers are a soft lavender blue with blotches of white on the fall. There is also a white form, alba, listed in van Tubergens' catalogue in 1936.

Lilium x marhan 'Ellen Willmott' (L. martagon x L. hansonii)

This cross was awarded a First Class Certificate when shown in 1898 by van Tubergen. There is a letter from John Hoog of van Tubergen to Ellen Willmott asking her permission to have the lily named after her, but according to Woodcock and Steam's Lilies of the World 'Ellen Willmott' was one of several selected seedlings from the original cross. It is said to have a slightly clearer orange colour and bigger flowers (red-brown spotted) than the F.C.C. plant.

warleyensis (now *davidii var. willmottiae*), RHS First Class Certificate, July 1912.

Collected by E. H. Wilson in western China, and reintroduced by him. Miss Willmott raised the award plant. A July-flowering lily, its flowers reddish-orange with numerous small brown spots covering the recurved petals, and with chocolate brown stamens.

Lysionotus

warleyensis (now pauciflora), RHS Award of Merit, August 1913.

willmottiae (now pauciflora). This second plant was shown to the RHS in 1914 by Miss Willmott and the Floral Committee recommended it for a Botanical Certificate, but the Scientific Committee ruled that unless a valid description had been published for this name the certificate should be withheld (and this is what happened). A dwarf shrub, with flowers resembling those of pentstemon in shape, white, streaked with dull crimson inside the tube, along which run two pale yellow ridges.

Both plants were collected in China by E. H. Wilson.

Appendix

Mysotis 'Warley' and 'Warley Blue'
These may be the same plant, but neither impressed the RHS Committees and were passed over by both, one at Vincent Square and the other at Wisley.

Narcissus
'Ellen Willmott', RHS First Class Certificate, March 1897.
This was raised and shown by the Revd G. H. Engleheart, of Appleshaw, Andover, Hants. The flower is now classified as a 1b (trumpet: perianth white, corona coloured).
'Great Warley', RHS First Class Certificate, April 1904.
Although shown by Miss Willmott, this was another of Mr Engleheart's seedlings. A 2b (large-cupped: perianth white, corona coloured).
'Miss Willmott', RHS Award of Merit, April 1907; First Class Certificate, April 1911.
Raised by van Tubergen and shown by Messrs Walter T. Ware of Inglescombe, Bath. A 3b (small-cupped: perianth white, corona coloured).
'Warley Magna', RHS Award of Merit, April 1902.
An Engleheart seedling, shown by Miss Willmott. A 3 a (small-cupped: perianth coloured, corona coloured orange-scarlet).
'Warleyensis', RHS Award of Merit, April 1906.
Raised and shown by Miss Willmott. A 1a (trumpet: perianth and corona coloured).

Nerine 'Miss Willmott', RHS Award of Merit, November 1899.
Shown by Mr H. J. Elwes of Colesbourne, Glos. A superb variety with large orange-scarlet flowers borne in large trusses. (At the same meeting of the Floral Committee *Nerine* 'Mrs Berkeley'—a distinct variety with pale orange-salmon coloured flowers—was also accorded an Award of Merit by unanimous consent.)

Paeonia willmottiae (now P. obovata var. wilmottiae), RHS First Class Certificate, May 1919.
Collected by E. H. Wilson in Hupeh in 1900, seed from this collection being raised at Warley Place. In the pan of seeds this plant was noted at the seedling stage as being different from the others, so it was pricked off and planted out next to P. *obovata*. F. C. Stern in his monograph on the genus *Paeonia* (1946) placed it as a variety of P. *obovata* with which it seemed closely allied. The flowers, pure white, have stamens with crimson filaments

and golden-yellow anthers, the foliage is a handsome dark green.

Parahebe 'Miss Willmott'. The origins of this cultivar are unknown but it has been grown for many years at Bressingham Gardens, Diss, Norfolk, and Mr Alan Bloom first knew it in 1923 as Veronica 'Miss Willmott'. It was grown in the early twenties by nurserymen R. W. Wallace and Arthur Charlton, both of Tunbridge Wells. It is described in the Bressingham catalogue as a rosy-lilac, very free, semi-shrubby plant, 15 centimetres high, May to July flowering.

Phlox

'Ellen Willmott', RHS Award of Merit, September 1910, when shown by Messrs Gunn of Olton.

A tall, strong-growing, late-flowering phlox of a pale ageratum-blue colour with a lighter zone round the eye.

'Miss Willmott' and 'Miss Ellen Willmott' are both mentioned as being grown in the trials at Wisley, but neither apparently merited the judges' approval.

Plagianthus lyallii 'Warley Variety' *(now Hoheria lyallii)*, shown in July 1915, but passed over by the Committee.

Potentilla 'Miss Willmott'. A herbaceous hybrid, probably with *P. nepalensis as one parent*. It appears in many nurserymen's lists.

Primula

auricula, see under Auricula

capitata 'Warley Variety', shown in November 1913 but passed over by the Committee.

spectabilis 'Warley Variety', shown in April 1913 but passed over by the Committee.

warleyensis, RHS Award of Merit, April 1912.

A pretty primula about 2½ feet high, the stems usually bearing four rosy-lilac flowers with orange-brown centres, on each stem. Collected in China by E. H. Wilson.

willmottiae (now *P. forbesii* ssp. *willmottiae*), a Himalayan species, probably not now in cultivation.

Pyracantha yunnanese 'Warley Variety' (now *P. crenatosenata*), RHS Award of Merit, January 1920.

A shrub with clusters of small white flowers on long arching branches, and orange fruits in autumn.

Rhododendron
warleyense and *willmottiae*
Both shown in April 1914 but both passed over by the Committee.
Rosa
blanda var. willmottiae (now included in *R. virginiana*). Miss Willmott in The Genus Rosa says this is a form grown in Warley
garden, raised from seed sent from America, which Mr Baker
thought sufficiently distinct to be given a varietal name. A pretty
rose, free-flowering and compact in growth, with red stem and
clustered, coral-pink flowers.
chinensis var. *indica* 'Miss Willmott'. A garden form, with orange-
pink single flowers.
'Ellen Willmott', Certificate of Merit from the National Rose
Society in 1935. A hybrid tea raised by Mr W. E. B. Archer of
Sellindge, Ashford, Kent. Its single pale golden-yellow flowers
are shaded pink at the edges, with petals peculiarly waved, making
an unusual bloom.
'Ellen Willmott', another hybrid tea, was raised by A. Bernaix of
Rhône, France, in 1898.
x warleyensis. A pink-flowered rugosa hybrid, raised at Warley
Place.
willmottiae. Raised by Messrs James Veitch & Sons from seeds
collected by E. H. Wilson in western Szechuan. It flowered at
Coombe Wood nursery in May 1907 and was named in compliment to Miss Willmott. It has rose-purple flowers, short-stalked
on orange-red lateral branchlets.
willmottiana. A white rose with long stems and no thorns, now
regarded as a variety of R. longicuspis.
Salvia warleyensis, RHS Award of Merit, 1916.
The flowers are violet-purple with a white lip, and the hairy calyx
is of a very dark purplish colour.
Scabiosa caucasica 'Miss Willmott'. A well-known cultivar of florists'
scabious, listed by many nurserymen.
Sorbus sargentiae var. *warleyensis*, named in 1933 when Miss Willmott
sent to Kew a specimen of Sorbus which she said had been growing
at Warley Place since before Wilson's Chinese expeditions, and
which she asked to be named after herself or Warley Place.
Syringa 'Miss Ellen Willmott', RHS Award of Merit, June 1917.
Shown by Mr C. Turner of Slough and Mr G. Paul of Cheshunt.

A double white lilac with large individual flowers borne in large trusses.

Tulipa

'Ellen Willmott'. A primrose-coloured cottage tulip, introduced in 1900.

willmottiae Collected in 1899 in the eastern mountains by van Tubergens' collector Kronenburg, and named for Miss Willmott, because of her great interest in the genus. Large clear yellow flowers, a blue-black basal blotch and yellow anthers. The following year when bulbs had been collected, John Hoog sent Ellen Willmott a few of them and wrote 'I hope they will please you and what is more prove worthy of bearing your name'.

Verbascum

'Warley Pearl', shown in June 1916 but passed over by the Committee.

'Warley Rose', RHS Award of Merit, June 1914.

Flowers of an old rose colour borne in a branched panicle.

Verbena

grandiflora 'Ellen Willmott', listed as being grown at Wisley in 1913 and 1914 but did not apparently receive an award. Sent by R. Veitch. A carmine-red variety with pale sulphur-yellow eye.

'Tresserve', RHS Award of Merit, August 1897. Shown by J. T. Bennett-Pöe of Cheshunt. Rose-coloured flowers in large trusses.

'Warley'.

At the show in July 1908 Miss Willmott exhibited a group of these plants for which she was awarded a Silver Banksian Medal.

Veronica prostrata 'Warley Blue', shown at Chelsea in 1914 but passed over by the Committee.

General Index

(*Note* Members of the British Royal Family are listed under Royal Family and all nurserymen are listed under Nurserymen)

Index of Plant Names

See also Appendix: Plants Named for Miss Willmott and Warley

[239]